Becoming Pastor

By

Jeffrey Kanode

For Kelly, my cherished wife.

And to my family: Greg K, Dianne, Monica, and Heather

Table of Contents

Foreword

Becoming Pastor tells my story, and I am petrified and as self-conscious as it is humanly possible to feel because of its publication. Still, I want my little book out there. I want it to be read.

I fear being accused of being a narcissist. I fear maybe I am a narcissist. I consider myself an incredibly humble, shy person. I have every reason in the world to be humble. I have nothing to be conceited about at all, believe me. I am shy, and I would rather be one-on-one with a loved one than I would in a crowd at a party. I am shy yet for a dozen years now, I have served as a pastor, speaking on behalf of God in a priestly, sacramental function in front of dozens, sometimes hundreds, of people.

I am shy, yet I have just composed a spiritual memoir, which in places is so self-disclosing I fear not being able to look people in the eyes for a while after I know they have read it. I don't think I am a narcissist at all, but still I fear: who can really write about themselves for over two hundred pages without being either, at best, self-aware and self-conscious, or at worst, incredibly self-consumed, and yes, a narcissistic?

I write because I love to write. Writing has always been a huge part of my life. Writing has helped me survive. Writing has kept me alive through some very dark periods of life. For years I dreamed of being a published writer, and I did publish articles here and there. I could never pull a full book together, though.

Those clichéd words from every creative writing class in every high school and in every college kept echoing in my ears, reverberating in my consciousness, *Write what you know.* After many years, it finally dawned on me. I am an ordained pastor who has served in rural Appalachian parishes for twelve years. I am an ordained pastor who has suffered from depression. I am an ordained pastor who has met some fascinating souls, some of them challenging, all of them beautiful even if in a challenging way. I am an ordained pastor who has a perspective and a story. I have to write to stay alive. Here it is then: *Becoming Pastor.*

In these pages, I don't just share life stories from my churches. I also spend a great deal of time telling stories, recounting narratives, and fleshing out feelings from my own heart. *Becoming Pastor* helps explain how the "me" who stood behind a pulpit preaching, or who stood at a bedside, holding a dying person's hand ever became a pastor.

I am just telling you a story, a story which is mine to tell.

Meaning, theology, instruction, didacticism, I leave to you and the Holy Spirit.

You can tell me later, if you like.

1 Foundations

Granddad

We all have the rocks and stones of the foundation of our humanity. First, I will tell you of my unseen rock, my spiritual stone. This story goes before me as it runs within me. Then we will turn to rocks and stones I do remember from my very beginning.

I don't think he was an overly religious man, my grandfather. At least, spiritual fervor and consuming Christian dedication weren't attributes that I ever heard roll off anybody's tongues when they described him for me.

I would ask people, anyone, about my grandfather when I knew they had known him.

I would ask anyone about my grandfather who had known him because I had not. I never knew my grandfather.

My grandfather, or Granddad as my sisters called him, died in January 1978. I was born in May of that same year. Granddad never got to see me or hold me, but at least he knew I was coming. I never got to hold Granddad's hand as he took me on a walk to the playground, but at least I know he was looking forward to me being in the world. I know that because my dad told me Granddad was in the loft of his garage, pulling down a baby crib for me the day he got sick. The last tasks Granddad accomplished before he went to his bed to rest, where he would be for hours until Grandmother knew something was wrong, was finding that baby crib: pulling it down, cleaning it up, and getting it ready for me.

Before I was born, my feeble granddad, who had suffered from a stroke years before, was climbing a ladder up a loft high above his garage to find a crib to shelter me, his unborn grandson. Throughout my life, I would see Granddad's face, and I would imagine what it would have been like walking hand in hand with him to the playground or having him there, alive and well, to take me fishing. He died while I was still unborn. Separated by womb and grave, denied the blessing of sharing life on earth together, we still were somehow very connected. Our lives somehow intertwined. Our souls allied in a way far beyond even the links of genes and blood.

I can remember seeing photographs of my granddad when I was a little boy, and to me, his countenance always conveyed a sense of great peace and lots of love. One photo, in particular, captured Granddad forever gazing into the camera with his nose playfully crinkled, his mouth childishly smiling. I sometimes got the feeling when I looked at that particular image of Granddad that the playfulness and that gaze was him saying, "Hello! I love you," to me.

Granddad was the oldest of five children. He had two brothers and two sisters. Uncles Raymond and Lake had also already died before I was born, but Aunt Eloise and Aunt Romaine were still alive. They lived far away from West Virginia: one in Arkansas and the other in Pennsylvania. At least they were alive! I did get to meet them and spend time with them on a few occasions in my early years. Still, I was too young to truly appreciate the treasure I had when I was in their presence. Lord knows I would cherish every second now. I would have held moments with them as precious time, in a sacred place, if they had just survived into my teenage years. They did not though. I was probably ten or eleven the last time I saw those dear ladies, those irreplaceable links to Granddad.

When I got older and could appreciate the priceless treasures of life more, God gave me echoes of my granddad's life that still reverberate in my own. I would meet grown men my dad's age who had been in Granddad's Boy Scout troop. Granddad was a Boy Scout leader for over thirty years.

In honor of Granddad's dedication to the Scouts, his old troop, the trustees of a local cemetery, and one of Granddad's best friends--who was then a county commissioner--dedicated a flagpole to Granddad. He was still alive when they dedicated it, and they placed it in a fine place — in a green field beneath a grove of evergreen trees in the cemetery just off US Route 52. For whatever reason, and I am not exactly sure why, many years later, the Scouts had another dedication service at the flagpole, although they may have called this one a remembrance service to Granddad. I was maybe twelve years old by then, and I got to attend. The event even made our local newspaper. A picture of Dad and me made the front page. The photographer forever captured Dad happily smiling while a teen Boy Scout hoisted an American flag up Granddad's flagpole. I, in deep contrast, looked miserable with deep melancholy evident in my adolescent frown. Anyone who saw that picture may have assumed I was just a bratty kid who resented being dragged out of the house, away from my Nintendo, to attend some stupid event. To the contrary, I was proud to be there. I was proud of Granddad. I just really, really missed him. For me, it was almost like attending his funeral. I was, and am, grateful for the event, which was a celebration of the human being my granddad was. I was just sad I never got to experience that humanity, eyeball-to-eyeball, face-to-face, for myself. The newspaper photograph captured those emotions in the little preteen me. All these many years later, those emotions still remain.

I would talk to some of Grandmother's friends from church who had also been Granddad's friends. The impression I got from Granddad's guy buds from church was that he was no saint, but he was lovable. I even got the impression Granddad was a harmless lady's man. He didn't betray his wedding vows with Grandmother ever, but he did enjoy flirting and hugging a pretty lady. What those old men told me about my granddad reminded me of Grandpa on *The Waltons*. I loved it.

Once I even met a delightful sister duo who had grown up with Granddad, Raymond, Lake, Eloise, and Romaine. Meeting them was a blessed occurrence where God took one of my goofy mess-ups and made a miracle out of it for me. This has become a habit of God's in the long annals of all the goofy mess-ups that have peppered my life.

I was probably sixteen or seventeen years old. I had only had my driver's license for a few months. I decided one Saturday afternoon, on a whim, I was going to take a little early evening, springtime drive to Athens, West Virginia. Athens was thirty country miles away from our home in Princeton. Athens is the ancestral home of my family, the little college town where Granddad and all his siblings grew up.

Granddad's mom and dad, my great-grandparents, were Elbert and Hattie Kanode. Elbert was a shoe cobbler. Evidently, he didn't make nearly enough money mending shoes, because he and Hattie opened up their home as a boarding house. Hattie cooked and cleaned, knitted and washed clothes for not only her own family but a whole passel of borders too, most of whom were Concord College students. The old Kanode house stood, and still stands, at the corner of the college entrance.

The old family house was my first stop in my spur-of-the-moment, hastily planned, solitary family-roots pilgrimage. I had no trouble finding it. I parked my car in the college parking lot just across the road from the main entrance very near the house. I crossed the road and stood before the house, the whitewashed, three-story house with the large front porch; the welcoming, very *home*-looking home, which had been home for my granddad. I stood out there standing for a while. I imagined my granddad as an eight or nine-year-old sitting out on the front porch, reading comic books. I could almost see him as a teenager holding a girl's hand, sitting on the porch swing, maneuvering closer to her, hoping for an opportunity for a kiss.

As clear as the fading West Virginia sunlight of that day falling on the façade of my family's old home, I saw Granddad walking out the front door in his army uniform, leaving for basic training and the war, World War II. I saw Hattie and Elbert walking out just behind him. Hattie's cheeks were stained with tears, and her hands and apron were smeared with flour – she was making fresh bread for supper for her family and her borders. Elbert looked stoic, but his eyes – I imagine them blue, like mine, Dad's, and Granddad's – were red and misty. Two teenaged boys, and two pretty preteen girls walked out right behind their parents to see their oldest brother leave home for war. They all knew he might never come home, and they were silent. Like Elbert, Raymond and Lake were stoic. Like Hattie, Eloise and Romaine cried quiet tears.

Granddad stopped, turned around, and waved one last time. His arms and hands silently trembled with emotions, and bravely like a soldier already, he fought not to cry. He then turned away from his family and walked down the very same sidewalk I was standing on fifty-four years later. I imagined this all in my mind, and within myself, I was there. I could have sworn I felt a little breeze as he passed by me. Despite the cooling mountain evening, the breeze felt warm. My reverie was interrupted by the loud burp of a young college kid coming out on the front porch with a beer –

yet another beer since the burp made clear he had already had at least one. My dad warned me about this. "Jeff, I am pretty sure the old home place is a fraternity house now. It was when I went to Concord in the mid-sixties." Apparently, in the mid-nineties, it still was.

The beauty of the Kanode home now ruined by the nineteen-year-old frat boy guzzling beer on the once holy ground where my granddad had long ago read comic books, wooed girls, and said goodbye to his family as he left for war, I left. My next destination was the old Athens Cemetery, where Elbert and Hattie were buried.

I don't know what possessed me to park my car so far over in the grass on a steep incline, on a hillside, that early spring evening. I don't know what good sense I didn't possess, which would have told me: *The earth is damp. We've had many spring rains lately. You need to keep at least one side of your car on the asphalt, so your tires can get traction.* I don't know why I was truly shocked when my car screeched and hollered; when my tires spun and gnashed rubbery teeth; when my rear end spun around very nearly hitting an eighty-year-old named Elsie Jones's headstone.

What did I think when I saw Elbert's and Hattie's graves? What profound thoughts raced through my mind poetically when I saw that he had been born in 1878, and had died in 1955; and she had been born in 1888, and had died in 1955? She was born ten years later, yet she only died one month later. Family lore, which I learned from Dad and Aunt Romaine, said Hattie hadn't been sick; there was no discernible medical reason for her to die. Elbert and Hattie's children and the family's friends and neighbors always maintained that Hattie just grieved herself to death over Elbert.

What did I think? Did I think any of these ponderous thoughts that spring evening with the sunset just over the horizon, a burning scarlet of promise, a flaming red reminder of living hearts no longer beating, and once coursing blood now ceased flowing forever? I can't remember. Knowing me, I probably did have some romantic thoughts on the occasion. Soon though, the narrative of this day would be the drama of my old 1987 Chevrolet Celebrity almost axle deep in West Virginia mud, as a teenaged me made a mug bog out of a sacred, pristine sanctuary of the beloved departed, including the bones of my own great-grandfather and great-grandmother.

Within not many minutes and many splatters of mud inundating the car from the spinning tires, I knew I was in trouble. As dusk fell, and I could see a pair of headlights approaching me, I knew I was potentially in much more trouble.

I expected one of two types of vehicles to belong to that pair of headlights. I expected, firstly, a town police car—one of those late model Chevrolet Malibu's with the *Smokey and the Bandit* paint job and sirens—driven by the kind of law enforcement agent best known for speed traps and pulling you over for the rolling stop at no-traffic intersection stop signs. If the headlights didn't belong to

Smokey, then I expected, secondly, a big, manly pickup truck — not a Chevrolet S-10 or a Ford Ranger, but a big 1970s Custom Deluxe or F-150 — with a Rebel flag bumper sticker and Hank Williams Jr. blaring from the aftermarket stereo system. In short, I expected to be ticketed or arrested by Buford T. Justice or Barney Fife, or I anticipated being beaten to death by a couple of barroom brawlers with Budweiser on their breath, Copenhagen in their mouths, anticipatory condoms in their pocket, and a modest criminal record in their background check. I expected a big bruiser with a Momma tattoo to open my car door, pronounce, "You ain't from here," and commence to beating the ever-loving life out of me.

I sat there with quickening breath and heartbeats about to burst out of my scrawny chest. I sat there as my parents taught me, with both hands on the steering wheel. My hands and arms and legs just trembled. I did not expect who actually did come to my car door.

"Sweetie, you really do need some help, don't you?"

With white hair and just a touch of lipstick; with just a hint of Ben-Gay aroma and a Methodist Women lapel pin, she could have been my own grandmother. I felt safe with her, safe enough to cry. So I did. "Yes!" I sobbed.

"And just who are you, exactly?" she asked in a patronizing tone sprinkled with just enough kindness that I didn't care. Besides, in those days, I didn't even know what *patronizing* meant.

I got enough control of my emotions to speak coherently

enough to answer the lady's question. "I am Jeff Kanode, ma'am." I fought back the tears. "I am an honor student at Princeton Senior High School. I really am a good kid. I didn't mean to come in here and tear up the cemetery. I just wanted to pray at my great-grandparents' grave!" I was sobbing pathetically again. What a stud! No wonder I didn't have a girlfriend.

The sweet little white-haired, Ben-Gay smelling Methodist woman smiled. "Well, I'll be. A little Kanode boy? So, you were here to find Elbert's and Hattie's graves?"

"Yes!" She spoke of Elbert and Hattie! I knew I was being rescued by a friend, and maybe even loved, too.

"And did you find those dear people's graves before you started making a huge mess of our cemetery?" Her tone wasn't at all harsh, just belittlingly amused. I didn't mind. I loved her already.

"Yes, ma'am," I replied.

"Well, my sister and I live just down the road a little way from the old Kanode boarding house. Perhaps you should leave your car behind. I don't think it's going to go anywhere, do you? And you can use our phone to call someone to help you. We may just have some chocolate cake and ice cream to share too." I was enchanted. They could have been septuagenarian serial killers, but I didn't care. They knew my ancient family. And they were offering to help me. And they had chocolate cake. Even if they were going to kill me, they were sweet old southern ladies.

10

Presumably, they would give me plenty of dessert, let me savor it, then kill me.

Indeed, they did! They gave me plenteous dessert that is--they didn't kill me. The white-haired little lady with arthritis and muscle spasm issues was named Beulah. Her sister was Nancy. Nancy was taller than Beulah, painfully skinny with black hair darker now than it had been, probably, when she was in her late thirties. Beulah abused the sports ointment, and Nancy clearly abused the hair dye, and I was falling in love with them both. As I ate my chocolate cake and ice cream, I was entranced by their stories. I was also amused at how they competed with one another for speaking time.

"Oh, I knew your grandfather, CH," Beulah began.

"Well, Beulah, I went out with him once!" Nancy interjected.

Beulah went on, and I regretted that because it sounded like Nancy may have had the more interesting side of the story to tell. Oh well.

"Your grandfather CH was the oldest of all the Kanode children. He wasn't that much older than Lake and Raymond, so the boys were all pretty much peers. His sisters were a different matter for your grandfather though. CH was a good deal older than the girls, Romaine and Eloise, and he was extremely protective of them."

"Some of the boys I knew were afraid to ask those girls out because they didn't want to go through CH," Nancy interjected.

11

"Yes," Beulah said, annoyed at what she considered an unneeded addition to her narrative. "Now, CH was quiet and studious. However, he was also something of the romantic. I heard he could be quite gallant."

"He was. He really could be," Nancy attempted.

"He dated the Baptist preacher's daughter once, as I remember." Beulah just wasn't interested in the possible enrichment and depth her sister could give to her narrative. "Then he started dating that little girl from McDowell County, Elkhorn. What was her name?"

"Lillian!" I shouted out excitedly. Particles of chocolate cake danced out of my mouth. "My grandmother!"

"Oh, of course," Beulah said. "That's the girl he did marry. Oh! And clearly, they did okay. Here sits their little grandson. You haven't mastered the art of driving a car yet, but you seem sweet and endearing."

"He has his granddaddy's eyes," Nancy said. "CH had dreamy blue eyes." The skinny elderly lady started piercing my baby blues with eyes as black as her unnatural hair. It started to feel a little creepy, so I buried said blue eyes deep into the texture of my disappearing chocolate cake and melting ice cream.

Beulah continued, "CH was the quiet leader, the dependable big brother of the lot. He just quietly lived his life without drawing attention to himself, but he did just fine. Ray was the athlete. He was the star of the bunch. Your great- uncle Raymond was a football star at Athens High, and at Concord too. He played college football until he broke his leg one year. That ended his career, and when it didn't heal properly—I don't know what exactly happened there—he wasn't accepted into the military. CH went, Raymond was 4-F, and Lake was too young. Now Lake was the comedian of the family. He could tell stories and come up with jokes. I remember how CH used to dote on him too."

"I went out with Lake the whole of our freshman year," Nancy tried.

Beulah went on, unfazed, "Those Kanode girls were sweet girls too. I didn't know them as well. Nancy and I were more the boys' age. The girls were a half dozen years or so behind us. They were cute growing up. Again, your grandfather was like another little father to them. He was so protective of his little sisters. Romaine was something a tomboy. She used to love to climb the trees, the large oaks and maples on the college campus. She could outrun any boy in school, too. She was a good little basketball player. I saw her play a lot during the young people MYF meetings at the church. Then there was Elouise."

Nancy had finally had enough. "Smart as any other kid in school! She could have gone to college anywhere and been anything. She did what many of us did, though. She fell in love young, got married, and started making a family, keeping a home. Elouise was so quiet. She was painfully shy. I can remember her little eyes just welling up when she would have to say anything at a party, among people. When she knew you though, you had a friend for life. I miss all the Kanode family. I miss Elouise the most though."

"Well, thank you, Nancy," Beulah said, not at all graciously. "Now, we kept up with all of your family over the years, mostly through Christmas cards and stories we would pick up. Your granddaddy, CH, has been gone a long time, hasn't he? You must have been really young when he died?"

I cleared a lump in my throat. For the first time ever, I understood a piece of myself I could never name—a piece of Aunt Romaine always lived inside of me. Now I knew the source of my shyness I worked so hard to overcome. "I...I didn't know Granddad. He died in January 1978. I was born in May."

"You poor boy," Nancy interjected before Beulah had a chance. "You and your grandfather would have been close. You have his eyes. I can see some of his facial features too. Surely you have his personality. You are quiet, like CH, and like him, you are engaged. I can tell you truly do listen, and you care, just like he did."

"Well, he probably is quiet, like CH, Nancy, but even if he weren't, how could he have a chance to say anything even if he wanted to, with us yacking away so? Now, your grandmother, is she still alive? Please tell me she is."

"Yeah," I said, "Grandmother is doing well."

"I never really knew her that well. I would see her off and on

14

at some district Methodist Women meetings, but we don't really go to those much anymore. We've become more stay-at-home and watch Dr. Charles Stanley on Sunday mornings here in our older age. Your grandmother always did have a humble, friendly personality. We like her."

Nancy nodded assent. I thanked them.

At some point shortly after that, one of the three of us remembered I had come home with the ladies in order to call my parents to get help.

Mom was not pleased, but I did think I could hear her fighting back chuckles under her breath. "You...you got your car stuck up...in the cemetery in Athens and you are at home with two little old ladies who knew Granddad? [Pause, while I imagine she composed herself.] We'll call Charley [my brother-in-law, the chief handyman and hero man of our family] and see if he can come with us to haul you out."

It would take my parents at least thirty minutes to reach Athens from our home in Princeton if they left right away. It would take them longer to call Charley, and longer still for Charley to pick up Mom or Dad and head to the cemetery to rescue the old mud-bogged Chevrolet Celebrity and me.

I knew I still had probably at least another hour with these elderly women who had known my granddad, my great-aunts and uncles, and my great-grandparents. I looked at Beulah and Nancy amusedly to be sure, because they were funny. I looked at them

15

with thanks, because they had reached out to help me, like two senior Good Samaritans, no doubt. I looked at them with a great deal of awe too, and respect, coupled with tenderness. These ladies had known my granddad.

Oh, Mom and Dad had known Granddad too, of course. Grandmother had been married to him all those years. They knew him deeply and profoundly within the holy bonds of blood, family, years.

These ladies had something very special not even my family had. They had known Granddad in a different way—a way I had never been able even to glimpse or imagine. No light had ever been cast, no playful sunbeams or dancing shadow had ever presented itself to serve as my epiphany, revealing the part of my granddad whom these ladies knew: CH, the doting older brother watching over his sisters; CH, the quiet but gallant young man in courtship; CH, the reliable rock who helped his younger siblings out, who helped his parents hold the family together. I felt a connection to these strange little old ladies; I loved them even, just because they had been there. They knew Granddad as CH. They knew about Lake and Ray and Eloise and Romaine. They knew about those Kanodes. They knew about those folks who were always a mystery to me, a sacred mystery; those folks whom I knew I had a mystic bond with—a bond of blood, family, and spirit.

I listened with the attention and reverence as if I were sitting at the Pope's feet as Beulah and Nancy (mostly Beulah) described the Kanode family home, Hattie's boardinghouse. Great-grandmother Hattie not only cooked and cleaned; she not only guided and cared for her own children, but she also opened her home to Concord College students and served as a stand-in mother for those young people-- as much as they asked her to do, anyway, Beulah was careful to mention. Hattie Kanode didn't push herself on her borders, or pry into their lives so long as they were obeying the house rules and not breaking any local, state, or national laws.

That boarding house on the corner of Vermillion Street, at the entrance of Concord College, was the place to be back in the teens, twenties, thirties, and early forties, those little elderly ladies said. The Kanode house was a happening place when Beulah and Nancy grew up. In that faraway time, any given day might bring the smell of Hattie's pies and bread wafting onto the soft breeze blowing on the large front stoop. To the sound of jazz, swing, and big band dancing from the radio, college students sat in rockers on the steps, or in one of two porch swings, innocently flirting around with the opposite sex, or joking around with buddies and friends. In the middle of it, all were those Kanode kids: Lake telling jokes; Raymond throwing a football out in the yard; Romaine dangling out of a tree branch like a monkey; Elouise in a corner, reading a book; and CH, my granddad, there quietly overlooking it all. In my mind, he was just smiling the same way I saw him smile in pictures of him as an old man after his stroke. Only now, his smile hinted at no pain or hurt; just joy at life and amusement at his siblings and peers gathered around him.

The ladies didn't have much to say about my great-grandfather, the patriarch of all that lovable chaos in the house and on the front porch, Elbert the shoe cobbler. No one in the family had much to say about Elbert, either. Everyone from Beulah and Nancy to Grandmother and my dad liked and loved Elbert. They say he had a sweet spirit about him. He was just incredibly silent. He was an incredibly quiet, large man. His nickname was Big 'Un, and he repaired the town's shoes. That's all anyone ever said. That's all there was to say, I suppose. I bet Elbert shared his world with Hattie only. I bet Hattie could have written a novel about Elbert, and vice versa. No one but Hattie could have written a book about Elbert, though. He kept his soul, the essence of his being to himself, for Hattie alone.

When nearly an hour had passed, Beulah stopped midsentence. She had been describing the leathery scent of Kanode Shoe and Harness, Elbert's shop. "We better get you back out to that cemetery, young Kanode," she said. "Your people are probably out there, waiting for you.

So, they were. Charley had nearly pulled my car out by the time the little elderly ladies and I arrived. He had taken a big old chain, and he tied it to his enormous Ford F-150 and my Chevrolet Celebrity. Only Charley had come, so there were no other biological Kanodes to introduce to the ladies. Charley just winked

18

at me and rustled my hair. "Someday you are going to get into trouble really doing something fun, I hope, Jeffro. I hope I can bail you out then, too." I loved my brother-in-law Charley.

I loved those sisters. I said goodbye to them, and I hugged them, too. I never saw them again.

As much as my family's history and lore mean to me, I never made the time in subsequent years ever to go back to Beulah and Nancy's house again. I never went back to their house again, even though in the soft twinkling of the rising moon that night, the ladies invited me to "stop by any time." I never went back to their house again. I never spoke to either one of them again, even though I would spend several years of my life as a student at Concord College.

Somehow, I knew even at my didn't-know-a-thing-really age that my evening with those ladies—the stories, the images, the humanity, and the love they fleshed out for me about my family—was a singular event in my life. That holiness could never be relived or repeated. The same stories probably could have and would have been, though. So, I walked away. I walked away with my holy evening with my granddad, his siblings, and his parents, my great-grandparents forever in my mind.

I was, and am, thankful to Beulah and Nancy.

Other Rocks and Stones

We lived in a subdivision called Lilac Hills. When I was a little boy, Lilac Hills was as magical sounding a name as Walton's

Mountain on *The Waltons*, or Walnut Grove from *Little House on the Prairie*. It was just a neighborhood, probably indistinguishable from most other middle-class neighborhoods anywhere in America. The magic was all inside of me and my child's heart. In my heart and in my eyes, Lilac Hills *was* magical and perfect. Lilac Hills was my home.

Several factors made Lilac Hills, my home, the epitome of perfectness.

For a child, no home means anything—there's no beauty, there's no wonder there's no innocence—without loving parents dedicated to making that home a sanctuary of love and protection. In a true home, a child can be a child, growing and learning with safe eyes always looking upon them, and nurturing arms wrapped around them. With my parents, I had that in our little home in Lilac Hills.

For the first five years of my life, my mom didn't work. She stayed at home to take care of me. She had worked her heart out before—as a surgery technician, and she would work her heart out later—as a church secretary, as a physician's billing service. Those first years of my life, before I went to kindergarten, Momma worked her heart out taking care of me. I loved it.

I had two older sisters, so there was typical sibling competition in the house for time and attention. For those five golden years, during the day, I had Momma all to myself. I was, theoretically, an only child. I don't know that I have very many firm memories of that sweet season of my life, whole days blocked off and remembered from start to finish.

I don't know that I have very many concrete memories like that, or an ability to recall whole days, period. What I remember of most of my life, and what I remember from those first five years with Mom are short glimpses of time, bursting forth with spring sunshine and a feeling of love and contentment.

I remember watching *Sesame Street* and *Mister Rogers' Neighborhood* every morning and then going outside to play for hours and hours and hours. I remember going to a restaurant beside Kroger in Bluefield with Momma for breakfast once. That event was something really different and special because it still stands out. Just down the road from that little restaurant was a somewhat ominous edifice for me: the redbrick, A-frame building that was my pediatrician's office. How many times did Momma have to take me to that building? I was such a sick little kid.

Pneumonia, strep throat, and finally allergies, plagued my early years. Dr. Robertson was a black-haired man with a very dominant Adam's apple, and he always smelled of what I would identify much later in life as Aqua Velva aftershave. I never disliked Dr. Robertson, and I can never say I feared him, either. I guess I never disliked or feared him, because his nurses did all the evil stuff, like sticking a swab down my throat to test for strep. That was awful. I also always hated taking off my shirt — a lifelong hang-up with me — for the requisite heartbeat check and tummy press.

It's possible Momma took me to that restaurant in Bluefield immediately before or just after a doctor's appointment. I can't remember for sure. I remember the happiness of eating out with Momma, and the dread I always felt when I saw Dr. Robertson's office. The staff always gave you a sucker too, after every appointment. I was never a big enough sucker fan to coronate a cherry-flavored candy-on-a-stick with the power to redeem a visit from bad to good in my memory.

My memories with my momma were always good memories. We played outside until it was time for *The Young and the Restless* and *Days of Our Lives*. I played with my Matchbox cars and Hot Wheels cars while Victor Newman, Nikki, and Paul; Roman and Marlena Brady, Stefano DiMera, and Victor Kiriakis lived their lives somewhere on the screen far beyond either my comprehension or my interest. Momma watched over me and protected me. I can remember when Momma's mother, Frankie, came to visit us. I can remember visits from the annoying neighbor Sharon, who was a chain- smoker and a chronic gossip, with an emphysema sufferer's course laugh, which punctuated much of the gossip.

Occasionally, Momma would babysit two kids from our neighborhood, my best friends, Mandy and Heath. The story of Mandy, Heath, and Jeff is a fortuitous one. Mandy was born in March. I came along in May. Heath, or Heathey as we always called him, entered the world in September. Our parents all became pretty good friends after we were born, the way parents of neighborhood children do, almost by necessity. Really though, they were just casual neighbors, acquaintances at best, and certainly not a circle of friends so emotionally close they planned pregnancies together. Does anyone ever really do that? Oh, in those early years of life, the three of us — Mandy, Heathey, and I — lived in Eden. We would play with Matchbox and Hot Wheels cars. We played school down in the basement of my house, with each of us taking turns being the teacher. We played out on the hillside in my backyard, sometimes rolling each other down the steep, mossy hillside. At Halloween, we went trick-or-treating together. In the summertime, we went to Vacation Bible School together. We were just really close little friends.

One incident in my memory — which happened a year or two after the first five years of life which I have been describing — details in thumbnail what happened to Mandy, Heath, and me as we grew and evolved as young human beings. Heathey and I had these two identical riding toys. They were probably manufactured by Fisher-Price; I think they were officially called Moon Rovers. You sat on it, used your legs and feet, and drove around on it. It had a steering wheel, a gear shift, and four little tires. There was even a little storage compartment that opened up underneath the seat. Again, I am almost 100 percent sure they called those darned things Moon Rovers, but for some reason — only two little boys' imaginations knew, once upon a time—Heathey and I called ours our milk trucks.

Now, over thirty years later, to me, tooling around the concrete back porch on a Moon Rover pretending you are driving around on the moon is exponentially more dramatic and daring than pretending you are driving around town in your milk truck. I suppose Heathey and I were just imaginative realists in our budding young age. Even then, our child's minds knew the two of us were far more likely to drive milk trucks than moon rovers. So, milk trucks they were. And Mandy had her Big Wheel. Mandy on her Big Wheel, Heathey and Jeff driving their milk trucks: the three of us were quite the convoy, and the three of us had hours and hours and hours of fun, again, mostly riding on my parents' large concrete back porch.

The day I knew everything had changed and nothing would ever, could ever, be the same ever again between Mandy, Heath, and I was the day I was lugging around on my milk truck by myself. I looked up, and in the distance, on Heath's family's driveway, there Heath and Mandy were joyfully, skillfully, laughingly riding bicycles. My friends were riding real bona fide bicycles, sans training wheels, mind you, and there I remained...on the back porch...on my milk truck. I saw their happiness. I heard their laughter. I looked down at my feet propelling myself forward on my milk truck. I felt aloneness for the very first time in my life. I felt ashamed for the very first time in my life. I loathed myself for the very first time in my life. Those first years with Momma, though, were incredibly wonderful years. In the years that evolved out of those foundational years, Momma always remained a beautiful, constant presence of love in my life.

The other sacred touchstone and safe harbor in my life is Dad. Dad gets his own whole chapter later on in this book, so I won't say a great amount about him here. For now, I merely want to begin casting paint on the canvas to convey Dad as a positive, bright, colorful life force. The winds of Dad's spirit propel me through the sea to this day, and I believe they always will.

My two big sisters are also two incredibly important rocks in the foundation of my soul. Monica, like Dad, is light and energy, vibrancy and joy — all wrapped up in a tiny frame that stands just under five feet. She has these big brown eyes and Van Morrison's "Brown Eyed Girl" will always be my sister's song, to me. My sister Heather is quiet and reserved, a person of dignity and silent sensitivity. Heather loves words, and she teaches. Though she is quiet by nature, she is the funniest person in our family. Monica is our vibrant, efficient leader. I've always said that the day some tragedy befalls our family, Monica will be the one to pull everyone together, and she'll keep us together through the passage of years. Heather stays a step behind Monica, and even me, in a happy, frenetic family mob scene. Heather is our conscience, our moral heart.

Growing up with two older sisters was almost like growing up with three mothers. Momma was a good mother by herself and completely equal to—no, surpassing-- the expected tasks and duties of motherhood. Momma got help, though, in mothering me, from both my sisters.

Because there is twelve years' difference in our ages, Monica was the most maternal toward me. She was grown-up, married, and moved out when I was just seven years old. Heather and I are separated by six years, so I had ample opportunity to be the bratty little brother to her—and I played that role to perfection. Poor little Heather! When I was early grade school age, she was a young teenager. When I was bratty preteen age, she was in high school. Our age gap made it perfectly possible for me to be the perfect epitome of the younger, annoying little brother. From decapitating dolls to trashing the dollhouse, I guiltily, with gusto, did it. From terrorizing her slumber parties with friends to using her waterbed as a trampoline, I was a horrid little snot sometimes to Sister Heather. Still, she loved me. Both my sisters love me. I love them completely.

I have gotten pieces of humanity from both my sisters. Monica's positivity and compassion are infectious. Many people who know us both have said we have the same personality, and even the same mannerisms when we talk, like pinching up our noses. As the years have gone by, no one next to my mom and dad has probably done more for me, lovingly and selflessly, than my sissy Monica. From helping take care of me when I was sick, and Mom had to work back when I was a child, to giving me, literally, all the furniture I have ever owned and lugged to all my Methodist parsonages I have lived in, Monica has been there. She and her husband, Charley, had their first child when I was in ninth grade, and they had their second the summer between my high school graduation and freshman year of college. Seeing Monica as a mother added an entirely new dimension to her personhood and my love and admiration for her. Witnessing her reading to Devon, her daughter, and watching her playing with Zachary, her son, I could see motherhood was a role and a life my sister cherished in a warm embrace.

Devon and Zachary's existence added layers to my own understanding and embrace of life and family. My niece and my nephew taught me how love deepens, and how bonds of blood and biology strengthen a human connection like nothing else can. I will try to explain. I instantly loved both Devon and Zach for who they are as people. As soon as Devon could talk, she spoke in this laborious Southern twang so cute, so pure, so seemingly primordial and untaught. Of course, I loved her from the moment I laid eyes on her in the nursery at the hospital, as I saw my little niece as she lay there, complete with dimply cheeks and wisps of blonde hair.

When she started talking, though, and that unique personality started blooming, I had an awakening: I loved Devon for all of herself, which was unique and new to the world. I could also detect whispers, reflections, pieces of my sister within Devon. It was then that I had my epiphany: I loved Devon for who she was and is. That love is authentic and lasting on its own. I also love Devon for the parts of my beloved sister I see living on within her. That makes my love for Devon a twofold love: I love Devon for Devon; I love Devon for echoes and flashes of Monica, who lives on in Devon, my eldest sissy's little girl.

The same can be said for my little nephew Zachary, who physically resembles his mother in ways not even her daughter does. Zachary has always lived in his own happy little world, the world of a boy: a messy world of muddy shoes and a trail of crumbs you can use to retrace all of his steps around the house. I love being "Uncle Jeffy" to Devon and Zachary. I love them for who they are. I love them for whom they resemble, whom they reflect, whose spirit carries on within them, body and heart.

I am a reader, a writer, a lover of words. I think much of that love surely comes from my sister Heather. Heather was writing poetry since the days I would raid her diary while she was at work slinging stinky toppings onto pizza at one of our local pizza joints. Heather's love for words would lead her to major in English and teacher education at Concord College. Heather was a reader, a writer, and a lover of words long before me. Not only did I follow my sister in becoming a voracious reader, a writer, a lover of words; I also followed her right up to the steps into academic walls of Concord College. While I didn't go the teacher education route,

I sure did earn a degree in English, just like my sissy.

Monica married Charley. Heather married Jeff. My brothers-in-law are integral parts of me too.

I was only seven years old when Monica and Charley married in August of 1985. They had dated through most of their high school years as well, which means Charley was a part of my familial surroundings when I was three, four years old. I don't ever remember meeting Charley. Charley has just always been there. He truly has always been there, too. Charley once drove three and a half hours to help me when my car was broken down when I was a student at Duke. That's only one example, the most extreme example, of how Charley has been there for me over so many years. He has been, he is, a brother to me.

My love of American stock car racing, NASCAR, came as a gift from Charley. When he came to the house on Sunday afternoons to see Monica when they were dating, Charley would turn on "the race." I fell in love with the driving personalities, the colorful cars, the roaring engines, the crowds, the living drama of racing, all because of Charley. Early on in my life, before I can even remember, and to this day, Charley is my brother. Charley is my bud.

Heather's Jeff epitomizes cool. They were married in 1993 or 1994 when I was in high school. They dated for a few years first too, so Jeff has been a part of our family, and a part of my life for a good chunk of that life. Technically, I have much more in common with Jeff than I do Charley. Jeff is a writer: he has worked as a newspaper reporter, columnist, and editor for years. His wit is abrasive and hilarious. His politics are conservative. We get into many debates, but we keep it civil and friendly. Jeff is my brother too. I love the guy, just as I love Charley. Jeff has always made humble, sweet Heather happy. If I couldn't stand the guy, I would love him for loving my sister and being good to her. It's extra grace that he's an interesting, intelligent, cool guy I really relate to and am happy to be around.

The last foundation of my life is not a person, but a part of the earth, a place, a mythic, looming place.

East River Mountain forms the border of Mercer County, West Virginia, with Tazewell and Giles County, Virginia. The big mountain posed a formidable obstacle to travel…The highest elevation along the Mercer County line is at Buckhorn Knob, 4,069 feet. Standing on the crest of East River Mountain, one may observe the parallel folds of the long, high mountains and wide valleys of the Ridge and Valley Province of Virginia to the southeast, a contrast to the Allegheny Plateau in West Virginia to the northwest with broad, flat summits and winding streams. (Raymond Thomas Hill, *The West Virginia Encyclopedia*)

That big blue mountain cradles both Princeton and Bluefield. That big blue mountain was always just above me, always right there, in the eastern sky, wherever I would go. At the playground in the summer, the mountain loomed. At my grandmother's house at Thanksgiving in the bleakness of November, the mountain loomed, still so blue in the distance, like in summer's height, though all the life of trees was dead. Winter's snow and frigid slaps of wind, spring's rains, and blossoming life all happened within the eternal clasp of her hands. She was like another guardian to me. She has cradled me my entire life, old East River Mountain.

I have lived most of my adult life away from my Princeton-Bluefield boyhood home. My work in the church has led me away, and the interstate always carries me back. There's another mountain, one called Flat Top, just outside of Beckley. The highway ascending and descending Flat Top can be a challenging stretch of road many travelers dread, but I adore it. I adore it because on the crest of Flat Top, if it's a clear day with no rain or fog, I can look straight outside my windshield, and I see it. It's the mountain mother, the Allegheny giant who could pass for one of her cousins in the Blue Ridge. It's my mountain, who forever watches over and holds close the land, and the people I cherish. It's sweet East River Mountain.

If I live to be in my nineties, like a dear old gentleman in my church now whom I love so much, I will still be standing on these rocks, these living stones, to borrow from Peter's first epistle. These will forever be the foundation of who I am, and who I will ever evolve to be.

2 The Calling

Every pastor can tell the story of their calling. Every pastor can tell the story of when they knew, beyond human doubt, God wanted them to dedicate their lives completely to the love of Christ in ministry. Every pastor can tell the story of when they knew Christ was calling them to follow, not just as Christians, but following in living completely for Christ, as pastors. Pastors are themselves very much little "suffering servants," to borrow from Isaiah, suffering servants living each day in the shadow of the cross, animated and directed by the self-giving love of Christ.

I call your attention to the word *ideal*. The ideal of Christian ministry, the ideal of the pastoral vocation, is to live a life reflecting the life of Jesus. The ideal pastor lets Christ live anew within her heart, within his words, within her actions, within his deeds. One could argue every Christian is called in baptism to lead such a Christ-centered, Christ-empowered life. One would be correct. No other Christian, though, dares to make such a life not only a matter of conscience or foundation, but the defining piece of their personhood, vocation, and lifestyle. That's the human being called pastor. That's the Christian called, and ordained, pastor.

I have never heard the voice of God. I know some folks say they have. I don't doubt them. I just wonder why God would let some people actually hear a real voice and let the rest of us just grope around merely on feelings, instincts, and gut. That is how

God has always communicated with me—on the real guttural, intuitive, heart level.

A question I have always wanted to ask someone who says they have heard the actual voice of God is, "What does the actual voice of God sound like?" I certainly don't want to miss it. I fear I may have been missing it all these years. I suspect if I did ever ask that question of someone who proclaims to have conversations with God, I would learn God has a deep, manly baritone voice. That, in and of itself, makes me highly suspicious. A baritone God-voice is almost as atrocious to me as all the blue-eyed Jesus paintings hanging up all over so many churches across America. He just didn't *look* like that. I don't think the First Person of the Trinity *sounds* like that, either.

As a guy with a forever high-pitched voice, I have always taken such pride, even comfort, in the sounds of Jack and Bobby Kennedy's tenor voices, to say nothing of Winston Churchill's squeakiness. The greatest of all though, is the plethora of written accounts reporting Abraham Lincoln had a voice thick with twang, vibrating with highness. Naturally then, I hear God the Father speaking in the voice of a Kennedy. Maybe the voice I hear isn't New England, but it certainly is high.

No, I have never heard the voice of God. I may be tempted to ask my doctor to up my antidepressant dosage if I ever thought I did. I do feel incredibly close to God. Like any relationship, like anything in life requiring cultivation and growth, I am not satisfied with where I am with God. I need to do better. I need to love more fully. I need to serve more energetically. I need to feel more of God's peace and less of my anxiety. I am realistic enough to know I will still be working all of that out someday when I am sitting in my room, alone in a nursing home somewhere, waiting either for a pretty nurse to come by and give me my meds or for a male orderly to wheel me to chapel or bingo.

I feel I am close to God, though. I feel like God and Jeff are indeed friends. I feel my life has been directed, even characterized, by a fairly natural, close relationship with God. No, I have not heard my divine friend's actual voice, and I am grateful for that. I would be disillusioned beyond description if that voice would indeed be a bass or a baritone. I am in tune with God in other more imaginative ways than the rather obvious way of hearing a voice.

I feel God called me into ministry when I was thirteen years old. The exact moment was rather mundane. I was not on a Boy Scout hiking trip thousands of feet up high on some pristine mountain, kissing the lowest reaches of heaven. I was not locked up in the bathroom, attempting suicide with a razor until I dramatically felt God freezing my actions, immediately saving me, body and soul. I was not at some high-intensity youth revival with a praise band and a charismatic young speaker with tattoos, giving a clarion call for Christian service. No. I was in my regular pew of my regular church, sitting with my regular parents on a regular Sunday.

It was in the late spring, early summer, those last sacred days of June when the season of new life becomes the season of that life radiating in heat and drowning in light. West Virginia is at its most beautiful then. All the mountains and hills were vibrantly alive with green. The meadows were bursting with life, from wildflowers to tall grass to buzzing bees. My soul was coming to life, too.

Listening to the pastor preach his sermon that sweet summer morning, I remember just looking up at him, looking up at the pulpit, and thinking, *That is what you are supposed to do with your life. That is what you are going to do with your life. That will be you someday.* In an instant, I saw thousands of Sunday morning sermons with me standing behind a pulpit, a congregation stretching before me. Of course, in every vision, in every flash, I remained my thirteen-year-old self behind that pulpit. I didn't see in my vision glimpses of the Rosacea scarred, thinning-haired young man I evolved to be, who would actually preach all those sermons.

I remember being awed by a tremendous sense of peace. *This is who you are. You are mine.* I knew then the stress, the confusion, the conflict of the teenaged years might get me down, but they weren't going to kill me. I knew, ultimately, where God was going to lead me. I just had to survive to get there.

Later that evening, I attended a picnic at our local park with the church youth group. It was a gorgeous evening, and I was happy. Usually, such social events freaked me out and left me feeling alone, emotionally exhausted and done. On this night, however, I felt really good. I interacted easily with my peers. Around a campfire, as the setting sun blazed crimson all over the western sky, I whispered to the pastor I had felt God calling me to be a minister. I told him it had happened during his sermon that very morning.

At this point, an important detail may need clarification. What exactly was the thesis of that sermon? From which passage of scripture did it emerge? I have no earthly idea. I have no recollection at all. Any memory of it may have been lost to my mind by that afternoon. The pastor, himself a pretty young man early in his own ministry, was thrilled at my news. A young kid in his church feeling "the call" under his pastoral care would be "a feather in his cap," to use a well-worn cliché.

I'm not at all pleased with what happened in the immediate aftermath of my announcing I felt God wanted me to be a pastor. At the time, everything that happened felt natural and good, but with the hindsight of some age, I question how healthy it was how events evolved. In short, I got put to work. Later that summer, I was preaching my first sermon at the church when the pastor went on vacation. I had long served as a volunteer at our local Salvation Army, and I was asked to fill that pulpit one Sunday, too. Within the year, I had completed the United Methodist lay speaker course, and I became — in the language of our denomination — a certified lay speaker. I was all of fourteen years old. It was all too much, too soon. I went from being an alienated, poetic, geeky little kid, to becoming an alienated, poetic, geeky little preacher-kid. For my healthy growth and development, I needed to be a normal little teen. That wasn't happening. It wasn't going to happen.

I don't want to dramatize the hurt of my teen years. Who doesn't suffer during that time of life? I don't know if I suffered more or less than you or anyone else. I just know what I went through and how what I went through made me feel. I also know the result of what I went through. I know what it did to me: my spirit, my mind, my sense of self and the world. I also know who I became as a result of what I went through.

I was different from all the other kids, that's for sure. Of course, we are all different. I guess our differences are magnified within ourselves, making our sense of *I am so much different* so much more pronounced. For me though, I had a couple of things going for me, or against me, depending on your perspective. First, I had my high, squeaky voice, which really started standing out when I was thirteen or fourteen years old, because so many of my peers were already baritone or bass with the dark line of mustaches already forming under their noses. I just kept nervously squeaking my way through life while my peers sang the low notes on The Oak Ridge Boys' "Elvira" when we sang it for the junior high spring concert.

Second, from probably around age eleven, I suffered from acne. I didn't just have a few blemishes here and there--you know, normal people acne. No, I had severe cystic acne. I didn't just get pimples, zits, or bumps (whatever you feel most cultured calling them). I got cysts. I didn't just get a zit on the tip of my nose. I got a cyst completely covering my nose. I didn't just have a little rash of little baby pimples on my cheeks. I got damn swollen, red, awful tumor-like things covering all of my cheeks. It truly was awful. There are pictures of me from that time period, which, to this day, are painful for me to see. Mom and Dad took me to a Garth Brooks concert at the West Virginia State Fair, and there I sit, in my little Garth Brooks t-shirt, a toothy, metal braces-filled grin on my face — a face which just looked like it hurt. It did hurt. My heart hurt worse.

The absolute worst experience of my teen years occurred one day in junior high school, in September. It was still summer-heat hot outside. Dad and I had just been to the NASCAR race in Martinsville, Virginia. With Dad, my ultimate hero, I screamed and yelled and cheered all day long for my other hero, Dale Earnhardt. Dale didn't win that Sunday. He ran second, as I recall. Harry Gant won. The trophy for winning a NASCAR race at Martinsville Speedway is, to this day, a beautiful grandfather clock made in the furniture factories of Martinsville and Basset. So Handsome Harry won his fourth-straight race that sun-drenched Sunday (tying a modern-day NASCAR record), and Harry won a

Virginia- made grandfather clock as his trophy. My trophy was a very intense sunburn. Throughout the day, Dad kept encouraging me to put on more sunscreen. I pretended to do it, but I didn't use much because I assumed the hot southern sun would help burn off my painful hormonal legions. My face was pretty red. The next morning, Monday morning, school day, my face was still acne-scarred. It was also sunburned and blistered. It felt awful. It looked worse.

In first period that day, I was to endure the worst bullying of my life. I was used to being called *faggot* by rednecks in Rebel flag shirts and skintight blue jeans bulging in the rear pocket with Copenhagen cans. Most of the time those taunts were in passing, like in the hallway between classes, or sitting in the bleachers before class started each morning. I could ignore those. I mean, I didn't ignore them. I heard them all, each time. They cut my heart to pieces. I didn't have to let on like I had heard though. I gained a little bit of victory. I retained a little bit of dignity in acting like I hadn't heard or engaging in the dramatization that if I had heard, acting like it didn't bother me enough to react. This time though, on that Monday morning after Martinsville, the picking was direct. The bullying was straight in my face. There was no running away from it. There was no pretending like I hadn't heard it. This bullying had witnesses — many, many witnesses.

One witness bothered me more than all of the others combined. The belittling was in front of a pretty girl. I happened

39

to have a crush on this pretty girl.

There was no walking on. There was no putting my head down, walking fast to the next class. This guy was there, right there in front of me, like a demon throwing flames of burning fire into my vulnerable defenses, which were already crumbling within the pressure of his horrible heat. I never ever crumbled completely. I always stayed strong enough to keep on fighting to stay alive. This was the closest I ever came though, to complete and utter surrender. This was the closest the brokenness, the darkness of this world, the brokenness, the darkness within the soul, came to completely ending me.

His name was Scott. Later in my life, I would meet great people named Scott who are wonderful friends. For a long time though, I loathed that name. This Scott, from my junior high school, was much older than typical junior high age. We were all thirteen or fourteen years old in this eighth grade West Virginia history class. Scott had to be every bit of sixteen or seventeen. Two years isn't a great age gap at all later in life, but in those developmental teen years, it's not a gap. It's a chasm! Much, much, much goes on between the near side of that cliff and the far side!

Scott had a beard. I don't mean he had peach fuzz like most of us guys were starting to sprout back then. This boy had a beard. He had a lather-up-the-shaving-cream, get-out-the-Norelco beard. Rumor had it that he had a car too. They wouldn't allow him a parking pass on the school grounds—a junior high school just didn't have a parking policy for students like a high school did. There was an "opportunity workshop" for special needs people down below our school, and Scott reportedly parked his car there. He would smoke a cigarette on his walk from his car up to the school. Now this, I did witness for myself. On multiple occasions already in the still young school year, I had seen Scott walking up the sidewalk toward the school, smoking a cigarette. I figured the car gossip really was true.

Bearded, driving, smoking Scott didn't talk so much as he groaned. He scared me. As I sit here and write this, I am a young man who just turned forty. I have been respectfully successful in my adult life. I am an ordained pastor. I have a master's degree from a prestigious university (Duke, the Harvard of the south. Or as we liked to say in Durham, Harvard--the Duke of the Yankees). I have published a book. I earned a doctorate. I fell in love with a beautiful, humane lady and she even fell in love with me too and we are married. And if I saw that Scott today — even today — he would still scare the ever-loving horse hockey out of me. I wonder if he is still alive? I wonder if he reads? I wonder if he is still alive, having not ever died in a gang fight? I wonder if he reads, and if he does read, I wonder if he remembers me? If he does read, and if he remembers me, I wonder if he will remember my name? If he does read, and if he does remember my name, I wonder if he will he ever stumble upon a copy of this book? If he does read, and if he does remember my name, and if he ever stumbles upon a copy

41

of this book, I wonder if he will take the time to read to read the book up to these pages and stumble upon his own name. Oh, Lord. Sweet, holy God, your loving protection I beseech thee for.

My hands are shaking now. I can feel sweat forming on my brow and rushing down my armpits. I am certain he is still alive. I feel equally as certain, though, he has been incarcerated for at least a decade. They wouldn't carry this kind of book in prison, I don't think. I am going to keep on writing about him. I don't think he will be up for parole before... Pen names. It worked for Sam Clemons.

The little girl I had a crush on in my first period West Virginia history class was named Stephanie. She was so quiet and so smart and, oh yeah, so pretty. Shy as I was, I would talk to her. I would force myself to speak to her. I just had to — love was worth the risk of awkward stuttering and embarrassment. On this day then, first thing in the morning, first thing in class, I was talking to my girl Stephanie. We were merely making easy small talk.

I said something witty, and she laughed.

My palms grew all sweaty. My heart was beating fast. My brain was churning even faster than my heart, trying to come up with the next cutesy little thing that would make my little auburn-haired beauty laugh, or at least smile.

Then suddenly, I heard it. The groan.

It was him.

It was Scott.

Jesus.

I offer that holy of all names right now just as I did that morning so long ago, not as a swear, but as a prayer.

"Oh, Jesus."

He towered over me. I could smell the cigarettes and the chewing tobacco on his breath. He had more stubble than my dad or my brother-in-law. Within his groans, I could make out the words.

"God, you ugly freaky faggot, what is that on your face? It looks like you fucking sneezed on your face, and there is snot all on your cheek. God, man, leave this poor girl alone and go wipe your face off. She'll sure as hell be glad. We all will!" I felt as if my entire face was going to burn off with embarrassment, shame, and yes, hate. I knew what Scott was talking about. It was the blister on my sunburn. Maybe it had busted. Crap, I did feel moisture on my cheek. He was talking like that to me in front of a girl I liked. He was talking like that to me — period. He was standing, looming over my desk. This wasn't just taunts passing me by in the hall. There was nowhere for me to go. There was nowhere for me to hide. I was in front of the entire class, and most importantly, I was in front of Stephanie. I was being belittled. I was being attacked. I was being bullied. I was being burned alive. I was being destroyed in front of the entire class, in front of *her*. And there was nowhere for me to hide.

He kept groaning at me. I could understand a few words

here and there. The longer Scott groaned, the more incomprehensible he became. I glanced over at Stephanie once. Her little brown eyes were round, wide, and red, like she was fighting back tears.

"I am going to buy you a pack of fucking Clearasil and sit down on your damn chest and put it on you, you damn ugly freak," he said. "I am going to buy you some Clearasil and smear it all over your ugly fucking face."

If I could have taken pills, or shot myself in that moment, I would have. I didn't have access to a quick, easy way out, though. I did have a girl I had a crush on, sitting beside me. Despite my nerdy demeanor, despite how beaten down I was in the pecking order of that school, I did have my pride. I did have my dignity. My voice may have squeaked the words, but dammit, as sure as the sun still shines on this planet, I spoke the words.

"That's fine, Scott. You buy me the Clearasil now. Someday, when I am a famous writer or United States senator, I will pay for your plastic surgery."

More people were listening to this conversation than just my little brown-eyed crush. I heard quite a few oohs all around in the class.

Scott's face turned a murderous glare I had never seen before and, thankfully, haven't seen since. He pursed up his nose and pinched his mouth in an ungodly, inhuman way. I could see him making a fist, and I closed my eyes. I knew I was going to die. Just when I could intuitively feel his fist almost bearing down on me, I heard another voice. "Scott, what the hell are you doing? Leave Kanode alone and get in your damn seat."

It was Mr. Bennett. I didn't like Mr. Bennett at all. He was old and bald. He was cranky and curmudgeonly. He wasn't at all friendly toward me. He wasn't at all nice to me. But he saved my life that day. God, I loved that old man. Scott groaned and walked away. I lived to write this to you. I never did get a date with Stephanie, but I lived to write this to you.

I that particular vignette with you in order for you to have some understanding of what my teenage years were like, the character of the context of my call. I was a lonely, acne-scarred, high-pitched voice, lost little teenager. My parents loved me, and I had a good, loving family and home. At school though, I was a little lamb, easy prey for the ravenous wolves who roamed those halls, the home of the Glendale Wildcats.

My life could have turned in many different directions. I suppose that is true of all of our lives. In examining my own life with some degree of self-consciousness and a self- critical analysis, I believe two things saved my life: words and the church. Those two things *saved* my life; those two things *became* my life.

My love of words ties into my calling. I always loved words, and I always read voraciously. One of my favorite moments in church was when the pastor read the morning scripture. When he did (and all of our pastors in my boyhood happened to be male), I would often close my eyes, and I would see the stories. I would hear the poetic music of the words. I used to love hearing the scripture read out loud, especially the ancient words of the Old Testament, and the gentle words of Christ in the Gospels.

I began writing stories at a very young age. The first full-length narrative I can remember ever having tried to produce was a very terrible synopsis/rip-off of the movie *Eddie and the Cruisers*. I loved that movie, and cheesy as it is, I still do. Something about the mystery of that plot captivated my imagination. Did he really die? Is he still alive? Oh my gosh, is that Eddie? Is that him in the storefront window, watching a documentary on himself?

My next memorable piece of writing was for a contest we have in West Virginia called Young Writer's Week. I was in fifth grade, and I wrote the story my great-grandmother, Pearl, or Mama as we called her, told me about when her husband, my great-grandfather Walter, was missing in action in World War I. Even at that young age, I was pretty frisky and precocious as a writer. I took all kinds of liberties with that well-worn, more than a twice-told little piece of family lore. I changed World War I to World War II. I changed 1918 to 1943.

In truth, ole Walter got knocked senseless when a German bullet hit him in his hardhat (To be sure, had he not been wearing that helmet, he would have been dead). The Germans found him before American medics did. In my little tale, Great-Grandpa had jumped in front of a Panzer in Sicily to carry a fallen comrade out of harm's way. His leg got caught up in the Panzer's path, and he was knocked unconscious. Taken for dead by both German and Americans, Walter was taken in by a Sicilian priest who nursed him back to health.

In reality, my great-grandmother received a letter from the American Red Cross telling her they had found her husband in a German prison camp: He was alive and well! That just wasn't dramatic enough for me, so in my fifth- grader's prose, on a cold, wintry night, with freezing rain beating the earth below to a pulp, my mama heard a noise on her front porch. She got out of bed, and rushed downstairs to see what varmint or prowler could be disturbing her peace. When she opened the front door — cue the orchestra! — there was Walter, emaciated and spent, but alive and well. There was Walter, in his American soldier uniform, standing there, dripping wet and cold before his beloved Pearl.

My story won Young Writer's Week, at least for my home county. It got overwhelmed by the competition, I guess, upstate. Mama was not impressed with my version of her story. She took a red pen and corrected all the inaccuracies, just for the record. That really hurt my feelings, but I can see now why an eighty-something-year-old wanted an important story from her and her husband's life to be remembered by the family correctly. Nor was the little children's magazine I sent it to for publication impressed either. Yes! I was attempting to be published even as a ten-year-old.

I came pretty darn close that first maiden voyage into the universe of writing for mass publication. It would take me many, many years to get as far in "the game" as I got when I was ten. An editor called me.

"Is this story true, young man?" she asked.

My mind kicked hard into overdrive. *What is the right answer?* Never mind the truth. What was the answer she wanted?

I stuttered and stumbled, "Y-y-yeah, it's a true story." I decided on the truth. Surely a children's magazine, expressly Christian, would want their stories to be true, right?

"Oh, well we cannot accept true stories for our publication. Only fiction."

"Wait! Wait! Wait! I made most of it up! I mean, it did sort of happen to my mama and my great-grandfather, but I lied about almost all of it! I changed the year. I changed the war. It could pass as fiction! My mama doesn't like or recognize most of it, and it's her life!"

My first editor was not impressed. I can't remember whether she wished me well before she hung up or not.

My junior high didn't offer anything to let a student like me shine. There wasn't a school newspaper. There wasn't a creative writing club. The only real recognition and joy I received in junior high was when we read *Rome and Juliet* in ninth grade. The teacher asked us to write a new ending for the play, the way we thought it should have ended. I can't remember exactly how I changed

48

Shakespeare's immortal climax and resolution to suit me. I just remember: a) nobody died, b) there was at least the allusion to "happily ever after," and c) my teacher lifted my work up as the best in the class. It was a very under-achieving class – I think I was the only pupil who hadn't simply scratched out a few simple lines of dialogue on tear-out notebook paper a few stressful minutes before class

My little creation was overall really well received by my peers. The teacher even asked several students in the class to do a reading of my work. It was the first time I had ever heard words I had created being read and breathed with life by someone else, and I found the experience profoundly moving. Over the years, a recurring dream of mine has been to enter politics – not as a candidate myself, but as a speechwriter.I don't want to be the person pressing the flesh, waving at parades, facing the cameras, or debating the issues. I'd love to be the person giving that person the words, though. I've thought it would be amazing to be Teddy Sorenson; I just need to find my Jack Kennedy. That *Romeo and Juliet* re-write experience was the high point of three years for me, and it happened late in the mid-spring of my last year in junior high. I've always been a late bloomer.

The high school years were much better to me than the junior high ones. Of course, within the immortal melody of the Beatles song "Getting Better," Paul McCartney wrote, "Yes I admit, it's getting better all the time," to which John Lennon just had to add the dose of realism, "It can't get no worse." That's how it was for me. High school was much better than junior high, but really, short of a nervous breakdown or suicide, it couldn't have gotten any worse.

I was a geeky little guy whom the girls looked to like a cute little brother, never as a potential boyfriend. I was a nerdy little dude all the jocks, and all the rednecks alike liked because I was quietly friendly to them, and certainly no threat to them and their kingdoms of ladies and bros, testosterone drenched ballgames and pick-up trucks. I was a friend to the preps. I was a friend to the hippies. They loved me in class and in the hallways, but the love ended on Friday afternoons. I was never invited to the hangouts or the parties. I was never included in the concert trips, to the cruising or to the mall. I had countless friends, but no real friends. I was embraced by all cliques and groups, but I had no group, no clique to call my own. Friday night found me visiting my grandmother. Saturday night found me at home with my mom and dad, watching, *Dr. Quinn, Medicine Woman*.

Geek that I was, nerd whom I was, there was one little niche, there was one little corner, there was one little cubby hole that belonged to me, a place in the school where I was in a class all by myself. I was the undisputed prince on the *Tiger Tribune*, our high school student newspaper.

The school newspaper gave me an outlet to express my humanity when I was in high school. Otherwise, I would have been a kid sitting in the corner of every class, every period, alone, silent, lost in the world of my own thoughts since the real world wasn't giving me much of a chance to thrive. The little newspaper staff did give me a place to thrive when I was in high school. I didn't have to fight mentally to survive, to want to stay alive, the way I had in junior high.

We were a good little newspaper, and we were an extremely competitive one, too. Our teacher registered us to compete in the state conference of high school newspapers sponsored by the journalism department of Marshall University. We cleaned up all three years of my high school career! I cleaned up too. For three straight years, I won first place in feature writing and column writing. I even got some second places and one first place for straight news writing too. I report my success on my high school newspaper staff not to brag — dear Lord in heaven, that was twenty years ago now — but to give you that piece of my personal narrative. Words were my safe haven. Writing was what kept me alive.

I wasn't a huge somebody or an extremely prominent somebody in high school, but I was made to feel like I did belong. I was made to believe I did contribute something to the life of that school through my work on the school newspaper. My teachers and my fellow students alike complimented me and thanked me for articles and columns I wrote. I mattered. My life meant something to the community. Just a few years before, it hadn't.

When I was in junior high, with spit wads and "loogies" spit into my hair on a daily basis, my life didn't seem to mean much to those around me, and it certainly was coming to not mean much to me. In high school, that changed. Words saved me. The Word, Jesus, saved me.

The power of words and my love for words became integral to my Christian faith, as well. In church, Sunday after Sunday, it was the words I was most drawn to, in wonder. Oh, I loved the hymns and the choir anthems. I loved the ritualized moments like the acolytes bringing the flame to the candles. I loved the constancy of the order of worship, which never changed week to week when so much else in the world, and in the world of my own life and body, changed daily. The words, though, were the most sacred things in the service to me. I loved to hear the ancient words of scripture read. I loved to hear the words of the sermons. I loved to hear the historic words of the creeds. I don't think it was an accident that God called me to ministry through the words of the sermon. The spoken word, which was also written words, in the pastor's manuscript, made me feel God's call. It wasn't a hymn. It wasn't a praise song. It wasn't even a sacrament, though I cherish the broken bread and one cup of Holy Communion, and the eternal waters of baptism. God called me through words.

I mentioned earlier I felt the church did me something of a disservice, regarding my own emotional and spiritual growth and development, by asking me to preach so soon after I had articulated my sensing God's call to ministry. I tried to do my own work in slowing the process down. By the time I got to high school, I didn't tell anyone I wanted to be a pastor. My life's ambition I would share with people was always to be a writer. Still, somehow, word got out into the student body that I was going to be a pastor. I can remember my fellow students asking me for help and wanting little counseling sessions. Once even old Stephanie — my eighth-grade crush — came to me, wanting sage Christian wisdom. That was hard. She wasn't articulating a desire to go out or even to hang out. She just needed some "Jesus help."

I didn't really want my peers to know I was going to be a pastor for that very reason. I didn't want Stephanie or any other pretty girl to see me as a pastor. I wanted them to see me as a guy. I wanted them to see me as a guy they could potentially maybe go out with if they were lonely and desperate and needy enough. I was geeky enough as it was. I didn't need my classmates to lift me up like some kind of little high school pope. I just wanted to fit in. I just wanted to have fun. I just wanted to hang out. I just wanted to date. I just wanted to be a normal teenager. I especially wanted to get away from Mom and Dad and Dr. Quinn on Saturday nights.

Despite the fact I didn't publicize the fact I was going to be a pastor, and even though I often resented people knowing that about me, the climax of my high school life occurred because my fellow students did see me as a young little pastor in their midst. My fellow students asked me to be the baccalaureate, religious speaker, at our graduation. I was so overwhelmed. I was so honored. I am still awed by how it all happened, and I still rank it as one of the coolest things I have ever gotten to do in my life. I used Jesus's words from John, "Greater love has no one than this than to lay down one's life for one's friends." I built my little speech on the idea that when we are true friends to someone, we are following Christ, whether we are even aware of it or not. I equated being a true friend to being a truly good person.

My little speech got a standing ovation. It was a special moment of beauty in my life. I don't have any specific memories of it. It was such an intense time, the singular memories have all somehow melted together to form just a unified memory of a feeling, really. I do remember it happened though. I am grateful it did.

Throughout my senior year in high school, my classmates were all abuzz about the various colleges they were applying to and then getting accepted to attend. Most of my peers were WVU bound. A few went to more prestigious places like Wake Forest, or Sarah Lawrence College. We had some to go to Marshall and Virginia Tech. There are several colleges though, just within driving distance of our hometown. One of them, Concord, had a wonderful reputation as being one of the best, if not the best, small public college in our state. Concord also happened to be my family's college. My granddad, as you recall, grew up just outside the gate of the school in Athens. My grandmother got her teaching degree there. My sister Heather got her teaching degree there, too.

I was drawn to Concord for very familiar, familial reasons. I was also drawn to it because it was only thirty minutes from home. Concord College was my way to go to college and still live at home with my mom and dad. When I was eighteen years old, I was in no way mature enough to leave home. Emotionally, I had no desire to leave home yet.

In retrospect, I wonder if my maturation into adulthood would have been speedier with less pain for me in my later years if I had forced myself to leave home when I was just out of high school. So much of the growing up most people do in their late teen years, as they live in dorms far away from mom and dad's house, I had to do when I was much older: in seminary in my early twenties, and in the parish as a pastor in my mid-twenties. I think I may have been better off intellectually, socially, and professionally if I had left home right out of high school. That thought, that possibility, just wasn't in my mind or my spirit at the time. It wasn't in my parents' consciousness, either. I don't think it ever dawned on them I would want or should even endeavor to leave home for college. I guess they assumed I would leave home soon enough, someday. They wanted to keep me home, safe and sound, for as long as they could. I don't blame them.

I didn't get much growing up in my college years, then. Socially, college was no different for me than high school was. I went to class. I came home to my parents. In my last year of college,

I was going out here and there with a girl, so that was something of growth. I didn't see as much *Dr. Quinn, Medicine Woman* that last year of Concord. Again though, what I was doing as a college senior — taking a pretty girl out a few times a month for dinner and a movie — most of my peers had been doing since early on in high school.

While my undergraduate college life lacked much personal and social growth, I believe I was wealthy beyond good luck in how I evolved academically. Intellectually, Concord was a rich feast. The consumption of that feast though, the eating up of all that food, which was totally new to me, did come at a huge cost to something very dear to my heart, something completely integral to my very identity. The banquet of college coursework left my faith shaken and bleeding.

I entered Concord still pretty sure God had called me to be a pastor. Like in high school, however, I wasn't going to advertise the fact. In the United Methodist church, fully ordained pastors have to have an undergraduate degree. The degree could be in anything, theoretically. Many would-be pastors majored in religion in their undergraduate careers.

Concord didn't have a religious studies program, but it wouldn't have mattered to me if it had. I was determined I was going to use my undergraduate years doing what I loved doing the most — writing. I was determined my first four years of college would broaden whatever skill I had and deepen whatever talent I possessed as a writer. Also, because I loved history, I wanted to study it more extensively. I declared as a double-major. I would earn degrees in English and history. I would spend four years reading great literature and then write about it. I would spend four years reading American and world history and use what I was learning to help make my writing more realistic and grounded.

Before I could get to classes on the Lost Generation novelists and the Beat Poets, before I could earn a seat in an advanced class on the American Civil War and Reconstruction Era, I had to get through all the entry-level courses and general studies classes everyone was required to take. I had earned a year's worth of Advanced Placement credit in high school, so I entered my English and history classes as a sophomore. I still had to take World History 101 though.

In the science and math department, I entered the hallowed halls of higher learning at total bonehead status. I always got A's in the classes I loved (English and social studies), but my practice had always been to just do enough to survive the classes I didn't care for (all math and all sciences). I got my share of Cs in high school math and science, and in some treacherous classes I snuck out with happy Ds. Because of my below average academic record in those critical areas, I was required to take all the basic college math courses and science classes. That included Biology 101.

I had World History 101 and Biology 101 in the same semester, the fall semester of my first year of college. It was the autumn of

1996. There were many things I didn't know, many things I hadn't gently learned over time, which now were violently thrust upon a mind connected to a soul which just wasn't ready for such revelation. For instance, I never knew there were other religions besides Christianity with a suffering, self-giving deity like Christ. I never knew many other cultures besides the ancient Hebrews had stories about an ancient flood like the Noah I had learned about in Sunday School. This new information jolted me a bit. Nothing created an earthquake in me like evolution in Biology 101.

My biology professor was a gracious man. Having taught for over thirty years at Concord, the doc was fully aware he was teaching undergraduates who had been born and bred as deep in the Bible belt as was culturally (if not geographically) possible. In his very first lecture, he told the class, "Now for those of you who are people of faith, I don't expect you to accept everything I am presenting to you today. I do expect you to learn it, though. I don't expect you to abandon your faith, and I don't ask you to. I do ask you not to try to convert me or argue points of your faith with me in class. Just sit in class. Take notes. Pass my tests. Leave with your faith intact, with a decent grade in your hands, and we can all have a beer together somewhere after finals." He couldn't have been more of a gentleman about it. I sat there in silence though, feeling my faith start to crumble.

Darwin coupled with *The Epic of Gilgamesh* left me an empty shell spiritually. Suddenly on Sunday mornings, it didn't seem so important to get up and go to church. Actually, by the time the dark green leaves of summer had turned to the lush ambers and yellows of autumn, my faith had evaporated to the point that going to church would feel hypocritical. I had been in college long enough to know one of the worst things any person could ever do was to be a hypocrite.

For weeks I stayed away from the church. My parents didn't think there was anything critical going on in their son's soul. They just figured I was finally becoming a normal teenager, including the growth of a propensity to want to sleep very late and be lazy generally. In reality, I was in deep suffering. All my life I had suffered from (at the time) undiagnosed depression. The combination of my loss of faith and the subsequent alienation from the rituals and atmosphere of the church, which had given my life so much meaning, left me in a depression deep and dark.

As if all of this weren't enough to paralyze me in a corner in the fetal position, there was more. I was terribly, profoundly, achingly lonely. I had never had a girlfriend. I had never had true friends I could go to, hang out with, be with. I loved every pretty girl in every one of my classes. How did I define a pretty girl? If she was a she, then yes, I loved her. If she was a she, then I just knew she was destined to be my one true beloved. My stomach turned, my palms sweated, my face grew red. I loved her, and of course, the first step was that I needed to ask her out. Then, hand in hand, heart-in-heart, our forever could begin.

Any guy in class talking about NASCAR, poetry, politics, or any variation thereof, was profoundly cool in my estimation. I wanted to be their friend. I wanted to hang out with them. If any guy had ever talked about NASCAR *and* poetry *and* politics, I probably would have fallen on my hands and knees and begged him to be my friend. I overheard so many conversations: the easy talk of friends; the giggly whispers of lovers; happy, laid-back banter; tender talk of plans being made. All of it was said, and all of it was done, all around me. I was hearing, and I was seeing, life. I was accidentally eavesdropping, and I was unintentionally gawking at life. Deep within my soul, deep within my bones, with every crying heartbeat, I just wanted to live my life. I just wanted a life to live.

Autumn yielded to winter. Winter finally let its cold hand slip off the earth, so spring could be born again.

One Sunday morning while Mom and Dad were at church, I took a mug of coffee into the den and sat down to watch C-SPAN. I was such a hopeless nerd. That morning they were broadcasting the opening ceremony for the United States Holocaust Museum. Elie Wiesel had just started to speak.

I was mesmerized by Wiesel. I had read *Night* in high school, and the poetic, humane way Wiesel wrote, even about the most inhumane, violent time in human history, was in and of itself redeeming, saving, for every soul, living and dead of the human race. Before that morning, I had only read Wiesel and seen his picture. I had never before heard his voice or watched him. His small frame, his   body, his soft-spoken voice speaking as poetically as he wrote, drew me in, with love. What Wiesel said that day changed my life forever.

Wiesel described how he had lost his faith in God in the Holocaust. How could he not have? He described how he had been such a devout, godly little boy. His Judaism had been everything to him. It was everything about him. When the Nazis murdered all his family, Wiesel said the devout, God-centered Jewish boy he was, died. With a trembling voice, Wiesel said God had died with all of his loved ones in the furnaces of Auschwitz.

I already had tears in my eyes as I sat there, watching Elie Wiesel on that sun-clothed spring April Sunday. I didn't know that good man, that gifted writer, was about to give my soul the epiphany I was crying in the night to experience. Wiesel said one day he just made a rational, stubborn decision. The Nazis had killed his family. He should not let the Nazis kill his God too. Wiesel said he began attending synagogue again. At first, he entered the doors of the Jewish community in faithful worship, without faith himself. Still, Wiesel said, he went. Without faith, he attended the worship of God with his people. Before long the ancient words, the precious songs, the eternal rhythms of his faith made God come alive again for him. Before long Wiesel was a writer, entering into his long, distinguished career as the memory of the Jewish people, and a major conscience for the world.

Wiesel didn't believe in God, but even in disbelief, he went to the synagogue to worship.

Within the worship of God, Wiesel found God again. Within the loving presence of his people in loving prayer and devotion to God, Wiesel found the loving presence of God again.

Thanks to him, so did I.

I wiped the tears out of my eyes and finished my coffee. I knew this was going to be my last Sunday out of church.

It wasn't instantaneous. It did take some time. In time though, within the words of the Communion liturgy, within the verbal reading of scripture, within the faithful preaching of pastors, within the faithful, if not melodious singing of the congregation, I found God again.

I found God's love again.

I found God's calling again.

As I prepared for my last semester at Concord a few years later, I applied, and I was accepted into Duke Divinity School. I was still conflicted and confused about a great many things, most of them internal to me. I knew though, God and I would work those matters out in time. I knew God wanted me to become a pastor.

3 The Voices

I believe we all live with monsters inside of us, and we hear voices no one else can hear. Rihanna and Eminem sang about becoming friends with the monsters under their beds, and the voices in their heads. I so completely understand. I had quite a few voices in my head, and any number of monsters under my bed. I had to learn to silence the voices and tame the monsters before I could become a humane person, let alone a person becoming a pastor.

"Get away from me, you faggot!" We were in the darkness playing Laser Tag. We had just met each other, so perhaps he thought I wouldn't recognize his voice. Maybe he just didn't care whether I knew who it was who called me that.

We were together in a group of college kids who had all received scholarships from the same community service foundation. We were together that night to build friendships and to build bridges to each other. We were there to build a team. We were there to get to know one another . I had never played Laser Tag before. I really didn't know what I was doing. I think we were on the same team, and I was getting in his way. And he called me *faggot*.

We were together as community minded, community service-oriented young people. We were together as young humanitarians bound together by a want to make the world a better place, both as college students, and later, as adults. We were together as colleagues in this scholarship program who hopefully would become good friends, brothers and sisters in the next four years. And he called me *faggot*.

I hate to admit this, but I must admit it because it is true. That hateful kid, and his hateful words to me, truly ruined that scholarship program for me. Oh, I spent my entire undergraduate college career as a scholar enrolled in the program, exchanging the foundation's payment of my tuition for community service. But I never really identified myself with the program. I never really let my guard down long enough to make friends in the program. I never did anything extra in the program beyond going to the required meetings and putting the hours in I needed to in order to maintain my status in the program. That hateful kid, those hateful words, ruined what could have been a beautiful opportunity and a wondrous time in my life.

In four years, I never found the strength to silence that voice.

There were other voices.

I was in junior high school, just a skinny, squeaky-voiced kid just trying to keep my will to live. To fit in better, to try to become more involved and find a life, I decided to play basketball. I was in seventh grade. I had never played any sport at any point in my life. Most all of my peers, of course, had been together playing sports since they were in early elementary school. Even though seventh grade is still very young, and despite the fact seventh-grade basketball isn't so far advanced, still I was behind. I was woefully behind everyone else.

I didn't get to play very often, even in practice. The coach, a very old, curmudgeonly chap named Mr. Bowler, who, you may recall, saved me from Scott that unforgettable Monday after the Martinsville NASCAR race, kept me on the bench for as long as he possibly could. More than once, my fellow players had to remind the coach I was even there at all. "Aren't you going to let Jeff come out for even a few seconds this practice, Coach?" my old buddy Heath once asked him. The old coach just sort of groaned, blew his whistle, told Heath to sit down, and called for me to come out.

I played in a real game only once. It was twenty-two seconds on a Saturday morning at Athens Junior High School. The ball had been knocked out of bounds. When the whistle blew, Coach called for substitutions. We were so far ahead, he pulled all five second-stringers off the court and told those of us left on the bench to go on out. When the whistle blew, I ran like the wind. I ran harder than I had ever run in my life. When I got down to the other side of the court, I wondered why I was there all alone. *Have I run so fast I have gotten down the court first, faster than anyone else?* Then I heard the laughter, and I saw the game was being hotly contested on the other end of the court. I took off running again with my ears buzzing and my face burning with embarrassment. By the time I got down there, the buzzer rang out, mercifully ending the game.

The next week at practice, as I rode the bench waiting for

seventh grade practice to begin, three or four eighth and ninth grade boys were laughing at me, and as they laughed, they spit on my head and on my neck. I just sat there, pretending not to hear, pretending not to feel.

I did hear, though. I heard every word. I heard all of their voices.

I did feel too. I felt the wetness of their saliva running down my neck. I felt the humiliation and the alienation their words and their actions were designed to make me feel.

Coach Bowler invited me to come back next year as the manager of the team. I served as basketball manager for my eighth and my ninth-grade years. I was proud to fold jerseys and collect basketballs after practice and games. The varsity won the county championship both of those years. I felt much more at home, much happier on the sidelines with my manager shirt on. I still heard voices though.

"Look at Jeff down there. He makes too many As to be special education, right? He's not 'short bus,' is he?"

Yes, I still heard voices.

In high school, I was the only guy on the newspaper staff who had been on staff for the entire three years of high school. Per the custom of the staff then, I got to be the boy representative for the newspaper staff on the homecoming court. The young lady I got to escort was Dee, our editor. Dee was beautiful. With the occasional short shorts and skimpy shirts, Dee was, in the parlance of every teenage boy of that era, just plain hot. I was so excited to be escorting Dee in the homecoming court. Dee was very popular. She had a real shot at being queen. Maybe I was escorting our queen onto the field, I thought to myself. Maybe if I work up my courage, when it's all over with, I will ask her out on a date. Maybe, just maybe, she will say yes.

It was Friday. The homecoming game was that very night. The homecoming court was practicing, midafternoon, during the school day. I was behind Dee in a huge crowd of students, walking toward the field. She didn't realize I was behind her.

"I get to walk with my own girlfriend in this thing," Clint said to Dee. Clint was a deep-voiced, hunky football dude.

"Yeah, you guys are so lucky. Just look who I get to walk with," Dee replied to Clint. She sighed heavily after she said it, and for some reason, she turned around. There I was, right behind her. I pretended I hadn't heard her. Of course, I had heard her. Dee looked at me very sheepishly, all red in the face. I just looked away. I couldn't bear to look at her.

I didn't have the heart to speak to her throughout the practice, or for the entire homecoming court ceremony. She didn't have the heart, or the audacity, to speak to me either. I was glad when it was over. I was glad Dee didn't get elected queen.

I never asked her out. I had heard what she said. I couldn't forget that voice, those words.

As I contemplate all of these voices from across the landscape of my life, I must say, one voice pains me more than all others.

It is my voice. It is a high-pitched voice. It is a voice that gets even higher when anxiety attacks me. It is a voice, often over the years, mistaken for a female voice. To this day, I don't know who I feel more embarrassment for: myself when I pull up to the first window to pay for my fast food, seeing the shocked look of the high school fry cook kid who just called me ma'am, or for the poor kid himself, whose face is obviously blushing, seeing the ma'am who just bought a chicken sandwich and a diet soda has a sprouting beard and a receding hairline.

My dad worked in radio, and because I idolized my dad (and still do), I wanted to work in radio too. Even as a squeaky-voiced thirteen, fourteen-year-old, I didn't give up on my radio broadcasting dream. I was just waiting on puberty to kick in and make me another Shadoe Stephens, or at the very least, Casey Kasem--you know, big-time radio broadcasters with national fame.

In the autumn of 1991, I did make it to the big time. I was on national, syndicated radio. For thirty to forty-five seconds, I was on a talk show with Mark Garrow of the Performance Racing Network (PRN) and one of every southern boy's heroes — Jeffrey Kanode very much included — Richard Petty, the most winning, most celebrated NASCAR driver of all.

Petty, or the King as we NASCAR fans call him, had just announced his retirement from racing. He would race the 1992 season and then end a career, which dated all the way back to 1958. He was appearing on this national radio talk show as part of a big media blitz accompanying the rollout of what he and his public relations team were calling the coming year's Fan Appreciation Tour.

The radio station where my dad worked featured NASCAR programming prominently in its schedule, broadcasting races and support programming, including this show featuring Petty.

I decided to call in!

Holy goodness! I made the cut! I was placed on hold by the PRN call screener to await my turn to ask my question of King Richard live and on-the-air to all of America.

I don't know what possessed me. I don't know if I was trying to be cute. I don't know if the self-consciousness of my high-pitched voice made me intuitively feel it was necessary to say what I said to Richard Petty and America that night. I think maybe it was my old belief, one I learned from another one of my heroes, David Letterman: it is far better to point out one's own flaws oneself, and gain laughter and retain dignity with self-deprecation, than it is to give other people the benefit of the first laugh.

"Let's go to Jeff in Princeton, West Virginia," Mark Garrow said. "Jeff, you are on with King Richard Petty. What's your question?"

And Jeff from Princeton, West Virginia, yours truly, said, "Mr.

Petty, forgive me if my voice is very high pitched. I am extremely nervous to be talking to an American legend, and I am still waiting for puberty."

I said that to all of America who happened to be listening. I said it to the King. On the other end of the receiver, also on the microphone to three hundred radio affiliates, I could hear Mark Garrow trying, but failing, to suppress laughter. I truly could see from the receiver of the phone all the way to the PRN studios in Charlotte, Mr. Garrow's face exploding in a fit of laughter. "And what is your question for Richard, Jeff?" he asked after he finally pulled himself together.

My face was burning. Cold sweat dripped from every pore of my skin. "I was just wondering what Richard Petty does to relax, you know, when he is not racing?" I choked out. There was a dead air on the radio for like eight seconds.

Finally, Richard Petty, who is partially deaf from years of racing banshee-crying stock cars, said, "Mark, can you help me out, buddy? I didn't catch that little girl's question?"

I wanted to die. I didn't blame Richard Petty. But I wanted to die.

Incidentally, the King's answer to my question was *racing*. He said the only place on earth no one could ever really get to him, or bother him, was when he was strapped down behind the wheel of his blue Pontiac, number forty-three. I was too mortified and too suicidal to appreciate his answer. In retrospect though, it was a good, very interesting answer to a damn good, very interesting question.

I just prayed to God with all the strength, with all the will to live which I had left, that no one else on earth had heard what had just happened—Richard Petty mistaking me for a girl on worldwide radio.

A little guy in my grade at school, Jamie, was an avid Richard Petty fan. It just so happened he recorded the entire radio program on his home stereo because he recorded all things Petty, be it on television or radio. Jamie had heard, of course, "Jeff from Princeton, West Virginia." Jamie knew beyond a shadow of a doubt "Jeff from Princeton" was me.

By the end of eighth period that day in school, Jamie had played "Jeff from Princeton" on the air with Richard Petty to each and every one of his classes.

Another haunting voice belonged to a little eighty- something-year-old retired Methodist pastor named Ruth. In her retirement, Ruth attended the same church my family did. One summer, after I had announced I felt God calling me into the ministry, my pastor asked me to preach for him one Sunday while he and his family vacationed. I was eager to get as much pulpit time as I could, so I readily agreed. It dawned on the pastor later, however, the Sunday in question was the first Sunday of the month. Our church was accustomed to celebrating Communion on the first Sunday of the month.

We needed a fully ordained pastor to preside at Communion. In retrospect, I wonder if dear old Sister Ruth was offended, or put off when she learned a snotty-nosed teenaged kid would be preaching the sermon instead of her. Today, I believe beyond certainty the politically correct move for the church's pastor to have made would have been to give the entire service to Ruth's capable hands. She should have been asked to preach as well as preside at Communion. The pastor had already asked me though, and I suspect it simply slipped his mind he was about to miss the first Sunday of the month, the Sunday our church always celebrated the Lord's Supper. I am betting he scrambled at the last minute with the phone in one hand, begging Ruth to administer Communion for the church, probably while he had one foot out the door where his wife and kids waited in the running car with their beach gear in the trunk, ready to go.

Due to what happened in that church service later, because of the words from that voice of Ruth's I heard and still hear, I suspect retired Reverend Ruth entered that service that Sunday with a bit of a chip on her shoulder. She shouldn't have. Presiding at Communion is a far bigger deal. It is a far greater sacred gift than preaching.

I tried. I tried. I tried. I was up there behind the pulpit, preaching my little heart out. I stuttered. I sweated. I strained. I droned. I went on and on and on. I paused for a breath. I looked down at my manuscript to see where I was. Behind me, in the choir loft, a voice emerged. The voice was loud. The voice was old. The voice was irritated. The voice was sighing. "It takes a long time to have Communion. Are you about done, little boy? You really should be."

The voice belonged to Ruth. She was up there behind me, like two thousand years of church history and tradition keeping their eyes on this dumb kid attempting to make sense of the universe of faith and mystery when he hadn't even begun to live and understand his own humanity yet. The voice was not graceful and gracious, though. The voice was cutting and condescending. The voice is one I still hear, especially when the Sunday just isn't my best, and I can feel the tension or the weariness from the people sitting before me.

It takes a long time to have Communion. What makes you think you have the right to be up there anyway, little boy?

The voice didn't say those words, but those words were behind every word the voice did say.

I remember looking back at Ruth in stunned disbelief for a few seconds, and then I turned around again to face the congregation. I had to somehow finish the sermon in some dignified way.

There are a thousand other voices too — voices without specific names, voices without recognizable faces for me to latch onto, to remember. How many telemarketers have there been over the years who called me Mrs. Kanode? How many times have I had trouble with the person on the other end of the phone when I call my credit card company, trying to fix a problem, and because of my voice, they doubt I am who I say I am?

I am not proud to admit I have literally screamed at a few of those folks over the years. I can still hear my own voice, all shrill, throaty, and raw, yelling out in tired frustration: "Dammit, I am Jeffrey Kanode! I have given you my address! I have given you my three-digit security code! I have given you my Social Security number! I can even give you my blood type if you need it! Please just believe me when I say, I am a guy with a high-pitched voice! I am who I say I am! I am Jeffrey Kanode!" And I can still hear the voices on the other end, and I say voices because this has happened so many times.

"Yes, Mrs. Kanode, please hold while I transfer you to our fraud department."

I can still hear those voices. I will always remember those voices.

While I still get aggravated to the point of yelling and even cursing on the phone with telemarketers or call center experts who can't believe my gender, I have learned to simply enjoy fast-food drive-thru windows. Oh, it used to bother me tremendously, but now that I am older, I have fun with it. I think age is the reason why. I am now in my mid-thirties, pushing my late thirties, and most of the kids working the drive-thru windows at these fast-food places are mostly little high school or college kids. I take mercy on the girls because, well, I just like girls. The guys though,

I just have unmerciful fun with them.

I will drive up to the intercom of a drive-thru. If it is a female voice, I will know to behave. If it is a guy's voice, all bets are off. Often, the voice of the attendant will tell me, "Thank you, ma'am. Your total is eight dollars and twenty- three cents. Please drive to the first window." Again, if I am dealing with a lady, I just feel bad when they look and see I am a guy. I can see the embarrassment in their little faces. I just flirt with them a little to try to ease the tension. I am just really friendly, and we get through the transaction. They get their money. I get my food. If it is a guy though, I do my faux-macho, bad impression of Tom Brokaw or John Wayne. This just throws the guy completely off, and many times I have seen their faces contorted in total confusion. This makes my day, and with joy, I give them their money and take my food.

I hear those voices. I have learned to live with those voices. I try to make peace with those voices. It is never easy. Those voices can come back in the blink of an eye, in the falling of a leaf from a tree, and they come back with the power of thunder, with the electric destruction of lightning.

Even primordial voices from far too long ago come shouting back. When they do, I have to follow them into the dark crevices of my consciousness where they forever lead.

When I was in the first grade, around Thanksgiving, we were making scarecrows. My hands were tiny — I still have really small hands for a man—and my hand/eye coordination, which to this day is not very good at all, was at that time still woefully undeveloped. I struggled mightily to cut out the parts of the scarecrow with those little safety scissors they give you in elementary school. The construction paper was thick. My hands were shaky with nerves. My hands would slip. I started crying, and my salty tears made these ugly blotches on my already deformed scarecrow. But what else could I do but keep trudging along to finish the damnable assignment of making this wretched scarecrow?

The teacher, Mrs. Culson, was making her rounds around the class. I had my head down low on the desk. I was in the zone. I was working so hard. I was so intensely focused on finishing the creation of my fledgling scarecrow. I didn't see Mrs. Culson coming, but I smelled her perfume right over me. I looked up. She smiled politely, but I was not to be calmed by even that usual reassuring gesture. My scarecrow was a blamed mess, and I knew it. I also knew I was doing the very best I could.

Mrs. Culson started examining the as-yet unglued parts of my scarecrow. She didn't say anything, but even at age six, I was astute enough to see she was no longer smiling. My hands trembled. Finally, she asked to see my scarecrow's legs.

I knew I was holding the legs on my lap because I had run out of room on my desk. I reached down and pulled up these two mangled little legs for my teacher to see. They were really rough looking, I admit. The left leg was nearly as thin as a toothpick and had it been a real leg and not art, it probably could never have held even the weight of an ant's body up. The right leg was a little fatter and sturdier than the left leg, but it looked pretty ragged as well.

I can remember the reaction. I can remember the voice. "I just don't see how something like this could ever be done by a first grader," she said as she stood over me. She put my scarecrow's little legs down on my desk, and I watched her walk away. The smell of her perfume grew fainter, and as I put my head back down low on my desk to focus on creating my scarecrow, yet another warm, salty tear hit the blue, cone-shaped head I had just started cutting out.

It is funny, or it is sad. Today, as a thirty-something-year-old man, every time I am asked to do a craft, be it at church, or be it once upon a time when I was married with little stepdaughters who were quite crafty, as my hands still stumble and fumble with paper and scissors, I hear that voice of Mrs. Culson. As she held up my little scarecrow's deformed legs, that voice said, "I just don't see how this could be done." The voice said those words only once, but the voice and those words have echoed inside of me forever since.

When I was in seminary at Duke, I availed myself of the services of a speech therapist who was on staff, who helped in our preaching class. The therapist was a lovely lady named Chrissy, and when I asked Chrissy for some extra help with my voice, she told me that she was grateful that I had.

"When I first heard your voice, Jeff, something told me I could really help you, if you wanted the help."

I told her I really did. I told her I had been looking for her and for her help since I was a thirteen-year-old in middle school.

I made an appointment to meet with Chrissy in her office on the other side of Durham. To start with, she wanted to actually see my vocal cords. She ran a scope partway down my throat. She showed me the picture of my throat and vocal cords on a screen. She then had me do all kinds of voice exercises. I went "ahhhhhh" probably a thousand times.

"Well, Jeff, I have made a definitive discovery about your voice already," Chrissy said to me later as we sat in her office. She had long brown hair, and she was very beautiful. I was grateful to God the woman who was going to finally bring salvation to my voice also looked like an angel. "At first, I wondered about your vocal cords. I wondered if perhaps, developmentally, they hadn't grown properly, if they had been stunted somehow. Your vocal cords are as developed as any healthy as they should be. Your problem is, you are only using maybe a third of your vocal cords. I think what is happening is, you get so tense, you get so nervous. Most of the mass of your vocal cords are just all tensed up, and you aren't using all of them at all."

I intuitively knew Chrissy was right. All my life, day in and day out, I have been living with a very nervous, very tense little guy named Jeff. I knew she was right. I could feel the tension and the anxiety right there in my throat. I was only too happy then when Chrissy suggested, as part of my treatment, nice long massages, which she hoped would relax me.

She was too attractive for a massage from her to relax me. Still, I enjoyed them. I also took very seriously the therapeutic work she asked me to engage in. For about two weeks, Chrissy had me talking in a deep, baritone voice. It sounded like the voice of a stranger.

"Oh no, Jeff, that is your real voice," Chrissy reassured me when I articulated my stranger notion to her. "The voice you hear now is you using the entire length of your vocal cords. This is how nature intends for you to sound."

I remember one of my homework assignments from Chrissy was to call a trusted person on the phone and talk to them for thirty minutes or so, exclusively in the new, deep voice. I called my sister, Monica. She was shocked to hear me sound so different. She was loving and supportive, though.

Somehow, someway, in the length of those two weeks, I started getting very depressed. First of all, the entire length and breadth of my emotional, mental framework was focused on keeping my voice way down low each time I spoke. It was exhausting. Second of all, to my ears, it sounded like I was doing my Tom Brokaw impression, twenty-four/seven. One day in the shower, it just dawned on me. Chrissy hadn't told me anything I

79

didn't already know. I knew my voice could go down deeper when it needed to. After all, I did many impressions like my Tom Brokaw voice, which required me to dip my voice into lower ranges. It wasn't that I couldn't talk lower. It simply was that my voice was most comfortable, most *me*, in the higher ranges. It was then I discovered the source of my depression. *In trying to talk in a constant, deep voice, I was losing myself. Jeff was losing Jeff.* As low as my self- esteem sometimes dipped, I discovered then I actually did sort of like the person who was becoming me. The voice was a huge part of that personhood.

Here and there over the years, I have also taken great comfort in what I read in history, and what I can hear for myself from historic archives. Although he played Abraham Lincoln once, Gregory Peck did not make an accurate Lincoln. Those who heard Lincoln speak described the high-pitched, nasally sound of his voice. Sam Waterston and Daniel Day-Lewis both made perfect Lincolns! John F. Kennedy's voice was pretty high too, and Winston Churchill's was extraordinarily high tenor in tone. Though I will never be in the same class of those gentlemen, in this or in any other universe, the fact I share a high-pitched voice with such great men has helped get me through.

Now as I approach middle age, God has blessed me with another voice or two. These voices can never drown out all of the negative voices who have inhabited my mind for so long. They can and do temper those voices though, and make them less potent, their powerless destructive.

I left full-time Methodist ministry for a couple of years. Some life circumstances happened to me — life circumstances whose story will be told in another book, on another day. During those two years, I taught high school. I really missed being behind the pulpit, preaching on Sunday mornings. When the opportunity came to preach a couple of Sundays a month at a couple of little Presbyterian churches, I thankfully leaped at the chance.

Both of those churches were gracious and loving toward me. Again, those are stories to be told in the future. One of the many gifts of grace the people in both of those churches gave me involved my voice.

After church one Sunday morning, a middle-aged woman named Toni approached me. When she began, "Your voice, Jeff, your voice..." I immediately prepared for my heart and my soul to be assaulted. All the voices came rushing through my being like hot wax on tiny fingers holding a burning candle. I was already preparing to respond graciously to someone after they hurled an arrow at me. The woman continued, "Your voice is unlike any other male voice I have ever heard. It is so unique. It is so beautiful. It just rings out, and it is beautiful. Something just told me to tell you that."

Toni was probably not prepared for my eyes to well up with tears. I choked a thank-you as I gave her a quick hug.

A week later, in the other church where I was guest preaching another lady expressed the same sort of appreciation, even admiration--dare I say, love?-- for my voice.

Now when I hear my voice: when I am praying, when I am preaching, when I am talking to a friend, I don't always hear a beautiful voice myself. Now I know though, at least one or two other people on this earth hear my voice as something beautiful. That helps. It helps. Those voices help me want to keep my voice speaking, still living, still existing, still dancing out there, somewhere on the air for others to hear.

4 Genesis

The spring of my freshman year of college was also a springtime for my Christian faith. College courses revealed layers of the universe I never knew existed. This new weight of knowledge in my brain caused my faith to crash like a baby bird with a crushed wing. By the end of the second semester, I had started doing the hard mental and work of the heart to reconcile my faith with undeniable facts of science and history. I no longer had a baby bird faith. It was a hard journey, but one I will always be thankful for. I believe the faith in God I still thrive on today rests on the solid foundation of my rebuilt, renewed faith of that spring, and not on my earlier, thin baby bird faith.

I would have the same experience, though not nearly as traumatic (owing to this earlier journey) when I entered seminary at Duke University.

Before I got there, there was the matter of my completing my undergraduate education. I also needed to begin the official process of becoming a candidate for ministry in the United Methodist Church. By my last couple of years at Concord, I felt I was ready. I had ignored my call. God kept on calling. My faith had been gutted. God let my faith rise again, stronger and more alive in creative resurrection. It was time for me to make some major life decisions for myself.

Degrees in English and history weren't going to be worth

anything except as an entry point for further graduate studies. I briefly flirted with the idea of getting a teaching degree so that if I wasn't really certain about God's call upon my life, I could at least support myself for a few years as a public school teacher while God and I continued to figure things out. One of my English professors strongly discouraged me from doing that. He told me he had been a public school teacher for a season in his life, and he had been miserable. I reminded him of himself, the professor said. "You have a great mind, Jeff, and you are a very good writer. You are a natural at this stuff. I think you would be very successful and happy as an English professor. You will be eaten alive, and you won't be happy at all, in the public school system."

I really loved the professor who spoke those words of advice and encouragement to me, and I took those words to heart. So much to heart did I take his words, I didn't enter into the education program. By my senior year, if I wasn't 100 percent rock solid about the validity of Christ's call to ministry, I would go on to nearby Virginia Tech and do my master's level and Ph.D. work in English.

It was an easy decision, but it was also a difficult one. It was an easy decision because by the time I felt decisions really needed to be made—the fall of my senior year of undergrad—I had no doubt God wanted me to enter the ministry candidacy process and apply to seminary. It was a difficult decision because I had always been a homebody with a deep soul yearning to know, to feel, to continue putting down roots. I don't mean the issue of leaving home made the English professor path versus Methodist pastor path a difficult decision. After all, I would have had to leave home for my graduate studies whether or not those studies were in English or theology. I am talking about my need to call a place home and the critical necessity of being able to love the place that life would take me to after my academic work was done and I was ready to start work.

Because I had always loved my childhood home so much, I yearned to have my own home someday with the same stability, with the same consistency, with the same gentle flowing of time, season to season, year to year, of the home and home life my parents always gave their children. There were rituals of the home. There were traditions of my hometown I cherished. Every June, there was the Mountain Festival in Bluefield. Every December, there was the Christmas parade in Princeton. Every fall, our church went to our city park for our picnic, and it was always at the same shelter, overlooking the same green, joyful meadow.

A college professor could get a job at a college or university, and if the work was solid, if the chemistry was right, that professor could eventually earn tenure and spend the rest of her or his life in that town, in that job, in that house. Many of my Concord professors had taught there for thirty or more years. Their spouses had established their own careers in the area. They had raised their families there. They had spent the best years of their lives there.

The roots of their family life were mighty and strong thanks to the stability of their positions teaching at Concord.

A Methodist pastor, on the other hand, could never know just one town as *home*. A Methodist pastor could never give his or her children Christmas in one house for all of their childhood. A Methodist pastor could never grow old talking to the same friends, at the same coffee shop, for many, many years. A Methodist pastor would have to itinerate. A Methodist pastor would spend a thirty- to forty-year career moving from town to town. I knew Methodist pastors who moved every five or six years. That was about the standard length of time any of my home church pastors were able (or willing) to stay. The longest pastorates I knew of in our conference were ten to fifteen years. Those were few and far between, too. They were the exception and not the rule. Even a ten- to the fifteen-year pastorate in a church was still nothing compared to the vibrant home life, the hometown connection made possible by staying in one home, staying in one workplace, for decades. Even the longest tenured of my Methodist colleagues hadn't put down roots to compare to others who lived their life in a town, in a home, in an institution they cared about.

Even as a twenty-one-year-old, I agonized about my vocation decision in large part because of the issue of the Methodist custom of itinerancy. I just didn't know if my fragile spirit and needy soul could take not having a real home, a real community, which I could cherish as sanctuary forever. I also worried about my future wife and the children we would create. How could I ever ask any lady I loved to pick up, pack up, and move on every few years? What about her dreams? What about her career?

The thoughts of what "the Methodist moving" would do to my children scared me most of all. If any children I fathered were anything like me, they would be shy, quiet, possibly depressive, and surely subdued at heart. I had a hard-enough time surviving school, and I went through grade school, junior high, and high school with the same bunch of kids. By the time I was in junior high, as rough a time as it was, at least I had known the vast majority of my fellow students for most of my life.

What would my son be like if he had struggled mightily to make friends only to be plucked from his school and his town as soon as they finally became comfortable and comforting to him? What would my daughter be like if she was always having to prove herself again and again, scholastically and socially in schools where teachers already had their picks of who was top, and students already had a well-established social order before my girl ever walked through the door?

How could I ask my children whom I had helped bring into the world, whom I was given the holy task of helping to raise in love and humanity, to never have real bearings, to never have a central home the compass always pointed north to, to never have any real hometown, which would always be their *home*?

Young as I was, I agonized over this. Despite the fact I had no steady girlfriend and no prospect to get one anytime soon, I agonized about what my vocational decision would do to the family I was certain God would someday give me.

My experiences working in a United Methodist Church in my hometown during my last year as an undergraduate at Concord helped me clarify God's calling upon my life and solidify my plans, which it was nearing time to make.

God blessed me with me about nine months—the length of time it takes a human embryo to grow to be ready to enter life in this old world—working with a very loving, very gifted pastor who embodied for me exactly what, and what kind of human being a pastor is. Ultimately, I chose the journey of becoming pastor for myself based in large part on the pastor it was my honor and privilege to be mentored by during those formative, learning days.

Rev. Dustin Jenkins came to Princeton to pastor Bolt United Methodist Church. His previous appointment had been his first placement right out of seminary at Francis Asbury United Methodist Church in Lewiston. Dustin was an African-American, and Francis Asbury UMC was one of the few historically predominant African-American Methodist churches in West Virginia. He was there for seven years—a very solid, respectable length for any pastorate, especially for a first one. After nearly the length of a two-term American presidency at Francis Asbury, Dustin was appointed to Bolt UMC.

It was one of West Virginia's first experiments at a cross-racial pastoral appointment. Dustin was black. Bolt UMC was predominantly, if not totally, a white congregation. Bolt was a predominantly white congregation in a predominantly white town. Bolt was a predominantly white congregation in a predominantly white town of Princeton, a very southern town in predominantly white southern West Virginia. Let me explain.

I don't know much about other states. I know quite a lot about West Virginia because I am one of her sons. I am also, quite proudly, a son of southern West Virginia. Southern West Virginia is very different from other parts of West Virginia. Culturally, southern West Virginia has far more in common with southwest Virginia—think of Roanoke, Bristol, and Wytheville—than it does with Charleston, Huntington, and Wheeling. Part of this fact goes all the way back to Lincoln's founding of us in 1863. The northern counties of western Virginia very much deplored secession and slavery and very much wanted to be a new state. The southernmost counties of western Virginia were very Southern in sentiment, politics, and practice. The economies were agrarian. There were some slave owners, though most folks lived on small farms without slaves, and many of the men who went off to war (including my own great-great-grandfather) wore Confederate butternut gray.

The town of Princeton itself held a small Confederate arsenal. When Union troops under the command of future president of the

United States Colonel Rutherford B. Hayes entered the town in 1862, the retreating Confederates set fire to the arsenal, a fire which, of course, spread throughout most of the rest of the downtown. Little Princeton, my hometown, and Dustin Jenkin's second parish, is one of the few towns to be burned by Confederate troops. Think burning towns in the Civil War, and most folks think of Vicksburg, Atlanta, Petersburg and Richmond, all set ablaze by Union siege and the subsequent looting that occurred after. Princeton was burned by Confederate hands yet still remained a deeply Southern, deeply Confederate town.

Lincoln's proclamation gave birth to the new on June 20, 1863. The southern counties of the new state of West Virginia were included in the state, not because the citizens living there were deeply Union in sympathy, but because they were conquered territories occupied by Union troops. This included Mercer County, whose seat of government was, and still is, Princeton.

Southern West Virginia, then, was Confederate during the war which created West Virginia, and to be honest, to this day, southern West Virginia is still more rebel, more southern in sentiment and politics than Union. One is far more likely to hear Hank Williams Jr. blaring from the speakers of cars racing down a country highway than to hear the jazz of Eric Dolphy resonating out of open windows. Sadly, Robert E. Lee is still more revered there than Martin Luther King. In my lifetime, no Democrats but southerners—Jimmy Carter and Bill Clinton—could ever carry these counties in a presidential election.

Into this area, the West Virginia Methodist hierarchy sent still quite young, black Rev. Dustin Jenkins to pastor all- white, aging Bolt United Methodist Church.

From gossip I picked up later on — and there's nothing quite as juicy and as tantalizing as hometown gossip shared from one native to another — a few members of Bolt UMC actually wrote letters to the bishop and district superintendent, begging them not to send a black man to pastor their church. I am not sure whether this happened or not. I don't doubt it did though, to be honest. I am sure the letters were polite. I am sure the prejudice, which spurred their writing was perhaps totally unconscious and buried deep under layers of civility and reasonableness.

"It's not that we have anything against black people. It's just that we are a white congregation, and we need someone who can understand us. We need someone we can understand. We need someone like us, so we can grow spiritually and build up our church."

Thankfully for my hometown and thankfully for a church I grew to dearly love, but with apologies for those who love the drama, I report there were no crosses burned in the yard of Bolt UMC. There were no ritual cross burnings with the hateful shadows and moonlit silhouette of men in white sheets in the front yard of the parsonage. There were those aforementioned minor protests in the form of polite, useless letters to the bishop. There were many raised eyebrows. There was lots of curiosity. And

Dustin Jenkins came to be pastor of Bolt United Methodist Church.

And in pretty short order, Rev. Dustin Jenkins became the beloved pastor of Bolt United Methodist Church. It didn't take long, at all. It didn't take long, at all, for this compassionate, dynamic, educated, Spirit-filled, Christly young pastor to be accepted and loved by his congregation because he possessed all of these attributes, and so much more. It didn't take long, at all, for that basically good, godly, loving church to get over its ancient assumptions and irrational prejudice to realize it had a good pastor, a special shepherd who loved them, a pastor they soon were not afraid to love back.

I came into Dustin Jenkins's and Bolt's universe five or six years into their relationship. I was still a student at Concord with basically one academic year to go. When someone decides God has truly called them into the ministry, the United Methodist Church requires the person to enter into a long, somewhat vigorous process—ideally, a spiritual journey. This journey begins at the candidacy stage and ends many years later, at full ordination. The first part of that journey, the candidacy process, involves getting the approval of an oversight board who then assigns the aspiring pastor a candidacy mentor. When I was approved by the board to be a certified candidate for ministry, the board assigned Rev. Dustin Jenkins to be my mentor. Even more than the board's approval of me as a candidate, the naming of Dustin as my mentor represented a sign to me from God: "Hey, kid, you are going down the road I want you to go down."

You see, I had been an admirer of Dustin's for years from a distance. I didn't attend his church, but many of my cool friends from high school--my beloved hippy soccer player friends, and fellow nerdy newspaper staff students--attended Bolt. Those kids always spoke so highly of their hip, relevant, spiritual, articulate pastor, Dustin Jenkins. In Dustin's first few months in our area, he spoke at a lay speaker's course, which I attended. He was brilliant, poetic, and inspiring. I was immediately drawn to this young pastor, this young black clergyman who was quickly becoming beloved everywhere he went. Even the Bolt members who resisted his appointment came to love him in those first fruitful, life-filled summer days. I wasn't a member of his church, but I loved him just like everyone else did.

From a purely nonspiritual perspective, it just so happened Bolt UMC and Rev. Dustin Jenkins were looking for a new staff person at the exact same time we began our work together as candidate/mentor. From a solely spiritual perspective, it seemed to me, God saw to it that Bolt UMC and Rev. Dustin Jenkins were looking for a new staff person at the exact same time we began our work together as candidate/mentor.

Dustin asked me if I wanted to work with him in the church. When I spastically, heartily yelled, "Oh yes!" he just grinned and said he would start the process of getting my employment approved by the church personnel committee.

I really don't know what my job at Bolt was ever supposed to be. I really don't remember even what my job title was, if I even had one. I wasn't the youth pastor because the church already had a middle-aged married couple coordinating the thriving youth group. I wasn't the associate pastor because Bolt wasn't really a large enough church to have or need a second clergyperson. Besides, I couldn't have been considered the AP of that church when I hadn't even started seminary yet. I wasn't the Christian education director because I wasn't responsible for Sunday school or Bible studies in the church.

Looking back on my work at Bolt with Dustin, I would define my role as the assistant to the pastor. My day-to-day work consisted of tasks the pastor had for me to do. I helped visit people. In the beginning, I accompanied Dustin on some of his visitation, and as time went along, he would give me my own visitation assignments. I filled in for Dustin on Wednesday nights for Bible study when he had to be out of town. (This was fairly frequent since Dustin's statewide commitments in the Methodist conference were growing, and he often had to travel for meetings in Charleston). Every week I served as liturgist, and I would do the children's sermon. Twice that year I preached the Sunday sermon when Dustin was on vacation. He let me organize the entire worship service those Sundays, as well. I was barely twenty-one years old, and instead of getting my first glimpses into darkened bars, rather than getting my first legal (or for me, ever) sips of alcohol, I was getting more than a glimpse, I was getting a crash course on life inside a mostly stained-glass tinted sunlit Methodist church; I was getting my first sip of the sometimes sweet, sometimes sour elixir called church life, and leadership therein.

Dustin was a pretty laid-back dude, so the workload, stress level working with him at Bolt UMC was normally minimal. In fact, there were some days when Dustin really wouldn't leave much in the way of instructions for me. Sometimes he would leave work early, being long gone before I came into the office after my school day was complete. There were days then when I was left to invent work to do, myself. I soon learned a great truth about pastoral work and work in the church. While there are laid-back days that can tie together to make for a laid-back week or two, the workload can pick up, and life can get really intense, really quickly.

A church member, or a close relative or friend of a church member can have a health crisis at any moment, day or night.

A church member, or a close relative or friend of a church member can die at any moment, day or night.

A mundane day, a day finding yourself sitting in a pew in the sanctuary, all alone with God and a book and a cup of coffee, can become a critical, stress-filled day in just a few seconds when that phone rings and the voice on the other end echoes distress and the silent sound of tears. I learned this truth working for Dustin at Bolt, and it has remained true for me in all my years of ministry, in all the various churches and communities I have served. There can be more relaxed days within the typical nine-to-five workday for a pastor than for other professionals. We typically set our own schedules and aren't required to punch a time clock.

For instance, on days when I know I will be working late, spending evening hours at the church in meetings or teaching classes, I will give myself a more leisurely morning, or I will block out an hour or two in the afternoon for a walk or a nap. Within a moment's notice though, the pastor may need to be at his or her absolute professional, spiritual, human best when a need arises in someone else's life. When those days dawn, when those moments come, when those needs arise, the pastor has to be there with all the grace, all the love, and all the humanity he or she can muster. It makes no difference what kind of day the pastor is having personally. It makes no difference where the pastor is spiritually, whether the pastor's interior life with God is healthy and vibrant, or if he or she is experiencing emptiness, edginess, or an absence with God. None of that matters when the phone call comes. A pastor goes. A pastor goes for Christ. A pastor goes with Christ. A pastor goes to give Christ. The person, the family, the friend in need on the other end of that phone will expect, will need, sometimes will absolutely demand, nothing less than the pastor's Christly best.

There were days when my employment at Bolt consisted of

sipping cappuccinos from McDonald, reading from my devotional book Dustin and I were reading and discussing together. I would do a home visit or two, maybe make a run to the hospital if we had any church members there, and that was it.

Then suddenly, one day, I learned how quickly human life can change. Then suddenly, one day, I learned how quickly a pastor's work can get intense and completely consuming in time and energy--both physical energy, and the more sacred, fragile emotional energy.

Three tragedies struck the family of Bolt UMC nearly simultaneously that spring. Spring, normally the season of new life and newly dawned hope, became for that good church a season of uncertainty, a season of impending doom. In so many ways, the leafed-out trees seemed to weigh us down like the drama going on within our community, instead of making our hearts glad about the promise of new life. That spring, our hearts fixated on the looming shadows of death, not the new life our faith assures us will dawn.

At nearly the same time, within no more than a week or two of one another, two young women in the church discovered they had terminal cancer. They were both mothers of little girls.

Christy and her husband Bobby had a little girl named Lucy. Christy was a stay-at-home mommy for Lucy, who wasn't quite school age yet. Christy had a sweet, friendly personality. She had curly brown hair, and she was a little plump. I always found her easy to talk to and a positive lifeforce. At a follow-up test after what had been a regular check-up with her doctor, Christy discovered her body was ravaged with bone cancer.

Leah was a tiny lady, short in stature and painfully thin. She would bring her little daughter Tessy to church each and every Sunday. I always assumed Leah was a single mom because I never saw her with a guy at church. As it turned out, she was indeed married to a really good guy, Mike, who just wasn't "the church type." Leah had recently enrolled in college, just as she was sending Tessy off to kindergarten. Just a few hours after she had been playing with her little girl in a green field filled with daffodils beside their house, Leah discovered from her doctor, her test results were not good. Her liver was ravaged with cancer, and her doctor feared cancer had probably spread to other vital organs.

Just as we were beginning to process the deep sadness enveloping the church over Christy and Leah, Dustin got a phone call from a young couple in the church.

"Come on, Jeff," he said to me as he poked his head in the main church office where I was working on the coming Sunday's bulletin. "We need to go to the hospital and visit with Jimmy and Tracy. Something is wrong with Baby Kyle."

Over the years in my work as a pastor, I have been in quite a number of hospital rooms. Some of those rooms have been places of healing, some of those rooms have been places of great pain. A few of those rooms have been sanctuaries of death. No hospital room I have ever been in was as stifling and as tortured as that hospital room at Princeton Community Hospital which Dustin and I rushed to, to pray with Jimmy, Tracy, and their child, Kyle.

Moments before Dustin and I entered that room, Jimmy and Tracy had learned that their son had leukemia, and Princeton Hospital was planning to airlift baby Kyle to Duke University Medical Center.

As we entered, Jimmy was clutching Tracy's shoulder as Tracy held Kyle. Her salty wet tears were rolling off of her face onto her baby's mop of hair. The baby looked around the room nonchalantly. He smiled and reached his hands out for a large Tigger stuffed animal sitting on the nightstand. Jimmy wasn't crying, but he looked like he could curl up and die. Standing there helplessly, touching his wife, staring at his very sick but normal-looking little boy, Jimmy looked like a little-lost boy himself.

I observed Dustin, tall and muscular like the high school and college basketball star he had been, gently, unobtrusively going over to stand with the heartbroken daddy. Dustin placed his hand on Jimmy's shoulder, mirroring for the husband the exact support he was giving his wife. I awkwardly and slowly made my way to stand beside Dustin.

Jimmy's own tears started to fall freely when he saw and felt Dustin's presence.

"Thank you, Dustin, for being here. It means so much to us. Thank you too, Jeff," Jimmy said between anguished sobs. I was grateful Jimmy mentioned me. I could tell, just from the touches, the gestures, the knowing way Tracy now looked up with moist eyes and a grateful smile to her pastor, how much history, how much of a relationship Rev. Dustin Jenkins had with this young couple. This young couple who were in such a sweet spot in life, blessed with a beautiful young child, now so suddenly and unexpectedly cast into such a dark void of unknowing, certainly needed their young pastor to be with them. And he was. I felt-- if not utterly and unconditionally welcome--my presence was at least tolerated. These moments, these sacred moments had nothing to do at all with me. My heart felt as if I was intruding in some way. For a brief, fleeting moment, I thought maybe I should step outside, excusing myself into the hallway. My instincts told me though that my leaving the room would be a greater distraction than my silently remaining.

Dustin would later teach me the actual term of pastoral caregiving that he was practicing in those moments with that young, beautiful, bleeding family. The term which he was then modeling for me and allowing me to enter into with Jimmy, Tracy, and Kyle was, he said, "a ministry of presence." I would hear the term later on in my seminary education, but long before I heard it explained academically, I had witnessed it practiced humanely.

"When you have a ministry of presence, Jeff," Dustin said to me later on that day, "words aren't necessary. Sometimes they can be a hindrance. Just your being there makes all the difference in the world to people who are hurting. We didn't need to say many words to Jimmy and Tracy. All we needed to say was that we love them, their church loves them, and most importantly Jesus Christ loves them. More than the words spoken though, our presence with them conveyed all that love." We were having a debriefing session, sitting in the soft light of the evening sun dancing through the stained-glass windows of the sanctuary of Bolt. I appreciated the fact Dustin wanted to take the time to counsel me, his young mentee and protégé, after such an emotional pastoral emergency. I could also tell though that Dustin himself was very shaken up by all the upheaval we witnessed in a young family's life in that terrible hospital room.

I never asked him, but I wondered then, and I certainly wonder now, so deep into my own ministry as I write this, if Dustin had ever encountered such sadness before in the life of his church. When I really think about it, Dustin was probably about the age way back then as I am now. I bet the weight of the moment was just as new to him that day as it was to me. The difference was, he had been in other hospital rooms. He had witnessed other family members breaking down. I don't think he had ever been with the young parents of a tiny child as they broke down, though. The pain was in his own deep baritone voice as he reflected with me, sitting in the beauty of dusk in the sanctuary of his own church.

"When Jimmy told us the doctors said Kyle has leukemia, it

was hard to take. When Tracy's crying made the baby start crying, that was hard to take, too. It was hard to witness all that and stay strong within it." I saw a tear fall out of one of Dustin's dark brown eyes then, and it reminded me he also had tears in his eyes after we had prayed with Jimmy, Tracy, and Kyle.

We hadn't been in the room with them for very long, but we knew the helicopter was coming posthaste to take the baby to Duke. Dustin had asked us all to join hands in a little circle. We formed a circle around Tracy who remained seated on the hospital bed, holding her baby boy. Dustin put his hand softly on one of Kyle's little hands. I held Tracy's hand, and I could feel the strength of her grip slowly weakening as the magnitude of what was happening to her child, to her little family, descended upon her being. Dustin's prayer was moving and brief, as it needed to be.

"Jesus," he began in a soft voice, a voice which gained volume and strength, but which never lost any tenderness, "Kyle is your child, and we know you love him. We know the waters of Kyle's baptism continue to pour over him and surround him. We know those waters continue to carry him, and will, forever. God, I know you know how much Jimmy and Tracy love their son. May they all three feel your love for them now. May they also feel the love of their church family and may that love help support and sustain them. Holy Spirit, love is a miracle. At this hour, we put our total faith and reliance in the miracle of your love: your love for all people, your love for us in this circle, and your love especially, for Kyle. Amen."

There were tears. There were hugs. Dustin and I left that hospital room as a baby gently cooed to his mother, and mother and father desperately clung to him.

There were many treatments and long hospital stays for baby Kyle at Duke. Dustin would go down and visit them at least once every couple of weeks. I never journeyed down there during my employment at Bolt UMC, but when I became a student myself at Duke less than a year later, I got to visit Kyle and his parents.

Baby Kyle died at Duke, with his parents holding his hands, within a year of that first terrible day of his illness. Their pastor, Rev. Dustin Jenkins, was there with them.

Christy and Leah both began their chemotherapy and radiation treatments around that same time period. Christy and Bobby weren't wealthy by any means, but they were more the upper crust economically at Bolt UMC. Bobby coached women's basketball at a nearby college, and both Christy and Bobby had popular, well-to-do parents in the community. Having more means and good insurance, most of Christy's medical care occurred down south at Wake Forest University in Winston-Salem.

Leah was poor. Her husband Mike worked, but they struggled to make it. Before she got sick, Leah cleaned houses and worked through a temp agency doing secretarial and janitorial work. She got all her medical care in Princeton. Leah was already so tiny anyway, I worried that when all the cancer treatment started kicking into her little body, she would just be blown away by a strong mountain wind whipping down our blue mountains.

Bolt UMC loved both Christy and Leah and their families. I was proud of the people of Bolt, and I learned much from them as I witnessed them rallying around two young families, families living through storms, traumatic events which could potentially make their lives crumble and forever change. I remember feeling then, and I still feel now, more than a decade and a half later, that Christy, Bobby, and Lucy probably got more attention and care than Leah, Mike, and Tessy. Christy got mentioned first and more often in the prayer concerns in church than Leah did. While the women's group prepared meals for both families, Christy and her family always received meals first, and I noticed more of the ladies volunteered to prepare those meals.

Leah was cared for. She was cared for, though, only after Christy received care.

This was true even in the pastoral care work of Dustin. Dustin was already close to Christy's husband, Bobby, and I assumed their friendship was based, in part, on their shared love of basketball. Dustin tended to really dote on doll baby Lucy when her parents brought her to church. Every few days I noted Dustin would go and visit Christy. He never mentioned visiting Leah. I did. I took it upon myself to mention Leah in conversation and prayer every time Christy came up.

Overall, Bolt did take good care of Leah, too. Dustin did finally begin making visits to Leah part of his pastoral routine. It only happened after I had left my position at the church to attend seminary, and I told him Leah had gotten accustomed to a weekly visit . I don't know for sure, but I always suspected economic and social standing had a tremendous amount to do with the care level and attention between Christy and Leah. If Leah ever realized she got less care and attention than Christy, this gracious young lady never mentioned it to me. She never would have. Christy could never be blamed either. She was a dear soul, as well.

I learned a lesson at Bolt I never forgot. I have seen the same type of scenario unfold in other churches I have worked in over the years. Folks, including pastors, only have so much time. Folks, including pastors, only have so much energy. Folks, including pastors, only have so much compassion. We all have only so much time in our days. We all have only so much energy in the machine of our bodies, in the spirit of our souls. We should have an unlimited well of compassion for our fellow human beings, but like any well, there are seasons when the bucket coming up isn't always weighed down, overflowing with water.

When there are multiple sufferers, when the suffering of souls requires organization and intentional care from church and pastor, more often than not, I believe, care isn't extended on an equal, humane level. One soul always gets more. One soul always gets less. I just pray the soul who gets less never realizes it. When it comes to the distribution of the water coming out of that well of compassion and care, I am afraid "who knows whom, who is connected to whom, and who has more wealth" becomes a factor, bringing tears to Christ's eyes. I try not to judge. I have been guilty of it, too.

When it came to the two sick young ladies of Bolt, I wasn't guilty of giving the one more care because of who she and her family were in the community, and what they had. When I saw Leah was receiving less care, I decided I would shower her with my own. Christy got far less from me than Leah did. I don't know. I suppose I have always had a deep, native love for the underdog. I am sure it comes from having been an underdog myself all my life. In many respects, I think my "underdog mentality" and "downtrodden, left-behind radar" has served me and the Gospel of Christ, which I try to serve, well. There can be a downside to it, though.

My propensity for showering with love the left-out and left-behind can leave the popular and the prosperous just as impoverished of Christian love and care as the left-out and left-behind usually are. Dustin Jenkins saw this within me, and he cautioned me about it.

It was in reference to the youth group. I was voicing concern to him that several of the nerdy and overweight young people were not being included in the life of the group as they should be.

"Just remember, Jeff," Dustin said, "the popular kids: the football stars, the cheerleaders, the class officers, need your love and attention too. Believe it or not, the kids, the people who do well in the world, still have problems. They need Jesus, too." Those were gently corrective or red flag words that I have tried to remember. With those words in my mind, I did begin visiting Christy more often even though I knew Dustin was going over there very often.

Christy was a joyful soul. Even in the middle of the worst of cancer's ravaging pain, she would smile. She would laugh at three-year-old Lucy's exploits. When I visited Christy, she sat on her couch with Lucy playing with her Barbie dolls on the floor, safe by her mommy's feet. Lucy was stuffing Barbie into the little Barbie car headfirst, and still, the car would move and drive despite the fact its driver was ensconced headfirst into the driver's seat. Christy laughed, and I laughed. Lucy giggled, and Barbie motored on.

Lucy's ill mother looked like any normal mother that day, except for the bandana she wore on her head and the paleness of her face. She spoke of the future with as much certainty as any mother and wife would. Christy spoke of the travel plans she and Bobby were making for the summer. She spoke of Bobby's excitement for the freshman class coming onto his basketball team the following fall. Moving her hand through Lucy's hair as Barbie stopped her car momentarily, Christy spoke of her anxiety but pride that Lucy would be starting preschool in months and kindergarten in just over a year. I forgot I was visiting a very sick person. I forgot I was in the presence of a dying woman.

My frequent visits with Leah revealed a very similar, sad, sacred scene of life.

Leah's sweetness and humility could not translate into resolve and fight. Already somewhat frail in body before she got sick, Leah didn't have much bodily strength in reserve. Her heart was so strong, though. She was holding her four-year-old Tessy in her arms, reading her little one a *Poky Little Puppy* story, while she herself received an IV at the doctor's office. Her eyes seemed to hint at tears when she looked up and saw me.

"Oh look, Tessy. Here's our friend Jeff," she said.

Tessy buried her head in her momma, hiding from me.

I laughed.

"How are you, Miss Leah?" I asked softly. All was silent but the click of the IV.

"I am making it, Jeff. I have to, with my beloved one here." Leah kissed the top of her daughter Tessy's head. Tessy had definitely inherited her mother's long black hair.

I nodded. "Yes, you have a lot to live for, friend."

"I do," Leah said. "Come on and sit down if you want. If you don't care to listen to little *Poky Little Puppy*. She laughed. "Tessy will be upset if I don't finish. Then we can talk."

I did indeed sit there as a frail, loving young mother read to her little girl — a little girl who could have been nearly an exact copy of her mother, a little girl still just clinging to her mother. I could feel the love, as well as see it, between Leah and her Tessy. As I listened to Leah's voice — a voice with a deep Southern twang and a certain vulnerability, an audible trembling to it — I closed my eyes for a few moments and prayed this good young mother and this needy little child would have many more stories, many more blessed moments to hold each other so tightly.

Leah died quietly in her sleep a few months later. Mike found her when he came in from work. I read scripture at her funeral. I watched helplessly during the service as a grieving husband silently wept. I wondered how life would unfold for the little girl who loved her mother so. I prayed Tessy would somehow remember her mother's gentle voice, her mommy's comforting touch, but I wasn't certain if she ever could. I was certain, though, that Tessy would always hold within her heart her mother's sweet, good soul. I was equally as certain Tessy would somehow always be able to feel her mother's endless love forever upon her.

Christy died about a year later. I was already gone, living and studying at Duke. She died in the hospital in Winston- Salem. Lucy was there, and there were Barbie dolls scattered around the room. Christy got to stroke Lucy's hair a little bit before a family friend took Lucy back out to the waiting room. The little blonde-haired girl had no idea then she would never see her sweet mother again. Christy asked Bobby how basketball practice was going. He described for her a new play he was devising. Then she asked him what he planned to pull out for Lucy to take to Show and Tell the next day at school. Christy reminded Bobby she couldn't take a Barbie doll again. She had taken that last time—Daddy had to help her think of something new, something a little more creative to take this time. Morphine began kicking in to relieve Christy of her pain. She fell into a quiet, peaceful coma. The next day, after he picked Lucy up from school, Bobby breathed deep, choked back tears, and told his daughter her mommy had died.

In seminary, I was required to take many classes in pastoral care. They were good classes, too. I gleaned so much from them, and I enjoyed them immensely. However, I learned more from one fleeting moment with Rev. Dustin Jenkins than I learned from any book, or any lecture, no matter how good the books and lectures were.

It was just one moment in time.

It became for me though, a moment locked forever in my being, a moment that became eternal.

Callie Baxter was an elderly lady in Bolt UMC. She and her husband Edgar had been members of the church for nearly sixty years, dating back to their marriage right before he left to serve in World War II. Callie and Edgar raised their children in the church, too. By the late 1990s, there were grandchildren as well, but none of the rest of the family attended Bolt. Like so many mainline Protestants of the era, Callie and Edgar's sons and their families left the family church for a larger, nondenominational church with a Pentecostal flare.

In the summer of the year I worked at Bolt, Callie had grown very sick, a combination of cancer and severe dementia. She was under hospice care and had grown unresponsive. Dustin and I were taking turns, checking in on Callie a couple of times a day between the two of us. We knew we were on a death watch, and all of the Baxter family-- Edgar, their two sons, their wives, and several of the grown grandchildren — were there. Dustin and I had just finished lunch at a fast food joint, and he suggested we go on to the Baxter home and do a visit together.

When we arrived, Edgar met us at the door in tears. The bald, frail little man couldn't say a word. One of his sons, Jay, came up and spoke to us. "It won't be long now. Mom is slipping away," he said in a hushed tone. "Why don't you all go in and pray with her."

Callie's bedroom was packed with family and the hospice nurse who sat quietly on a stool beside the bed. Everyone made room for Dustin, and for me in his wake. Callie's pastor reached down and took her hand, and he began to pray. When he was done, there was silence and subdued cries throughout the room. Edgar, who was standing beside me, very nearly leaning on me in his feebleness, broke the silence.

"You know, Dustin, Callie loved to hear you sing. She loved your sermons and your prayers. Lord, she loved to hear you sing though. It meant so much to her, that Sunday several years ago when you closed your sermon singing "Blessed Assurance." She cried because that was her favorite hymn. She sang it to her own mother as she lay dying in the hospital in Bluefield, oh those many years ago."

I reached up and squeezed Edgar's hand, which rested on my shoulder. The next thing I knew, within just a few holy seconds, the sound of Dustin's deep baritone voice and the brush of angel's wings and sparks from the Holy Spirit's fiery love all filled that bedroom, making it a sanctuary, such a holy place.

Blessed assurance,

Jesus is mine

O what a foretaste of glory divine

Heir of salvation, purchase of God

Born of his Spirit.

Washed in his blood.

This is my story

This is my song,

Praising my Savior,

All the day long.

This is my story,

This is my song.

Praising my savior,

All the day long.

Dustin held Callie's hand, and he leaned in close to her face as he sang. We were all there as part of the sacred experience, but Dustin was singing for Callie alone.

I knew I was witnessing holiness. I knew I was seeing pastoral care and pastoral love at its very best.

Callie didn't die that day. Her heart beat on for a few more days after that. Thanks to her loving pastor, I have always felt like she died with a hymn in her heart.

Callie's death was one of the last events I lived through in my nine-month employment as Dustin's assistant at Bolt. Shortly thereafter, the church was having a reception, saying goodbye to me. The last Sunday of my employment, Dustin had a special time in the worship service. Folks came up and make a circle around me. They placed their hands upon me as Dustin led them in prayer, a special blessing as I left their loving circle to attend seminary.

They knew I would come home someday, as a pastor. They knew their patience and love in letting me serve them had gone a long way in beginning to mold me into a pastor.

No single person has ever taught me more about being a pastor than Rev. Dustin Jenkins. Dustin came and visited me a couple of times while I attended Duke, his alma mater. Yes, my love and admiration for Dustin led me to Duke. In fact, I applied nowhere else. Had I not been accepted there, I had no other school on my short list to consider.

Dustin's time at Bolt UMC was the high point of that church's life. Attendance and, most importantly, the Spirit and the love within that church peaked during his remarkable nine-year run. The church, which had in some small corners, in whispers, and in letters, doubted and resisted a young black pastor coming to them, fell in deep mourning when the time came for Dustin to say good-bye.

He received a major promotion in the Methodist world. The bishop named Dustin, a District Superintendent. DSs, as they are known in the circle still following Wesley's ways, have supervisory responsibility for a large area of churches, and all the DSs together comprise the bishop's cabinet. The bishop and the cabinet make all the personnel decisions in Methodism--they decide what pastors serve what churches. In our profession, being a DS entails great responsibility, great power, and at least in our little circle, great prestige. Dustin was District Superintendent of the area of West Virginia including Morgantown and Fairmont. For a young man just in his mid to late forties, it was a major career advancement.

We stayed in touch some during those years. The end of my seminary education and the first few years of my ministry coincided with Dustin's years as a DS and on the cabinet. I wasn't sure how a young pastor just getting started was supposed to maintain a friendship with an old friend who had reached the upper power structure of our church. I loved Dustin and never stopped caring about him. I called him rarely, though. My e-mails to him became sparse because I didn't want him to think, or anyone else to ever think, I was trying to use an old friend to advance myself. How sad that I let a system so poison my thinking. How sick the system is, which could encourage such thinking. During this era of our lives, Dustin and I really never hung out or reached out to each other. When we would see each other though, maybe a couple of times a year at the yearly Methodist conference and perhaps another statewide church meeting here or there, we were both extremely warm and gracious to one another. I always thought Dustin seemed as happy to see me as I was to see him.

Dustin served as a DS as long as our church law says any one person can serve, eight years. When Dustin hit the prescribed maximum time for the superintendent's position, the bishop assigned him to another church. Dustin was assigned to a very prominent church in Charleston, our capital city. I was so glad when Dustin became just a regular old church pastor again.

For one thing, I and many other people thought Dustin was being wasted as a district superintendent. While he did a solid job and while the position is a highly important and loftily regarded one, everyone who knew anything about Dustin's ministry and his service was keenly aware that he was the most tender and humane of pastors, with one of the most articulate and effective preaching styles of anyone our church had to offer. Very few of us could love our people as much as Dustin did. Very few of us could preach as good a sermon, week-in and week-out, as he could. If anyone needed to be the pastor of a church, lovingly leading the congregation's life together, strongly administering it to do the right thing in the name of Christ's love, joyfully teaching it to reach out to others in the name of that same love, it was Rev. Dustin Jenkins.

For another far more selfish reason, when Dustin became a parish pastor again, I felt like we could have a normal friendship again. When Dustin was just another pastor like me (albeit in a far larger church), I would no longer feel self- consciousness or insecurity about e-mailing or calling my old friend. I really looked forward to contacting Dustin and sharing a cup of coffee together like we had so many times in the past. I longed to share a meal and talk for hours about the various church people we had together loved at Bolt and the church people in our current churches we now loved.

I had it in my mind to call Dustin soon that first summer within a few weeks of his taking over in his new church.

Summer seamlessly yielded to the fall, and I still hadn't made the phone call or written the e-mail yet to reconnect with Dustin.

One Sunday morning early in that fall, Dustin didn't show up for Sunday school. When their new pastor, who they were already growing to really love, hadn't shown up within ten minutes of the beginning of church, a few of the trustees decided to drive over to the parsonage. Dustin's car was there. When he didn't come to the door, one of the trustees decided it was appropriate to take his own key to the parsonage and unlock the door.

They found Dustin, dead in his bed. He had died peacefully in his sleep the night before. I never actually heard confirmation anywhere, but the assumption I picked up from everyone else was that he had died of a massive heart attack. He was barely in his late-fifties. He was handsome, still young, still and forever a bachelor.

He was, still and forever, the best pastor I have ever known. He is still the model, the measure for me. As I continue to hopefully grow and evolve, always, perpetually "becoming pastor," Dustin Jenkins was authentically, intuitively, long ago all I ever pray to be.

5 New Dawn

The nine or so months I spent working for Dustin Jenkins at Bolt United Methodist Church entailed perhaps the most fruitful and holy season of my preparation and education for becoming a pastor. In saying that, I intend to in no way diminish my divinity school education. My years at Duke were seminal in my spiritual development and human evolution, and the education I received there is not, to paraphrase William Faulkner, *was*. The education I received there still *is*. Not a day goes by in my pastoral work or even in my life in general when I don't remember something I learned there or pick up a book on my bookshelf dating back to those years. Perpetually I gain new insight or remember a forgotten jewel which I first encountered either in a classroom of that brownstone castle or sitting solitarily with the book in the Gothic Reading Room.

The time spent working under Dustin, though, was the early springtime of my being. It was then, through that work, that God plowed the fields of my intellect and imagination and sowed the seeds of my spirit and my soul to prepare me for the growing season of seminary.

Work with Dustin didn't just involve the Bolt UMC. There was actually another small Methodist church Dustin Jenkins was pastor of: New Dawn.

New Dawn was an African American church "yoked" to Bolt

in what the United Methodist Church refers to as a "charge." Sometimes charges consist of two or more churches of equal size — usually pretty small, say twenty to forty people — who share a pastor because on their own, they can't afford one. In other cases, the Methodist leadership will yoke a small church with a larger one, with the larger church sharing a pastor with the smaller church. It's one of the most Christian acts within the Methodist system: a larger, healthier church being willing to share and sacrifice some pastoral labor to give a struggling church a chance to either make a comeback or die with dignity. In the case of Bolt and New Dawn, Bolt was willing to share Dustin with New Dawn, a once thriving congregation then down to fifteen to twenty members.

Dustin never required me to attend worship at New Dawn. I was employed strictly by Bolt UMC. Still, New Dawn UMC fascinated me. I really wanted to go. The problem was one of time. In order for Dustin to be present at Bolt for both worship service and Sunday school the hour prior to worship, New Dawn's morning worship service was held at the ungodly hour of 8:00 a.m. Many a Saturday night, I went to bed with the intention of waking up early enough to get ready to attend worship at New Dawn. Most Sunday mornings, it never happened. I was three months into my nine-month employment with Dustin before I made it to worship at New Dawn UMC.

How do I write this poetically? I don't think there is any way to write it poetically. New Dawn was in the "black part of town." I was a sheltered little white boy from the burbs, and I didn't even know where the "black part" of my 90 percent white southern West Virginian, Appalachian town even was. I figured out it was High Street. High Street was where New Dawn United Methodist Church was. I was twenty-one years old. I had lived in my hometown my whole life. I had no idea the street, the neighborhood, and the church even existed.

I promised myself I wasn't being a racist when I made sure all four of my car doors were locked solid when I left the house that Sunday morning. High Street was two blocks over from Mercer Street, the main downtown drag of Princeton: Mercer Street, where the high school kids "cruised" on Friday and Saturday night; Mercer Street, where alcoholic veterans congregated outside the VA; Mercer Street, where the prostitutes walked. (Local legend, or should I say scuttlebutt said that if the soda bottle she carried was closed, she was just on an errand. Leave her alone. But if the lid was off, she was, how to say this poetically, open for business.) In other words, getting to High Street required traversing a pretty questionable little old neighborhood, the old downtown drag, itself.

We West Virginians value realism far more than we do imagination. When I saw a steep grade off Thorn Street, I had a hunch. The green sign told me I was right. This was High Street. Just up the road, maybe five hundred feet, I saw a little redbrick church, which reminded me very much of my own home church. Sure enough, the old-time sign, dating back before the branches of Methodism reunited and united with the Evangelical Brethren in 1968, read "New Dawn Methodist Episcopal Church. Est. 1865." My heart raced at that, and a shiver coursed up and down my spine. Being the geeky American history aficionado, I am, I was moved with the realization: New Dawn was started the year the Civil War ended. Princeton had been a rebel town. Those spring blue mountains cradled a small piece of the Confederacy. In all likelihood, former slaves had started this church just after they were liberated. It looked like my home church, a church, ironically enough, which had been Methodist Episcopal, South, before the first Methodist reunion in 1939. It was clothed in history just by the very sign on the front wall. Before I even entered the doors, New Dawn UMC welcomed me.

That first Sunday morning I worshiped there, the people of New Dawn clothed me with welcoming love and hospitable grace. Dustin looked surprised to see me when he looked up from his bulletin and saw me when I first walked in. He smiled though, and he introduced me to the twelve or so people who were gathered for worship. Dustin's smile grew even broader when Mary Alice Dreasey and Dotty Hensley enveloped me in hugs. They were huggers at New Dawn. I loved it. I was too.

"Honey, you can just sit here with me," Miss Dotty said to me. She moved her little fan, compliments of Waverly Funeral Home, so I could sit. Dotty was a very pretty elderly lady who looked refined. Like all the other ladies in that church, she wore a dress, and Miss Dotty had a fur hat.

I noticed how adoringly Dotty looked up at Dustin as he began the worship service. Unlike at Bolt, Dustin did not wear his robe at New Dawn. In fact, he just had on his shirt and tie, having discarded even his dress jacket, I suppose, because of the early spring heat already collecting in the century-plus old sanctuary which had only open windows and a soft mountain breeze to provide climate control.

Worship at New Dawn made my spirit soar. I loved it. To be honest, worship at New Dawn was nothing like I expected. Of course, as you can well imagine, I was, God forgive me, expecting the worship service to mirror a stereotype of African American worship I had seen on television and in the movies. I had never experienced a worship service in a black church for myself until that sacred spring morning.

To my shock, surprise, and delight, the worship service at New Dawn was deeply traditional and deeply liturgical. We prayed a morning prayer responsively. We joined our voices in a call-and-response call to worship. We recited together the Apostles' Creed. We sang the Gloria Patri. We observed tradition with the recitation of a psalter, including a sung response. New Dawn United Methodist Church's worship service was far more liturgically *at home* for me than worship in the much larger, much more contemporary Bolt UMC. In those days, Bolt was experimenting with new modes of more upbeat, youth-friendly worship—you know, Amy Grant songs and praise and worship choruses. I hated all that. (I still do.) My little old home church, New Hope UMC, was as old-school Episcopal as you could get, and I loved it. New Dawn was just as "high church" as New Hope, maybe even more so, and worshipping there, my heart found a new church home. From that first Sunday, I loved New Dawn deeply.

It struck me during that first worship service I experienced at New Dawn that the folks who so lovingly welcomed me to worship with them lived a far different human experience than did I—different and yet the same. We recited the same creeds with our voices. We knew the same creeds in our hearts. We heard the same stories about Jesus; we listened to the same theology from Paul. We believed the same stories about Jesus; we accepted the same theology from Paul. When I knew them, the church members from New Dawn were mostly in their late sixties and early seventies. This was the late 1990s–early 2000s. Dotty, Mary Alice, Doc, and the other members of the New Dawn family had come of age in the 1940s and '50s when inhumane Jim Crow laws defined southern society.

These ladies and gentlemen were just a decade or so older than my parents. My dad vividly remembers the "separate but equal" society as he grew up beneath those same mountains, along those same streets, as the New Dawn congregation. "I never really understood what people went through before I had my own children," Dad said to me on more than one occasion. "After I became a father, it hit me: how would I explain to my little boy, 'We can't use that bathroom son,' or 'We can't sit down there. We have to go up to the balcony to watch the movies, girls.' I don't see how dads and moms ever explained that to their children."

My new friends at New Dawn *were* the children whose moms and dads had to tell, "We can't go there. We can't sit there." Of course, facilities and services segregated by race were outward expressions: visible faces, hands, and feet witnessing to deep heartbreak, sorrowing souls, the ancient disease of the people called American—the disease of racism that kept America from being everything her ideals called her to grow to become.

I had read about segregation, Jim Crow, the scourge of white supremacy, and the holiness of the Civil Rights movement. I remember crying in high school when I read a book about Dr. King, and I saw a photograph of a crowd at a peaceful march centering on one young black man carrying a sign which said simply, "I Am A Man." I read, I listened to the lyrical cadences of "I Have a Dream" until I knew whole portions of the speech by heart, and I discovered the text and video of King's last "I Have Been To The Mountaintop" sermon he delivered so passionately the night before he was murdered. My dad told me stories about his segregated boyhood. I read the history myself. I saw pictures and watched documentaries. The people of New Dawn lived it. It occurred to me all those years ago that they lived it and they endured it, perhaps because "new dawn" wasn't just a historic name for their church. It had profound meaning for them.

The folks of New Dawn believed in the hope the name of their church family conveyed: through the prejudice, past the discrimination; distancing the hate, leaving the alienation, Christ would bring them to a new dawn. I could never equate the sorrow of my young life to the struggle of my black friends at New Dawn, but the sores and scars of my past had led me to believe in a new dawn, too. Without faith that Christ's love would make tomorrow better than today, I would never have had the courage to survive the hell of my teenage years. Though I never articulated these words to any of them, whenever I worshiped at New Dawn, I felt so at home. Feeling safe and secure at home, my heart resonated with words from John Denver: "Yet as different as we are, we're still the same."

Just as I loved New Dawn deeply from the very beginning, from that first Sunday on, I loved Miss Dotty deeply too. She was such a classy lady. She was such a Spirit-filled lady, too. When Dustin was preaching, every so often Dotty would punctuate his thoughts with exclamation: "Well," she would say when her young pastor made a unique, or relevant, or deep, or soulful point. She would say it this way, lengthening the life of the *l*: "Welllllllllll!"

Probably about halfway through the sermon, Miss Dotty retired her *well* for *all right.*

I can still see Dustin's young, handsome countenance up there behind the pulpit of New Dawn—his pulpit. I can still hear his strong, poetic baritone voice. "When we feel overwhelmed in this life, when we feel overcome in this world, when circumstances make us feel unimportant, not counted, in the shadows, we need to remember scripture teaches us our God works in the lives of ordinary people . . ."

"All right!" Dotty proclaimed.

"God promised Abraham and Sarah a new family and new land. God promised Abraham and Sarah their family would be God's family. God made a miracle within Abraham and Sarah. Abraham and Sarah were ordinary people. And they were God's people."

"All right!"

The eloquent, inspiring young black pastor went on, with me as transfixed by his words as my new, elderly friend was. "Mary: Young, little, unmarried, unimportant Mary. God chose her to bring God's son, God's presence into this world. Mary would give birth and give motherly love to Jesus. Joseph would be his daddy and help protect him and teach him. God moved, God still moves. God used, God still uses. God loved, God still loves ordinary people."

"All right!" Miss Dotty took a piece of tissue from her

pocketbook and patted the tears dry, coming out of her eyes. "And on this earth, from the Sea of Galilee to Jerusalem's gates, Jesus taught, and Jesus healed ordinary people. From the grass and the flowers of the hillside where he preached his Sermon on the Mount, to the waysides and the side streets where lepers and prostitutes found a friend in him, Jesus forgave, and Jesus befriended, ordinary people. To Gethsemane so dark and hopeless, to the cross so lonely and loveless, from drops of sweat like blood, to wounds so bloody and violent, Jesus died out of his love for ordinary people."

"Well all right!" Miss Dotty said as she openly wept and smiled. It was the first of many times I would hear Miss Dotty combine her two affirmations, *well* and *all right*. *Well* meant the preacher was on the right track, taking the congregation on a good road to a better place. *All right* meant the preacher had us to a place where we could feel the first light of resurrection hope shining on our clothes. "Wellllllll, all right!" meant the preacher had us at the foot of the cross as Christ breathed his last sacred breath: God's love was pulsating through the words; Jesus's holy presence was radiating from the word being preached, the Word visibly and tangibly come alive through the words of the faithful preacher.

"And on that first Sunday, it was the women first, and then Peter and John, who rushed to that tomb that was cold and empty, that cave that was dark and lifeless…God allowing the greatest miracle of all, the miracle of eternal love to first be witnessed by ordinary people..."

"Welllllll . . . All right!" I didn't say a word, but my heart sang.

There were some wonderful folks in that New Dawn congregation.

Besides Dotty and Mary Alice, I remember a little man named Doc. Doc was a retired postman who had spent his working life walking the streets of Princeton, our hometown, delivering mail. Now a diminutive bald man, back in his youth Doc had been a soldier in the Korean conflict. "I was a kid during World War II, but I remember it all from the perspective of being home," he told me one sun-drenched Sunday morning in the parking lot after church. "I remember when Mr. Roosevelt died too. Lord, we wept. We all wept around here. In Mr. Truman's time, when Korea came around, I was of age, and I went," Doc said.

When I asked him what the war in Korea had been like, Doc just got a faraway look on his face and maybe the twinkle of a tear just starting to collect. He quickly turned to me and smiled. "I was glad to get home. We all were — those of us who got to come home. After being shot at and scared, hungry, and homesick, every day delivering the mail around here was heaven, a real blessing. Then love came, and kids came, you know, a family of my own..." This tear, Doc could not suppress. As a gentle tide pulled from his lively brown eyes, he said to me, "Time claimed my wife, Gladys, and a car accident my little girl, Eleanor, and Vietnam my son, Woodrow. The family's gone except in here." He gently punched his chest. "And in there." He pointed up to New Dawn.

Marty Alice was as slight of build and usually sparing of words as Miss Dotty was grand of person and overflowing with talk. I visited her house once. I learned that in the comfort of her own home, within another sanctuary, this one of her own space, Mary Alice could let the words flow, too. As I recall that day, she was irritated because her neighbor had called her to babysit their children again. Two little children, a boy and a girl, maybe eight and eleven years old, sat in her living room, watching a cartoon on television. Mary Alice had the same type of TV my grandmother had: an old Quasar on wooden legs with bunny ear antennas sitting on the top of the flat top, with one arm pointed due north, straight up, and another stretching to the west to pick up some far-flung signal beyond the mountains. Arranged around the bunny ears, as if insisting that this television was a piece of living room furniture, which could have redeeming value, Mary Alice had — just as my own grandmother had — pictures of family: a husband in uniform circa World War II; a young lady in a wedding dress whose face bore a striking resemblance to Mary Alice; several little baby pictures, and a teenage girl in a tank top uniform holding a basketball.

"I can't keep up with those kids, so I just let them watch that all day. At least I know they are in here, and they're safe. There's not much you can do when the kids aren't your own, or even your grandkids. I just feed them and keep them safe until their mommy gets home from work," she said.

I asked Mary Alice about her family, and she told me she did have children. The little babies in the picture frames on her television were her daughters. They were both grown now. The one who lived closest was two hours away in Winston Salem, North Carolina. The other, her namesake, Mary, lived all the way out in California. The young basketball player was Mary's daughter, Mary Alice's California granddaughter. Mary Alice said that indeed, the photograph of the soldier was indeed her husband. In World War II, her beloved one somehow survived both Guam and Iwo Jima, and, Mary Alice said, had it not been for the dropping of the atomic bombs, he would have been part of the American invasion of Japan.

Mary Alice poured me a glass of iced tea and handed me a cookie she had made just within the hour for her little visiting neighbors. After taking a slight sip of her own tea, she said, "You know, Jeff, I grew up at New Dawn. I received Jesus there. I was baptized right there. I received Communion there, every month of my life. Joe and I got married there. I said a million prayers in the darkness of my closed eyelids there. I have seen the light of Jesus piercing into the darkness there too, every time I have prayed there. My baby girls were baptized there too. I can still see Joe lying there in that chancel, in his casket." She closed her eyes and paused. When she opened her eyes, I could see years of hope and years of love emanating from them but what I saw was the manifestation of hope and love now salted with the distance of years, conditioned by the march of time. "Now, there's just a few of us left in that good old church. We really do appreciate Dustin. We really do appreciate you, too."

Miss Dotty was just a joy. I remember one day she called Dustin as he labored at the computer, trying to finish Sunday's bulletin. With a wink to me, he put her on speaker phone so he could go on typing while she talked.

"The Lord's been good to us, and the Lord is being good to us. I really do believe that, Reverend," Dotty said as Dustin murmured agreement. "I believe we do have to reach out more though, Reverend, don't you? There are some lost souls out there. Lost souls. Hopeless souls. There isn't any reason our little church shouldn't be full on Sunday morning. Full! Now I am not saying you aren't doing your job, Reverend Dustin, because you are. We are the ones who live on High Street. We are the ones who need to reach out more, give these broken people a hug, and draw them inside where God can love them whole."

This time it was Dustin's turn to exclaim, and in the call and response of the conversation, he offered to Dotty's exhortation, "Yes!" and "You are right! You are right!"

As time went on during my almost year working with Dustin at Bolt, I also got to preach a time or two at New Dawn. I loved it. To this day, one of the highlights of my ministry was receiving my own *wells* and more than a few *all rights* from Miss Dotty. I knew I was truly walking with Jesus and saying the words Jesus truly needed me to say when I got the soulful, authentic *welllllll all right.*

The last time I ever worshiped or stood behind the pulpit of New Dawn UMC was for Miss Dotty's funeral. She died a year or so after I left home to attend Duke. Dustin invited me to say a few words at her funeral. Miss Dotty finally got a packed church again when everyone who loved her, everyone left whom she had loved, came out to say good-bye. I told the packed church my "wellll" and "all right" and climatic "wellll all right" story. The laughter, and the "yes," "amen," and "oh yeah, that's Miss Dotty" responses that story elicited told me I was saying the words Jesus needed me to say.

In just the first two or three years after Rev. Dustin Jenkins left Bolt and New Dawn for a promotion within the Methodist hierarchy, Doc, Mary Alice, and other dear souls from that church all died. New Dawn died with them.

6 Education, Part One

When it came time for me to decide where I would go for my seminary education, there was really no decision for me to make. Rev. Dustin Jenkins was an alumnus of Duke. Duke was the only place then that I wanted to go. Most people, most sane, rational, reasonable people, make a list of their school choices. They rank them. They visit them. Not I. For me, it was Duke or bust. I seriously contemplated my acceptance or my rejection from Duke as being an affirmation or a correction from God as to whether or not I was truly called to be a pastor.

I believed with all my heart God did call me to the ministry.

I still had my deep love for writing though, and my love for all the work I had done in Concord's English department. I loved being an English literature student. I loved reading the great works of literature; I loved gleaning meaning from the rushing humanity I felt in the rhythm of words from the masters. I loved writing academic papers on those works. It was nothing for me to produce a twenty- to twenty-five- page paper with a pot of coffee in a night of work. I am not bragging — I still can barely tie my shoes, and I am lost in most matters that really matter in the real world — but darned it, I could make an academic English major paper happen in a few hours, like magic.

My favorite piece I did in my years at Concord was a paper I wrote on Ernest Hemingway's wonderful short story "A Clean, Well-Lighted Place." It's a story seemingly about a couple of bartenders having a chat at closing time. In my paper, I argued the story is a deeply, profoundly Christian work in which Hemingway shouted down with all his literary strength the poison of Social Darwinism. I loved the paper. It did get an A. Hemingway's "A Clean, Well-Lighted Place" remains my absolute favorite short story, to this day. Hemingway is not my favorite writer per se, but lord, I love that story. I wrote a whole sermon once about how the church at its best is "the clean, well-lighted place" lost, lonely people look for in their dire, dark nights.

My Concord English professors encouraged me to pursue a Ph.D. in English. One professor in particular, who knew I was also contemplating seminary and a life's work in ministry, begged me until the day I graduated to apply to a master's programs in English literature. I was so very tempted. When the Concord's English department awarded me the Shrewsberry Award for the top English major in my graduating class, I was thankful, shocked, and scared. What if my winning that award was a sign from God? *"This is the direction I want your life to take, Jeff?"* I was good at the work, and the work did make me very happy. Surely those factors could be signs from God.

There was also the matter of my still being very much a homeboy, a self-aware and self-avowed homebody. A major university, Virginia Tech, lay just forty-five minutes from

Princeton and home. I could work toward my master's and Ph.D. in English, walk away in three or four years as Dr. Kanode, and never ever even have to leave Mom and Dad's house. I was sorely, sorely tempted.

Truly, there hasn't been a time in the last dozen years of my ministry when I haven't wondered what that other life would have been like. I especially contemplate on that subject when life in the parish gets hard, conflicted, lonely, and hurtful. That happens more than anyone outside of ministry, or anyone outside of the inner workings of a church will ever understand.

Every time the "Methodist move-around dance" comes, and the bishop and cabinet calls out my name, asking me to make like a little circuit rider and move on to another Methodist parish somewhere else in the state, I wonder about my alternate reality, my could-have-been self. I wonder about where I would be today as Dr. Kanode, the professor of English literature. As each move in the Methodist ministry takes me farther away from my family and my home, I see Dr. Kanode, my shadow-self, peering out from my eyes, piercing into my reflection each morning in the mirror. Each time, he asks: *"Where would we be now, Jeff-ro, if you had let me live?"* My plan was pretty simple: I would pour my heart, I would bare my soul, I would squeeze my brain, I would flex my intellect as hard as I could, into the application to Duke Divinity School. To use a sports cliché, I "wouldn't leave anything on the field." As the great NASCAR driver Rusty Wallace said in his championship battle with Bill Elliott in 1988, I wanted to come out of turn four on the last lap with all four tires on fire. There could be no question I hadn't given the Duke application everything I had, and everything I am. I would give the application everything I possibly could, of heart, soul, and mind.

Whereas Rusty lost the championship battle to Bill in '88 (but he would beat Earnhardt out to be champion the very next year), my outcome was positive. I got a victory. I was accepted to Duke.

I was so surprised that my hands shook, and my muscles quivered as I read the acceptance letter. I didn't get through the letter before my eyes were all fogged up, and my cheeks were salty and wet with my tears. My parents and my sisters were so proud. I think they were as shocked as I was that I got in. Dustin Jenkins was not surprised at all. He was almost lackadaisical when I gave him my news. "Well yeah, cool. I knew you would get in, Jeff." Either Dustin Jenkins had more faith in me, more faith in God, than either me or my family, or he had "an in" with the Duke admission's team. It could be Duke had a very liberal admissions policy too, and Dustin just knew that.

I took my admission into Duke as the sign of all signs from God: *"Yes, I have called you to be a pastor. Yes, this is the path you must take. Yes, there is another path open to you which would bring you happiness and fulfillment too, but I am opening for you the path I want you to take."* I never even reconsidered or spent any time in further contemplation. I never applied to Virginia Tech or anywhere else to pursue advanced degrees in English literature. I was going to seminary to become a pastor.

The journey away from my parents' home, the home of my childhood, the only home I had ever known, was without question the most traumatic trek of my young life. Leaving my parents was the most profound and the most painful step yet in my evolution, in my growth, in my development as a human being.

I was twenty-one years old. Many of my peers left home when we were eighteen. The fall after our high school graduation, they had left for WVU, for Marshall, for Virginia Tech, for a handful of other colleges and universities. By that same time in our lives, leaving home, leaving Mom and Dad, leaving our hometown, was something many of my friends, acquaintances, and classmates had done years before. My peers adjusted, they reoriented their lives, they grew up, they individualized, a long time before I did. Even my fellow Princeton Tigers who stayed home like I did to go to Concord or to Bluefield State in our sister city, Bluefield, had ventured out of their homes long enough to party with fraternities and sororities, to take exotic trips over spring break, to date and to build sustaining relationships both romantic and within the bounds of friendship. I really had done very little of any of those hard, essential tasks.

I was cursed with being someone who was well-liked by pretty much everyone, with innumerable acquaintances, but with very few, if any, long-standing, life-sustaining, lifelong friends. In college, I repeated the same pattern I lived in high school. I related easily between groups of people and types of people. The pretty girls thought I was cute because I was so sweet: They loved to sit with me and talk in the library, but I never crossed their mind as a guy they would ever go out with on a date. None of my Concord lady friends ever saw me in the potential boyfriend category.

In high school, my best friends were the hippy, probably pot-smoking soccer players, but the muscle-obsessed, testosterone-blessed football players made me a nerdy pet to protect from the rednecks. At Concord, the same thing happened.

In high school, I found my niche in the student newspaper. The dear old *Tiger Tribune* gave me an outlet for my creativity, and the audience it provided for my writing got me much-needed attention, recognition, and accomplishment. I wrote for the Concord College newspaper, too. My career at *The Concordian* was short-lived, as I only wrote for the paper during my freshman year. Although it was a college paper and theoretically should have been far more professional and deeply more literate than any high school newspaper, it wasn't. To be honest, the paper was so cursed with typos, bad grammar, and shoddy production that I was embarrassed for my name to be anywhere near it, let alone in it. I wrote some personal columns like I had in high school that first year, and when summer break came, I was happy to call my college newspaper writing career done.

Within that brief career, I wrote some straight news stories, which got me some great interviews with the president of the college and a few professors. I wrote some feature stories including one on all the twins then enrolled in Concord. That one I did because I had a crush on these twins in my Biology 101 class. I really didn't give a rip about any of the other twins at Concord. I just used the whole idea of researching how many sets of twins we had on campus as a clever ruse to have an excuse to get a shot at talking to that one particular set of twins. These girls were brown-eyed, brown-haired softball players, education majors bound for careers teaching PE classes, coaching sundry girls' athletic teams in high schools somewhere in southern West Virginia. I was hoping interviewing them for a story for the school newspaper would impress them, and I was hoping the gushing, favorable story about them appearing in print would woo them.

You see, I could never tell them apart, so I really was forced to aim my charm at both of them, hoping if I got both of them to have a favorable opinion of me, I could then focus on the one I really wanted to be with. I always thought I was in love with the quiet one and not the buck wild one, but since I could never really tell them apart, I just had to really give them both the old "stare into their eyes with my baby blues" treatment. I was never with them in a social setting because I never did anything socially, and thus I never could tell them apart, having never seen them really "in action" to tell them apart-- the sweet, silent one versus the wild, verbose one. Therefore, all I could *do was just hope and pray I handed the right one the love note.* Yes. As a college freshman, I was so immature that I wrote a "Will you go out with me? You are really pretty. Here's my e-mail" note like any other seventh grader in the county.

The love note didn't work.

The feature story on all the twins at Concord — with a particular emphasis on my biology class, softball playing beauties — didn't work either.

The Concordian just didn't do for me in college what the *Tiger Tribune* did for me in high school.

The best friend I made at Concord I made on that newspaper staff, though. The fun times I had as a college student — the few fun times I allowed myself to have as a college student — I had with those guys.

I suppose we had all been newspaper staff geeks in high school, so collectively, our social skills were comparable to one another — all comparably low. Every day we would gather in the pressroom to watch reruns of *Dallas*, then running on a now-defunct cable network. To this day, that tickles me. There we were, all of these eighteen, nineteen, twenty-something-year-old kids watching a drama/soap opera which had been popular when we were kids, a show which had been the cutting-edge, cultural landmark for our parents twenty years before. To this day, I love *Dallas*, and I will always consider J. R. Ewing the greatest television character of them all. We truly were a motley crew of English or communication major dweebs, all huddled up in our introvert's ghetto, watching a show made for our parents while our peers were transfixed with *Party of Five, Beverly Hills, 90210,* and MTV's *The Real World.*

One day when the rerun of *Dallas* was a re-rerun for us too, someone got the idea that maybe we should venture out of our cavernous pressroom and drive forty minutes away, to the mall in Bluefield. We could have a late lunch, early dinner together, and just hang out. I can still see the collective look of fear coming over all of our faces. Hang out? Just exactly how does one hang out outside the pressroom without J. R. to marvel at, without Cliff Barnes to loathe, without Sue Ellen to feel sorry for? Just exactly how does a group of newspaper staff nerds go out to the mall and hang out like ordinary college kids?

Despite great collective trepidation, we did indeed go for it. I have such fond, warm memories of that day. It was one of the only days I remember I ever truly felt carefree and happy, just a kid feeling the burning fire of youth in my blood. We ate Chinese, and then we raided the junky everything's-a-dollar store in the mall. We all bought squirt guns. I can remember this guy named Ryan holding his squirt gun bazooka just like an Al Qaeda terrorist in the backseat of the car. I can remember us all running through the green, grassy meadows dotted with daffodils back at school. For once in our lives, we were just part of the crowd of kids being kids, worshiping the sun and our juvenescence, donned in our shorts and T-shirts. We laughed and ran. Squirt guns at the ready, we shot each other, ran away from each other, took each other hostage. We scurried all over that campus, looking for cover, making charges, using ditches as trenches. It was so much fun. I felt so alive. I felt so close to all of those guys that day.

And that was pretty much it. I had one day like that. I have one truly awesome memory of the way things probably could have been all through my life as a college student, but the way things were for me for only one day. It was a golden day though.

In terms of dating in college, I made other awkward, tortured attempts very similar to the one I made with the twins. It was in this era that I learned one of the great strategies I used perpetually ever after in my dating life. This strategy has brought me great heartache over the years, but it has gotten me far more dates than I ever could have gotten without it. At Concord, I learned the trick of asking a girl to "hang out" with me as opposed to "going out" with me. "Going out" has clear dating, romantic implications. Hanging out is safe, sanguine, romance-neutral, expectations-limited.

I couldn't find any girls who would go out with me. I found several girls who were happy to hang out with me. I was sweet. I was safe. I could be funny. I had a car.

My first experience "hanging-out" with a girl foreshadowed all the heartbreak I would experience for many years afterward in my life. The cycle repeated itself ad nauseum, time after time over many years. She would be hanging out with me. I would be falling for her because my heart was interested in her from the beginning. She didn't know I even could be falling for her romantically because I had made the terminology for our relationship so safe from the dangerous, choppy waters of sexuality. I would finally come out with my feelings for her. She would be shocked I was falling in love because we were, after all, "just hanging out." My feelings would be as visible as a pulse on your wrist when you're stressed out, or the beating of your heart on your chest when you are silent and still enough to see it. She couldn't reciprocate my feelings of love because we were just hanging out as friends, and she loved me like a brother.

You'd think that I would have learned. Well into my thirties, though, I would ask a lady to "hang out" with me as opposed to going out with me. I just never thought she would go out. She could very well have agreed to hang out though. I wondered many times if I was cursed, if this cycle would go on forever. It didn't, praise be, but it lasted far longer than it should have.

This cycle began with my Concord College girl — well, I can't call her a girlfriend, I suppose, but she was the first thing even close to a girlfriend I ever had. We went out quite a few times, and I think anyone who saw us together assumed we were a dating couple. I can imagine people who saw us out saw a young little college couple out on a date, so young, so inexperienced, so shy — too shy to even hold hands or sit very close together in the restaurant.

Her name was Dee. She wasn't exactly beautiful (any more than I am handsome), but she was cute. She had short- bobbed blonde hair, blue eyes, and she was a petite little thing. Once one of our Concord classmates asked us if we were sister and brother — I guess we really did match-up physically. In the early days when we first met in class, we were always polite and friendly to each other. I never saw her talking to any other guys, and if so, never at all in a flirting way so as to suggest dating, or even interest. After several weeks of this classroom intelligence gathering, I got my courage all concentrated up in the tips of my fingers, and I e-mailed Dee. It was a Wednesday. I asked her if she might be interested in "hanging out" with me sometime during the coming weekend.

She was.

We went.

We went out many times that spring. We would go out to eat. We would go for walks in the park. We went to the movies. We were doing everything dating couples do together except there was nothing at all physical. We weren't even holding hands, let alone kissing. For my part, I did indeed want to do those things with Dee. I just didn't know how. I mean, I knew how; I just didn't know how to surmise if she wanted to do those things. In the movies and on television, there are always, to quote The Drifters, these "magic moments." The sun shines softly on her face. The wind whispers through her hair. She looks up with sparking eyes so bright and so full of life. Those eyes, in their lively silence, shouts out, "Come here now." There is no one else around. The strategically placed orchestra—just out of eye range (maybe they are down there in the trees) and filled with discreet professionals who are also rooting for love—begins playing a beautifully earnest plea for love, a tearjerker, which reminds girl and boy, "Life is fleeting. Love is here now. You guys need to kiss and dance away together, madly, deeply, relentlessly loving each other." That moment just never presented itself to me when I was with Dee. The moment for loving just never came. The moments we had together, all passing so swiftly by, just never ever felt right.

We were, after all, hanging out. I am so brilliant.

I always got the impression, I always had the general vibe, Dee felt the same way about me. I just figured Dee and I were both just two incredibly shy people being incredibly shy together. Someday, someday sooner rather than later, I thought, Dee and I would both just agree we needed to be boyfriend and girlfriend. Someday, someday sooner rather than later, I thought, Dee and I would both laugh and say, "Yes, really we have been boyfriend and girlfriend all this time. We were just too shy to admit it." Someday, someday sooner rather than later, I thought, Dee and I would agree it was time to hold hands, kiss, and start experiencing all the wonders of the mystery of love.

One Sunday night, Dee asked me if I cared to swing by a trailer park in Hinton to pick up her roommate, Annie. Annie couldn't find a ride back to school after a weekend home. She and her mother had a fight, and her father was drunk, Dee said. I told her I didn't mind at all. Hinton was thirty minutes away and in the exact opposite direction I was hoping to go (to an Italian restaurant in Bluefield) but being chivalrous, being a rescuer for my girl's roommate had to be almost as good as being chivalrous, as being the rescuer for my girl, I figured.

The oddness of the evening began right from the very beginning. For starters, Annie's trailer wasn't in a trailer park at all. It was up a high, rugged mountain road probably five miles up the main room, itself a serpentine monster that had made me carsick even from the driver's side. At one point, near the top of the mountain where the trailer lay, my car literally bottomed out in the tall weeds growing in the middle of the supposed road. The second really strange occurrence happened when Annie got in the car. Dee left the front seat where she had been riding beside me (I hadn't gotten up enough nerve to reach over and grab her hand, but my sweaty hands on the steering wheel were a testament to the fact I was thinking about it really hard), and she sat in the backseat with Annie.

Well, I thought to myself, *she just doesn't want her friend to be riding the back of the car all alone, lonely.* I did wonder why Dee sat in the middle of the seat, right up on Annie, and not in her own personal space. Again, I figured, it must have some personality quirk with Annie. Maybe since Annie didn't know me, she was nervous, and Dee was trying to comfort her friend.

The rest of the evening was like watching a television show for me, except I was playing a minor, though significant part in the show (as the driver of the car, I was, after all, advancing the plot forward). Dee and Annie talked nearly nonstop, both of them talking rapidly, feverishly, giggling like ten-year-olds, and occasionally whispering. I was glad Annie didn't normally go "hanging out" with Dee and me. I was hoping, borderline praying, this would be the last, as well as the first time, I was asked to participate in whatever this was.

I didn't learn what that evening really was until a good five or six months had passed. I will go ahead and kill the suspense for you. Dee and I never moved beyond "hanging out" to actual grown-up dating. Except for one evening when we were walking in the park too late in the evening and the darkness of dusk caught us off guard and I held Dee's hand to help guide her over the gravel road, we never got to any point of even the most innocent touch, or any hint of intimacy. I graduated from Concord — Dee had one more year to go — and went away to seminary at Duke. When I left, I still had the same basic impression of my relationship with Dee — we were boyfriend and girlfriend. We were a dating couple. We were just way too shy to really talk about it or do anything about it.

I came home from Duke for the first time in mid-October. I

decided to call Dee for a date. She seemed delighted to hear from me, and she was excited for us to get together again, she said. I hadn't been in real regular touch with Dee since I left. Mostly I had kept my distance from everyone from home for those first weeks, because it was so hard for me to be gone. Too much contact with loved ones from home would make me that much more homesick, that much more likely to just quit school and head on up the interstate, northward from the Carolina Piedmont to the Allegheny Front, and home.

Dee was waiting for me outside her dorm when I arrived on Concord's campus to pick her up. She looked more beautiful than I ever remembered her looking. I never really ever saw Dee as beautiful; I had always seen her as cute, and sometimes very cute. That chilly fall night though, she looked downright beautiful. Her jeans were pretty tight too, and her shirt wasn't not humble, but it revealed more of Dee than I had ever seen. I was ready to propose marriage. I was ready to hold her hand. I was ready for sure to finally kiss her at the end of our evening together. Dee was determined to go to graduate school and begin work on her Ph.D. I was convinced her Concord grades were good enough to get into Duke. Maybe we would even have a wedding at Duke Chapel sometime in the spring of the next year. That is how quickly my mind works, and how rapidly my heart falls. That was the direction my soul was heading in that night for what I had convinced myself was an actual date and no longer "hanging out" with Dee. I am sure you are wondering just what exactly I said to Dee, what words I employed to express my feelings toward her, and how she very gently turned me down.

It actually never came to that.

On the long drive from Concord to Bluefield and that Italian restaurant at long last, Dee just started talking. She talked to me for nearly thirty minutes, nonstop. She talked about how she and Annie had encountered some problems a few weeks earlier, but how they had worked them all out. They loved each other, Dee said, and they were committed to making their romantic relationship work. They had lived together as a dating couple for nearly four years now, Dee said. She figured they could make it work sharing a house or an apartment together the following year.

I moved my hand off of the gearshift. I had placed it there, trying to gently give myself strategic positioning to reach over and hold Dee's hand when the moment was right. That moment would never be right, I realized in an instant. I needed to use both hands to drive, anyway. Suddenly I understood why we sat the way we did in the car that night with Annie. Suddenly I realized why Dee and I never moved any deeper than "hanging out." Suddenly I realized we never would move any farther along; it would always be just hanging out. Suddenly I was determined this would be the last dinner Dee and I would have together that I would insist on paying for.

My Dee story ends rather anticlimactically. I guess when the climax of my relationship with a girl was the night I served as driver and meal ticket for her and her girlfriend, one should expect an ending with a lightning bug and not fireworks. The ending is this: I went back to Duke. Dee and I remained friends over the years. She went to Marshall for her graduate school, and she teaches college now. She and Annie did not work out, but Dee finally did meet the right someone, and they have been together ever since. I have seen pictures of Dee and her lady; they look beautiful and very happy together.

Needless to say then, I left home to go to Duke with very limited relationship experience, and what experience I had was pretty strained and conflicted.

You may be happy to know this and not at all surprised. I really didn't have any dating life at Duke. I had so much to figure out: about God, about myself, about the world. I really didn't have any energy or drive, and especially time left to pursue romance. Okay, had romance presented itself, I certainly would have taken her hand and asked her to dance. Romance was never that direct with me during those years, though. The internal work I was doing within myself was so hard that there were no resources left for me to try to go and find romance when she was being so coy, so mysterious, anyway.

It was a sun-scorching, hazy, hellacious August day when my parents, my sisters, and my brothers-in-law helped move me to my apartment down in North Carolina. It was a family project. It was a family event. The baby of the family was leaving the family.

At least that is the way it seemed to me. It seemed to me as if I was leaving my family forever. Maybe that is the way it feels to all children, all young people, when they leave their families and their hometowns for the first time. I felt like I was leaving, never to return, going to a place I didn't know and was sure I could never love. Strangers would remain strangers and never become my friends. I would never learn my way around this new country. My sister Heather gave me a carefully crafted, lovingly written paper detailing the directions from my apartment to Duke's West Campus, where the Divinity School was. I doubted I could, or would, ever learn where anything else was. I had directions from my new home to the school. There was a Foodland and a Walmart along the way, so I could survive. With just that one set of directions my sister had made me, I could survive. I was certain I wasn't going to be able to do anything more than that. I had left home. I was certain I would never make a home here or find my way home again.

This all sounds so melodramatic, I know. It is. I was. I was so melodramatic. I look at myself the way I was back then. I remember my thoughts. I recall things I was thinking and contemplating back then, and I am horrified. People go away to school, and people come back home. People have to leave home for a season, and the same people return, better equipped for the world, all grown and strong. I have that sensibility now. I didn't then. Then it just seemed as if my world was coming to an end. Suicide didn't enter my mind, but I don't think it was a thought completely out of the scope of my universe.

I suppose curiosity kept me going more than anything else in those days. I didn't give up; I didn't get suicidal because I was too curious to see what the next day and the day after that and the day after that would bring in the way of learning and in the possibility of new relationships. I was always so hopeful, if not certain, that I would meet my destiny, named Miss Whoever, one day at Duke. I kept getting up and I kept going on—even in the midst of loneliness defined in a dark, lifeless apartment in a complex where I could name not one friend—because I hoped I could meet Miss Thing just any day in the Gothic Reading Room at school. I just knew she would completely change my life into a miracle with just a smile she would send my way.

My mother told me later she cried the entire three-hour drive back to Princeton when she, Dad, and the rest of the family left me at the Strawberry Meadows Apartments that day. I don't doubt she did indeed cry the full length of that drive back up to the mountains to our home. I probably cried for the entire three hours, too. My family left me with a gently used living room suite, a tiny dinette, a bed and dresser, and the aforementioned directions to help me drive from Strawberry Meadows to Duke. In short, they left me with everything they could, but they had to leave me. For the first time in my existence, I was completely and utterly on my own.

So much of the learning I had to do in this phase of my young life had to happen there: in my apartment, in the darkness, in the confines of my own head, my own heart, my own soul. I had to learn I could make it on my own. I had to learn I was okay. I had to learn God truly was with me. Before I could preach and teach "God loves you. God loves us all!" I had to experience for myself, by myself that God loves me, as well. Before I could preach and teach, before I could be with people, before I could be with a church of people as their pastor, I had to be by myself. I had to be by myself to learn myself. I had to be by myself to experience for myself God's love — that holy love which saves, that sacred love which keeps alive.

A huge part of my education was my learning to be alone and learning to be me.

After my family left, but before the school year started, God and my best friend from high school gave me an unforgettable memory. I can close my eyes and still see the dark red velvet sunset of an evening I prayed would last forever. In high school, the Beatles saved my life. *The Beatles Anthology* came out in the fall of 1995 to the spring of 1996, right in the heart of my high school career. That anthology project, which consisted of albums and a television documentary, made a group who had been popular when my parents were in high school the most relevant group of *my* high school era. Everyone in my school seemingly loved the Beatles. It wasn't just newspaper, creative writing geeks like me, either. Even football studs, cheerleader beauties, and my hippy soccer dude friends were going around, singing "Yesterday" and "Let It Be."

At Concord, I discovered a new group though, and this group was destined to change my life and save my life just as the Beatles had done. They weren't a new group, but they were new to me. I watched the VH1 *Behind the Music* on REM, and I was hooked forever. After just one sixty-minute program, I had heard enough of his poetry to know Mr. J. Michael Stipe was destined to become the poetic laureate of my life. It didn't take me long at all to have all the words memorized to all the songs on *Out of Time*, *Automatic for the People*, and *New Adventures in Hi-Fi*. Then *Up* came out, and I also picked up *Monster* and *Green*, and before long, I was catching up with *Fables of the Reconstruction*, *Dead Letter Office*, and all their earlier albums as well.

To my twenty-year-old mind's eye, no writer had ever put the heart and soul of human life as I had so far experienced it, more succinctly and more truly, than Stipe had in the opening words of "Losing My Religion."

Oh life, Is bigger.

It's bigger than you And you aren't me

When I first heard those words, I cried, though I really didn't know why. I did know, without question, that I had found a new band, and more important than that, I had found a soul mate in

Michael Stipe.

I discovered almost all of my other peers had known about REM for a long time. One of my brothers-in-law had idolized them for years, dating back to his high school days. I was late for the REM party, but hell, what party in my life had I ever finally made it to where I wasn't far, far behind all the others? I may have been late coming to REM fandom, but I was convinced (and still am) no one appreciated them quite as deeply as I did.

In honor of that, my best friend, Lane, purchased two tickets, one for me and one for him, for the REM concert at an outdoor amphitheater in Raleigh the weekend before my Duke classes started.

To understand the beauty of that evening for me, in addition to my love for REM you also have to understand the meaning of Lane's friendship to me, as well.

Lane was the best friend I had ever had. He was really the only true friend I had in high school. I was well-liked, maybe even loved in high school, but I really had no true friends. I had no group, no posse, to belong to. Because I was not defined by membership into any one particular clique, folks from the hippy soccer stars to the stud football players felt free to like and adopt me. These guys adopted a brotherly compassion toward me, but that sense of fraternity only included asking me how I was and making sure the rednecks weren't picking on me. Their concern, and like of me, did not include--it never included--asking me to hang out with them, inviting me to their parties.

Then I met Lane. I met him in the autumn of our senior year. I met him in Mrs. Carnes's typing class. It was almost magical how we met. I didn't really approach him, and he really didn't approach me. We just sort of bumped into each other as we both stood along the back wall of the classroom and started talking.

Our speech impediments drew us together, I think.

Lane had the most pained stutter I had ever heard. Lane's stutter remains the worst I have ever encountered. My voice was plagued with being so extraordinarily high-pitched. Sometimes it literally hurt me to speak because I hated to hear the sound of my own voice. Especially when I was nervous (like when talking out loud in class, or most especially when trying to have a conversation with a pretty girl), my voice would go up so many octaves, to highest female soprano range, and I was powerless against the tide of nerves swelling up my vocal chords.

Lane remains one of the dearest, truest souls I have ever met. He was the star of the soccer team. Yet he dared to be friends with me, the star of the newspaper staff. We somehow were attracted to each other in friendship naturally, like magnets. We didn't know each other at all. We just started talking as we both stood there against the back wall, waiting for Mrs. Carnes to begin her typing class.

He was as wild and free as I was conservative and sheltered. He was as experienced with girls and romance as I was completely innocent and unknowing of both. He never got me a date although he said he really wanted to. Just listening to his stories was enough to at least give me some primitive idea about what that great mystery was all about. Lane drove his car super-fast, and he was constantly looking for a thrill, even when that thrill was simply driving through a curve fast, managing to hang on to reach the other end.

Lane had a paper route, and after we had been friends for a couple of weeks, he invited me to go on his paper route with him. Lane's voice was really deep, and if you can imagine Rocky Balboa speaking with a stutter, then you have captured Lane's voice in your mind.

"Hey, man, you wanna go on the paper route with me Friday?"

"Sure!" I squeaked back instantaneously.

"You may want to ask your parents first, man," Lane said. "I do the route early, like way early. Man, I will be picking you up at three a.m.!"

"That sounds awesome, man. Count me in!" I was so thrilled. I had a friend. My friend had asked me to do something with him.

I had lived in Princeton my entire life, but I had never seen my hometown as beautiful as it looks at 3:00 a.m. She simply gleams. Even the bad, dirty street, the crime-ridden street where the drug dealers and the prostitutes walked, looked hopeful in the shining street lights of 3:00 a.m. Lane's paper route ran through the heart of Princeton. It consisted of downtown, Mercer Street, and three or four streets up, running parallel to it. Lane's custom, being the physically fit athlete, was to park his car at the beginning of each street, grab a handful of newspapers in his arms, and jog to each customer's house until he ran out of newspapers. Then he would jog back to his car and get another handful and pick up where he had left off. Lane would point out to me the homes of his customers.

He would leave it to me to deliver three or four papers per street, while he delivered the rest—probably twelve to fifteen papers per street—by himself. Lane would be done delivering his load before I was done getting rid of my few. Other times he slowed the pace down a little, so I could keep up and accompany him. So it went for two hours. I was running. I was sweating. I was with my buddy, and we were having fun. Lane played the oldies on the radio, and I remember "It's The Time of the Season" and "Turn! Turn! Turn! (to Everything There Is a Season)" being part of the soundtrack of our bewitching hour adventure.

Along the route, at least three girls who had crushes on Lane had left little gifts outside for him. One girl left him a bottle of pop. Another left him an actual love note. One left him a box of Pop-Tarts. Lane just laughed when he found them, saying the girl's name as he picked up the treasure of love she had left.

Lane told me he had a tradition after completing his paper route, which was breakfast at the Omelet Shop. "You up for a little breakfast, man?" he asked me.

"You bet!" I said with a smile.

Around five o'clock, still a good hour before the sun would sprinkle specs of blood red on a dark sky just flirting with lightening up, Lane and I sat down to breakfast at the Omelet Shop. We sat around with a crew of insomniacs, truck drivers, a probable prostitute and her paid-to-be beau, and a guy who claimed to be an unemployed Ph.D. who kept feeding the jukebox to play Beatles songs. I couldn't remember being happier in all my high school years.

I got to do the paper route with Lane many more times over the next eight or nine months before we graduated from high school. We hung out other times too, and I started attending the home soccer games to see my buddy and all the other crew of lovable hippy dudes play. My oldest sister, Monica, went with me to a game or two, but I didn't care at all to go by myself. Even if I sat in the stands alone, I knew I had friends, and a best friend, down on the field playing. So I was never really alone.

Lane and I remained friends through college. He started with me at Concord, but Concord's pretty strident academic pace was too much for him. He transferred to a community college before dropping out of school entirely. He got a job with another friend of ours whose family owned a variety of small businesses in our area: Lane helped manage a gas station, an automatic car wash, and a pawnshop. Later in life, Lane owned his own pawnshop.

Just a day or two before I left for Duke, Lane surprised me with the REM tickets. His parents had been divorced for years, and Lane's mother had relocated years before to Durham. His dad was the custodial parent for him and his younger brother, but Lane had spent many summers and weekends in Durham at his mom's. On a recent visit to his mom's, he heard on the radio about the REM concert. The concert was on a Friday night. Lane would come in that afternoon. We would go to the concert. He would spend the night at my apartment and then go on to spend Saturday with his mother.

I was already desperately homesick, and the sight of my best friend, Lane, standing in the doorway of my apartment pretty well brought me to tears. I had never been happier to see anyone. I had been living there for about a week by then, and I had only managed to venture out of the apartment complex as far as the grocery store and the pizza place.

"Hey, man, you ready to rock it out tonight?" Lane asked me in his lovable, stuttering Rocky Balboa way.

"You know it," I replied. I hugged Lane, though I knew he wasn't big on guys showing too much affection, except for with their ladies.

Rarely in life do we experience moments of near perfection. I have experienced a few. The evening of the REM concert was one. As Buck and Mills played and Stipe sang and spoke to the crowd, the sun began to set, making the westward sky scarlet. As the first stars began dancing in a coal black, cloudless sky, a summer breeze whispered, and the concert crowd seemed peaceful, every soul tranquil and somehow every soul seemed as one.

That night Michael Stipe spoke to the crowd so lyrically his words could have been written in a book. He told the story rhythmically of a friendly person who purchased a sixteen-year-old a beer just so the concert would be that much more memorable. He told us his grandmother always insisted on shopping at Piggly Wiggly, even though she would drive past three or four other grocery stores nearer her home than the Pig was, because she said, "Piggly Wiggly is a southern institution."

I think Lane enjoyed himself though I don't think he was as transfixed as I was. Stipe was like a possessed poet that night — possessed with charm and humanity, possessed with the spirit of words and communal soulfulness. He walked the stage, riffing poetic stream-of-conscious thoughts connecting REM's rich catalog of songs with stories and sayings steeped in Americana. Mike Mills and Peter Buck and their new drummer who had replaced the retired Bill Berry played to perfection.

Surrounded by, I am sure, young lovers and college kids, as well as young adults whom I am sure had young children and very respectable careers, I sat there with the only true friend outside my family I ever had. My eyes got involuntarily teary as Stipe sang

Nightswimming

deserves a quiet night

161

I'm not sure these people understand
It's not like years ago
The fear of getting caught
The recklessness in water
They cannot see me naked
These things they go away
Replaced by every day.

Somehow, I knew that night was a moment of unique beauty and a point of transition in my life. I was there, listening to my favorite band with my best friend from my hometown. God was dancing in the blood and stars of the sky, and God was dancing in the words from the band, too. The Spirit enveloped all of us strangers, united by the crowd we made together, one in the music we all found meaningful. I knew I needed to let a great deal of my past go. I knew I needed to shed much of the pain, let go of many of the tears, and focus on the new adventure God was about to unfold before me.

I cherished the night I had with Lane, my first and best friend. I could feel REM's music sanctifying my past, cleansing my present for a future that I knew truly did not belong to me.

7 Education, Part Two

I began my formal education for ministry at Duke Divinity School in August 1999. In that first semester, I had a class on the Old Testament, early Christian history, pastoral leadership, pastoral care, and Christian spirituality. Duke also required all first-year "Div students" to belong to a covenant group, which met weekly for ninety minutes. That first semester of seminary nearly killed me emotionally and spiritually. It also saved me.

Cliché annoys me, but I don't know how else to put this: seminary, or a divinity school education, isn't Sunday school.

"It can't be. It shouldn't be," my heart cried out. In my Old Testament class, I learned *Adam* meant "human," so Adam and Eve probably weren't to be understood literally as the first people running around naked together in a perfect garden called Eden. They may well have been meant to personify the genesis of the entire human race. Moses may have had an actual experience with God on Mount Sinai, punctuated with fire and smoke, thunder and fog. The Sinai experience between Moses and God may have pointed not to an actual event though, but to a figurative description of how, and why, Moses became a giver of law. The events of Job and Esther probably never occurred. Job is a narrative poem written to give theological meaning to human suffering, and Esther is a novella meant to cheer up and give

163

courage to an oppressed community, both Jewish and female.

Today I can deal with all of these facts. From years of more reading, and from years of more teaching and preaching these texts in the life of local churches, I have a deeper insight into the debates forever swirling around those ancient words. I know that the meaning, the poetry, the holiness, the gift of God in these texts are not determined by the actual fact of their origins. Over a decade of ministry and life have taught me the scripture has meaning, power, and sacredness just because the scripture *is*. The twenty-one-year-old me who existed in the fall of 1999, couldn't take any of this.

I can still hear the internal dialogues within myself:

Holy crap! Did he just say Moses didn't write the first five books of the Bible?

There are two creation accounts in Genesis, and they are different?

The Creation accounts in Genesis may be more art than fact? The world wasn't created in six days?

Seminary wasn't Sunday School, and I expected it to be.

I got very depressed.

Two other factors added to my emotional, mental, and spiritual crisis. First, I found myself woefully behind my classmates academically. I discovered many of my fellow seminarians had religious studies degrees from their undergraduate years. All of the various forms of Biblical criticism, which were tearing the fabric of my faith apart, were not new to

164

these folks — they had been exposed to them years before. Church history and Christian theology were also completely new disciplines for me: I didn't know Origen from Orion; I didn't know Aquinas and Augustine from the Aqua Velva I tackily wore in those years (Is it any wonder I was single?) or from the Florida town where I knew they played tons of golf. Again, most of my peers had years of reading and study of the church fathers and church mothers behind them in their academic careers. I found myself very lonely then. The few people I felt comfortable enough to share my heart with couldn't relate because I was fighting a tide, nearly choking in waters those folks had navigated long before, waters they were merely wading through by that point.

The second factor battering my soul and bruising my spirit during those days was a factor that was perpetually the devil riding piggyback on my shoulder, pouring venom into my being as he unmercifully thrust his weight upon me. I was lonely. I was lonelier than I had ever been in my entire life.

Sure, I had experienced a great deal of loneliness when I was a teenager. It was horrid, and I never thought anything could be worse. I discovered it could me much worse though, living three hours from home, being three hours from my parents, my sisters, and what few true friends I had. To make matters worse, there were female divinity students: cute, sweet, beautiful, Christ-centered young ladies, and they were all already married. I was making a crew of pretty nice friends at Duke, but all of these young dudes, many of them exactly my age, were all married. It seemed like every future Methodist minister but me had gotten a memo from a bishop or maybe even Jesus: "Go ahead and find your mate, date, get married, and start trying to make babies between graduating from college and entering seminary."

I did truly like all these peers, ladies and gentlemen alike, but I found I had next to nothing besides our future vocation in common with them. They were not where I was in my struggle with our studies. They had discovered that key long before I knew I would encounter a lock. They had no idea what it was like being lonely in a new town, feeling completely alien in a new world, because they were not walking through the maze alone like me.

Something remarkable did happen to me among my new seminary friends, however. This was something that had never, ever happened to me in my entire life. I actually had a clique. I actually had a group of peers I "rode with," sort of.

My relationship with my little Duke clique never really extended outside of school. They were all married after all, and some of them had little children. We did hang pretty tightly at school though, and that meant lunches together. It meant all sitting together in class, often in a cluster close to the back of the classroom. It meant, in short, not feeling quite so alone, at least at school.

Simon was something of the leader of our little posse, I guess. Amusingly, Simon was the one non-Methodist in our friendship circle, and we all deferred to his gentle shepherding. He was a Baptist, and he was a Baptist with a mission. Simon wanted to take a seminary education — a Duke education, no less, pretty blue-blood — into a fractured church and a fractious denomination and use the theological and scriptural tools he would gain to help bring unity and balance to that church. Simon mourned that "Baptist" had come to meet Jerry Falwell, Creationism, and the inerrancy of scripture above and beyond all else. He was our witness. He was the witness in training to all the world--or at least eastern North Carolina--that a Baptist could agree with biblical criticism and make peace with postmodern approaches to Christian theology and pastoral care.

Roger was my antithesis in the group, and we loved the dualism our personalities and backgrounds brought to our friendship. Whereas I was the puny English major, Roger was the buff social work major. Whereas I had never really left West Virginia and had never fired a gun, Roger was a veteran of Desert Storm, and he still frequently spent time shooting at a local firing range. Our great commonality besides a perceived call to the ministry was Roger was a mountain boy, too. Where I came out of the Allegheny Mountains of southern West Virginia, Roger came from the high Blue Ridge and Smokey Mountains of western North Carolina. I knew East River Mountain on the West Virginia-Virginia border like the back of my hand. Roger knew Mount Mitchell and Grandfather Mountain just as intimately. Roger's mountains were much higher than mine, and he was much more of a man than me. Toned and muscled, married and content, Roger exuded a quiet confidence and a peace of self I really admired and was drawn to.

Turner was my favorite of my Duke boys. He was irreverent. He was wild. He was hippy. He was a trip. He was long-haired and male-model handsome. His wife, Erica, was as gorgeous as he was. Those two sure did belong together. Turner was just a few years older than me. He had gotten a degree in education in undergrad, and he had spent a few years teaching science in a North Carolina high school. Turner just had a way about him. He could flirt with all the married Divinity students, and it wasn't inappropriate or sexual harassment because Turner was…well, Turner. Turner could cut you down or insult you, and you laughed about it, and were not hurt at all because Turner was…well, Turner. A case in point: one day at the end of our school day, Turner and I were walking to the parking lot together. We had reached my car, a little red Dodge Neon.

"Well, Turner," I said, "this is my ride. I guess I will see you tomorrow."

"This is your car, huh, Kanode?" Turner asked.

"Yeah," I said.

"Yeah, these cars suck, don't they?" he said with just plain honesty and no meanness about it.

He went on to explain that he and Erica had one just like it and had nothing but trouble out of it. I had experienced quite a bit of trouble with mine too, but even before Turner offered his explanation of why he thought my car sucked, it was all truly okay with me that he had insulted my car. This may sound like a small thing to you, but as any southern West Virginia boy knows, insulting a man's car is closely akin to insulting a man's momma. The fact that I gave Turner a pass on this mortal sin just proves how special that guy was to me.

I have two other Turner vignettes which so vividly portray this young, handsome man's vivacious, audacious sense of humor and personality.

For months, Turner had been inviting me to the church he and Erica attended. I hadn't yet gone. It's not that I didn't want to. It's just that, on the weekends when I didn't drive home to West Virginia, I really enjoyed attending church at the gothic Duke Chapel, which was unlike anything I had ever experienced back home. Roger was serving an internship in a local church, and he had invited me to come and hear him preach his maiden sermon. He wanted me to then have lunch with him, his wife, and his dad. I could tell this was a really big deal in my friend's life. It was an honor he wanted to include me in such a milestone event in his life, and I knew there was no question but that I had to attend.

On the Friday before that Sunday when Roger was preaching, Roger, Turner, and I were walking to our very remotely located parking lot after a hard week of classes. We reached my car first.

When I said goodbye to Roger, without thinking about Turner being there too, I said, "I will see you at church Sunday, Roger."

Without seemingly pausing to think, Turner said with mock incredulity, "Hey, what about my church, dude? You've been putting off my invitation for weeks. You think we worship Satan, or what?"

Toward the middle of the fall semester of our first year, all of my friends were worried about me. They knew I was really struggling emotionally to even stay at school, and they all figured my grades had to be suffering. In actual fact, I was doing pretty well, but since I didn't feel like I was, the fact I was doing better than okay just hadn't really taken root in my consciousness.

Turner wanted me to come home with him over a weekend so we could study together for our midterm exams. "I will grill out some steak, man, and we will have a beer or two if you care to imbibe," he said. Then he said with a twinkle in his eyes and a mischievous thirteen-year-old-like grin, "Of course, the greatest blessing of going home with me for the weekend is that Erica lives there too, and she'll be home all weekend. She likes you, man. She thinks you're cute. Not as cute as me, but she still thinks you are cute. And Erica is a great kisser, man." I could feel my face burning, and I actually felt sweat popping out in my armpits, not to mention other more personal biological reactions to Turner's wife, Erica—whom I had met and who was a nearly perfect looking lady—being a great kisser, who thought I was cute.

The last member of the very first and only posse I have ever belonged to was Andy. Andy was a good twenty-five to thirty years older than the rest of us guys. He was a middle-aged, potbellied man who looked a great deal like the portrait of Martin Luther on the cover of one of the books on our required reading list for church history. Andy fascinated me, and I loved him. He wore me out though.

Andy was a second, maybe even third career candidate for ministry. In my experience, those are the best kind of candidates for ministry, and they make the best pastors. So often in my life, I wish I had some other kind of profession, some other life before ministry. Such life experience would have made me a fuller, better human being. Andy was both. He had worked as a newspaper reporter and as a political operative. Andy was well-connected and well-informed in politics, especially in the state of Virginia. He had worked for years as a Republican consultant to state-level candidates for various offices. Andy's biggest campaign was a primary fight for the GOP nomination for United States Senate back in the mid-1990s. His candidate lost the primary fight, but it was a big race, closely watched, with national implications. Although I was, and am, a "Bill Clinton Democrat," Andy and I still became fast friends. He knew my politics, and I knew his. Since we were both decently moderate—me walking in from the left, and Andy pushing in from the right—we found enough common ground to have conversation, not just debate.

Of all my fellow students at Duke, Andy was the most intense. This includes all the students I knew, not just the members of my own eclectic clique. He threw his heart and his mind into our schoolwork like no one else I knew. If a paper for a particular class needed to meet a twenty-five-page minimum, most all of us would come into class with the required twenty-five pages, maybe twenty-six or twenty-seven, including a bibliography, but no more. Andy appeared in his coffee-stained khakis and his button-down shirt, never stuffed into his pants but always hanging out in countercultural splendor, and Andy always produced papers fifty to seventy pages in length, written with poetic flair, researched with scholarly brilliance. More than one of our professors declared Andy's papers worthy of publication. I loved the guy for it. Some of my fellow students openly didn't like him because of it.

I loved Andy, but there were times I avoided him, times I evaded his phone calls. I didn't do so out of jealousy. I did so out of survival. Andy's intensity touched every aspect of his life, I suppose, including friendship. Often, he would call me on the phone, always with the same "Jeffrey Kanode. Andy Jones speaking." I would say hello, and Andy would lay out "the agenda for this conversation, including the following items." He would then enumerate the conversation items he wanted us to cover. "Then I will give you some brief headlines from my life and work. Then I want to hear your conversation items and your headlines, Jeffrey." Yes. Phone conversations and chats over coffee with

Andy were intense. I wasn't always emotionally and intellectually up for them.

I don't know if this is true in every denomination, but I suspect it is: we Methodists love holding hands, singing "Kum Bah Yah," as the old cliché goes, and sharing what is on our hearts. Another cliché goes that the line between love and hate is incredibly thin. Symptomatic of the Methodist love of sharing from the heart, I can't decide whether I was blessed or cursed in the fact I entered Duke at the time Duke was just embracing the concept of covenant groups, making them part of the academic requirement of the Master of Divinity program.

The founder of Methodism, John Wesley, was a great proponent of small groups. He and his brother Charles started what they called the Holy Club at Oxford, a group the guys on campus who didn't like the Wesley boys started calling, derisively "the Methodists." What the world knows today as the United Methodist Church began initially as a small group of dedicated Christian friends who gathered to study the Bible together, pray together, and hold each other accountable to their shared covenant with Christ. Wesley would often ask his friends in the group, "How is it with your soul?" He expected an answer! Methodism, then, has always been tied to and has a history with small covenant groups. That doesn't mean I can't call my own history with such groups a tortured one, and not be considered still a faithful Methodist.

We were all assigned to a covenant group. Each covenant group was provided a leader, most of them pastors from various churches throughout the Raleigh-Durham area. The groups met each Tuesday at the one o'clock hour. You had to go. You couldn't move up into the second academic year until you completed a year in a covenant group your first year. These covenant groups were not organic. They didn't create themselves. They were created, I guess randomly, by the admission's office. That first day I entered the room printed on my school schedule telling me where my covenant group was to meet, I knew no one sitting there, until — praise be to God — Simon walked in.

When Simon saw me, he gave me a wink. "Creed," he said. "Creed's in the big covenant group. This is going to be all right."

Yes, my friends in seminary didn't call me Jeff, or Jeffrey. Occasionally they called me Kanode, the way many people playfully call their friends by their surnames. My friends in seminary usually called me Creed, my middle name. I loved it. It came up in conversation one day during lunch.

"What does the C in Jeffrey C. Kanode stand for?"

"Creed," I said to the group. "Creed was my grandmother's

maiden name. I am Jeffrey Creed. My dad is Gregory Creed. Someday, if I ever have a wife and we have a baby boy, my wife can name the baby whatever first name she likes, so long as his middle name gets to be Creed."

My friends loved the name Creed. We were, after all, seminary students, students of church history and Christian theology, for whom creeds were taking on more and more importance. From the Apostles to the Nicene to the creedal formulation of the Barmen Declaration, we were all about creeds. So "Creed" I formally became, at least to my Dukie friends.

There were times that fall when covenant group wasn't so horrible an ordeal. Often our leader, an American Baptist pastor named Leon, would give us free reign, and we would commiserate on our opinions of this professor, or that book. It became more awkward when he insisted we share deep feelings with one another, become vulnerable with each other, always covenanting with one another that the group time and the group process we were in was holy: a sacred space, a sacred time, whose sanctity could not be violated by any of us by sharing "out there" what we discussed "in here."

By the early winter, I was buying into it. I was starting to feel a connection with my fellow covenant group peers, not just Simon. Some folks were starting to share some pretty raw, heartfelt, soul-deep stuff within our group. I started to open up and share more, too. I discussed how homesick I was. I shared how much some of our schoolwork really was challenging and sometimes shaking up my faith, nearly to the point where I feared it could collapse.

Smooth Simon started to become the natural leader of our covenant group just as he quite organically, with humility, assumed leadership of our little peer lunchtime gang. Simon spoke for all of us, I think, at our last covenant group session before winter finals began.

"I try to love everyone in this school, and I try to pray for everyone I see here," Simon began. "For the most part, I think I do. It is different for me though when I see any of you. When I see any of you, my covenant group, when I pass you in the hallway, or when I sit down close to you in class, it's different. It's a different kind of feeling I have for you guys. We pray together. We share together. We are just linked together in our group in here, and it is different than any connection I feel with any of the other students here. It's like when I see you guys out there, I know you are my family. You are my family within this school. I love everybody I pass in the hallways, but I love you guys more deeply."

Simon got a little choked up when he spoke those words to us. We all did. That's how well the covenant process was starting to work among us. That's how stressed out we all were. That's how raw all of our emotions, our intellects, and our souls were moving toward as we collectively approached our first week of finals as seminary, Master's level, students.

There was a young professor I just adored. I think all of us students adored him. I am confident to say I think a poll of Duke Divinity students that year, among first-year students anyway, would have revealed this young, red-bearded Englishman would have been the most popular professor on campus.

Dr. David Leslie taught us that first year of church history, which covered the early church period through the Reformation. He was super intelligent on all things ancient and holy, but he was also hip, culturally aware. Dr. Leslie could quote from *the Didache* (an ancient letter of instruction for the church, much like the Pauline epistles of the New Testament) and then after a semicolon, a pause mid-paragraph, he was quoting dialogue from *Buffy the Vampire Slayer*. He talked about Hippolytus and Homer Simpson. Dr. Leslie was wonderful.

Once, as Simon and I were chatting and walking down the hallway, we were passing Dr. Leslie's office. Unbeknown to us, the professor was in his office. His door suddenly burst open, and out appeared Dr. Leslie, hair disheveled, eyeglasses on the tip of his nose, necktie loosened up, and top button undone. Dr. Leslie pointed to Simon. "You. You are tall. I need you to get a book down for me. It's on the bloody top shelf." That's all he said. That's all he needed to say. Simon went in and got the professor's book down off the top shelf for him. I politely waited outside. Dr. Leslie just nodded as Simon handed the professor the book. Dr. Leslie held the book like a daddy about to cuddle with his baby kid. Simon told me later that from the point the professor got his hands on the book, he was oblivious to everything and everyone else. Simon very quietly took his leave.

It was a Tuesday in early spring. It was already a bad day for me because I wasn't feeling well: the pollen count in the North Carolina Piedmont struck earlier and harder than anything I ever experienced in southern West Virginia, and each morning found an icky yellow coating of nastiness on my bright red Dodge Neon. The same icky yellow nastiness found its way into my nostrils and into my lungs. I couldn't breathe through my nose. My lungs sounded like I had just inhaled a carton full of Marlboro Blacks, unfiltered. As bad as my health was making my day, it was about to get profoundly worse.

Everyone, even Simon, was profoundly silent and somber as we assembled for our covenant group. At first, I didn't think anything of it. We were about a quarter through the semester: it had been a long haul since Christmas break, and we still had a couple of weeks to go before spring break. We were all just tired and weary, I postulated. Maybe everyone else was miserable with allergies too, I added as an afterthought.

When Leon began to speak, I knew something strange was going on. I didn't have a clue what it was.

"I suppose we all need to address what is going on with Dr. Leslie," Leon said in a hushed tone I imagined he would use in his pastoral role at a funeral. "I am sure that, above all else, is weighing on our hearts."

"What is going on with Dr. Leslie?" I asked myself. I am sure my brows probably reflexively furrowed too. I didn't have a clue what was going on with Dr. Leslie. Oh, sweet Jesus! Did he just find out he has cancer or something? Did his mother die back in the motherland and now he has to leave us to go back to England to run the family estate and teach at Oxford? My mind raced in a thousand different directions. I didn't have a clue what was going on.

The silence in the room after Leon gave us our discussion prompt didn't last long. Vivian spoke up first. She usually did. She was a pretty young lady, but I didn't care much for her that way. She just wasn't my type.

"I am really hurt and let down by it all," Vivian began. "I mean, I still love the guy and all, but I have lost most of my respect for him. He shouldn't be teaching in a seminary."

Holy God! What the heck? Now my mind was racing in a thousand and one different directions. What had my bud Dr. Leslie done? Pinched Vivian in the butt or something? Why would he do that? All kinds of young women much more beautiful than Vivian were constantly buzzing around him. He could have had his pick of the...Oh, sweet Jesus. I danced — no, I wrestled with my thoughts. He hasn't done something like that, has he? He couldn't. He wouldn't.

"I think it is all being blown out of proportion myself," Ernie began. Thank you, Ernie. I was starting to feel better about things already. I really liked old Ernie. He was exactly my age, and a red head with a goatee much like Dr. Leslie's. Ernie wasn't in our clique. He was part of another clique, but Ernie and I had many good conversations before and after class. He had been a psychology major in undergrad at the University of Chicago, and the kid was just grounded. He was jaded and a little cynical, just enough to be really healthy, I thought, in the often self-righteous, incredibly full- of-ourselves world of divinity school. "She is a mature adult nearly exactly his age. They both made a conscious choice. He is still doing his work profoundly well. It reminds me of President Clinton during the Lewinsky mess. Who cares as long as the man keeps doing his job with brilliance and focus? Like Clinton, Dr. Leslie isn't missing a beat professionally."

"But they are both married!" Vivian interjected tearfully before I really had time to process all Ernie had said.

"Yes, I'm sorry, Ernie, but I have to agree with Vivian," Jake said. They were roommates. I thought Jake was a little strange. I didn't like him. Maybe I was jealous of him because he got to be roomies with Ernie, whom I thought was so cool. He was my age, with an already receding hairline (also like me), but Jake was a computer nerd, and I couldn't look at him without imagining he had probably downloaded tons of porn late at night in his time, and maybe still. That was an unfair, not at all Christian judgment based solely on stereotype I victimized Jake with, but only within the confides of my own head and heart. "Had they both been single and just sort of hooked up at work here, I wouldn't have had a problem with that. But, dude, they are both married. Two families are being broken up here."

The pace of conversation was now too quick for me to keep up with. I could no longer process or reflect upon anything being said by anyone before the next someone said something else. Now it was Simon's turn. Dear, good Simon.

"I still love Dr. Leslie," Simon said. "I would get a book down off the top shelf for him any old day. Right, Creed?" He gave me a light fist in the forearm, remembering the day Dr. Leslie burst out of his office, interrupting us mid conversation, imploring a tall man for help. "I think he is a brilliant scholar who could teach anywhere. I could see him at Harvard or Yale, even. I just don't know that he needs to be teaching in the context of a school preparing young Christians for ministry. Not now. Not after what he's done."

Not after what he's done. I still didn't know what the hell Dr. Leslie had done, and I was getting so frustrated, my internal dialogue consisted of just that kind of language, and much worse. It got worse for me. This already bad day was about to get worse.

I was the only one in our little covenant group who hadn't yet shared. We all had to share: it was a rule. It wasn't even so subtle, empowering, or consciously respectful of our adulthood as to be an unspoken, or an unwritten rule. It was both spoken and written in the expectations the school had for every covenant group. Everyone had to share, and our reverend Leon insisted everyone had to share every week. Therefore, Leon homed in on me.

"Jeff, you haven't shared yet," he said. Leon never called me Creed. Only the inner clique did that. I didn't want him to call me anything that day. I didn't want him to see me or think about me.

I was lost in a hurricane of thoughts and emotions, and I didn't even know yet what the winds and thunderclaps were trying to tell me.

"I...I...I don't know what to say," I began. Being a man of my word, I stopped right there. I didn't know what to say, so I didn't say anything else.

"Well, you have to say something," Leon persisted. "Everyone else has. You too must have thoughts. You too must have feelings on this matter."

"What matter?" I screamed inside myself. I was more diplomatic in my verbal expression. I at least wasn't having *that* bad a day. "I, um...I must plead ignorance, guys. Obviously, something is going on here, which I know nothing about. I suppose I am the only one in this room, and the only one on campus who doesn't know what is going on, but I don't. Before I can share, I have to know what I am sharing about. Even once I know, I don't know that I will be able to share. I am guessing whatever it is you all are talking about, you have had lots of time to think and to process. I haven't."

I was proud of myself for being able to articulate those words. My voice, of course, went up several octaves, as it always did when I spoke up in class or attempted conversation with females. My voice and my sweaty palms told me how nervous I was. Leon was in no mood to give me any slack at all. Dammit, I was going to be pushed to share.

"Dr. Leslie is having what is alleged to be an inappropriate relationship with one of his teaching assistants," Leon said. "They both insist their relationship is not sexual, but they are both insistent that they do love each other, and they are going to be together. Both are filing for divorce from their spouses. The dean has called a school-wide town hall meeting tonight to discuss this matter. So, Jeff, what do you think?"

I was stunned. I could feel tears welling up in my eyes. I looked up at Simon. He was looking at me in a very humane way. His eyes said to me, *Dude, I am sorry. I thought you knew. I thought we all knew. I know how much you love Dr. Leslie.*

Regardless of my love, my feelings, my shock, my state of mind, or my peace of mind, I had to share. I had to share because we were required to share. I had to share because my covenant leader was bearing down on me, hard, to make me share.

I have no idea what I said. I have no recollection exactly of what I shared. I think I tried to explain I loved Dr. Leslie a lot. In a pretty snotty school, I thought he was pretty human and humane. Obviously, he was human. I think I sheepishly talked about how sheltered I kept myself, how I truly had no idea any of this was going on. I think I said I thought the whole thing did sound pretty tawdry, but a school-wide town hall meeting sounded pretty "Jerry Springer," or Salem witch trial to me. And I am pretty sure that is all I think I said.

The end of Dr. Leslie's story is that he was dismissed from

Duke, but he and his new lady recovered nicely. They both got teaching positions at another very prominent divinity school, and their careers didn't miss a beat. I did not attend the school-wide town hall meeting. That whole bit just sounded insane to me. It still does.

Many years later, I would look back on the Dr. Leslie drama and see it was, for me, an eerie foreshadowing of events I would face at a later age, in a later stage in my own life. Some of the events are so parallel that it borders on unfathomably freaky.

At the time though and for most of my life, what happened with Dr. Leslie personally and professionally were not nearly as important as a life's touchstone as what happened to me in the course of that covenant group meeting.

I am fearful my language here may come across as being too strong, especially in comparison to what other people, particularly women, often suffer through. But here it is. Here are my words. I felt put on the spot. I felt embarrassed. I felt forced upon. I felt victimized.

In the context of that covenant group, I had been forced to share things—thoughts, feelings, words from my heart— which I wasn't ready yet to share. I learned later that day my suspicion was correct: Dr. Leslie's alleged affair was no new news to anyone but me in the student body of the divinity school. Simon told me later the professor and his pretty teaching assistant visibly sparked up as early as midway through the first semester. I never saw it. I guess, at that place of my own maturation and development as a person, I didn't know what two people becoming emotionally connected and entwined with one another looked like. Everyone else in that covenant group had been living with facts, rationalizing them or being in conflict with them, for many weeks, if not months. I had not. Nearly the very minute I even knew what was going on, I was forced to share how I felt about what was going on. I was forced to share from my soul before the embryo of my thoughts and beliefs on the topic had even had a chance to grow a spine or a brain.

It left bitterness in my heart, which to this day has never gone away. Our little covenant group was never the same for me. Oh, I went through the motions for the rest of the school year. I shared. I made myself vulnerable when I knew I needed to. I quickly evolved to be calculating, strategic, and artfully defensive with my vulnerability, though. I was selective with what I chose to be vulnerable and open about. Within the context of that covenant group for the rest of that school year, I kept a protective trench dug around my being.

Methodists still love covenant groups, and I have been required to participate in several others since. You'll never be in a covenant group with anyone as freely sharing, with unspoken, subtly silent strategic survival skills, as me.

My seminary friends were awesome, but those friendships

really didn't continue after we all graduated. Most of those guys were North Carolinians, save Andy Jones the Virginian. I found my early years of ministry in West Virginia so consuming that there was just nothing left emotionally to maintain friendships across states. As sacred as those friendships were, I believe they were for a season of our lives. Now I have memories of all those guys, and they are happy memories of brotherly love.

The most lasting gift God gave me through my years at Duke were the amazing professors I had the honor of studying under and the dewdrops and raindrops of God they shared with me. To this day, those dewdrops and raindrops coalesce like small, but deep, significant tributaries feeding into the river of my faith.

Dr. Peter Storey was my favorite. He was the holiest soul I encountered in my ministerial education. Dr. Storey had been a Methodist pastor and bishop in South Africa. He was active in the peaceful protest movement against Apartheid there. Dr. Storey told us many stories about beatings and imprisonments he endured in that great movement for peace, justice, and humanity. He also told us a story, which has forever shaped the way I pray aloud for someone in church.

"The good doctor," as one of my friends referred to Dr. Storey as, told us about a time in one of his churches where two young women, two young mothers, both fell ill with terminal sicknesses. Dr. Storey led the church in public prayer for God to heal both women. One of the young women was miraculously healed. She got to sit in church each Sunday with her husband and children. The other young woman died, and each Sunday her children and husband sat with her space in the pew forever empty.

Dr. Storey told us that he, as the pastor, along with the church itself, had done a grave injustice to the family of the young woman who died. What did it say to that grieving family about God when there had been two sick young mothers in that church: one had been healed, and their loved one was the one who had died? The good doctor told us ever after that, when he prayed pastoral prayers to his church, he never openly prayed for healing again. He prayed for God's mercy to be upon the person. He prayed for a great awareness of Christ's presence and Christ's love to bless the person. The rest, Dr. Storey said, should be faithfully left to God. He told us every Christian experience of prayer is like a "little Calvary," where we experience anew the suffering love of Jesus. We leave the people we pray for with Jesus at Calvary, and we trust Jesus knows what to do with their pain, with their needs, with their dreams, with their struggles, and with their tears.

I have practiced Dr. Storey's "little Calvary" way of praying for ninety-five percent of my pastoral ministry. The other five percent, when I have slipped and openly called for healing, I have regretted. I try to leave the people to God's care with no unneeded commentary from me as to what God needs to do. In remembering the ones who live, whom we pray for, I try to remember the ones who have died. More importantly, I try to remember the loved

187

ones of those who have died, who sit there in those pews, who pray with me.

While Peter Storey's name isn't exactly well known outside some select circles in South Africa and in and around the radius coming forth from Duke Divinity School, the name William Willimon is very well known, at least in Methodist circles.

After my graduation, Willimon was elected to the episcopacy of the Methodist church, and he served as a bishop for some years. Willimon's best years and his best work emanated from his nearly twenty years as dean of the chapel at Duke, and professor at the Divinity School.

One of my warmest memories of human contact and touch involves Willimon. It was a very simple gesture anyone would have forgotten about after all these years, but I remember. One day, I was deeply depressed, homesick, and running on little faith. Aimlessly I walked around Duke's West Campus. I wasn't looking for anyone. I knew no one was looking for me. I was just walking. As it happened, my path took me right along the path of Dr. Willimon. We met on the steps leading from the student union portico to the chapel. I looked up at him, and he smiled. As he smiled and as we passed, Dr. Willimon simply reached out and patted me on the shoulder. We exchanged no words. It was all a passing touch. The pat on the shoulder meant a great deal to me that day, and that human gesture of recognition means a great deal to me still. Dr. William Willimon, a famous Christian preacher, author, and dean of Duke Chapel, recognized me from the sea of faces in one of his classes. If not that, Dr. William simply saw within me that day a hurting kid, a kid who needed a little humanity. That day, Dr. Willimon, later Bishop Willimon, helped teach me I wasn't as anonymous as I felt.

Dr. James Crenshaw was the white-bearded, bald culprit who's teaching nearly killed my faith in those first weeks of my seminary education. Later in that same first semester, after I had grown up some, I recognized that Dr. Crenshaw was a deeply faithful, profoundly spiritual man. He was a poet, and his teaching was quite deliberately liberating God from the inhumanity, from the infamy, from the sacrilege a truly literal interpretation of the Bible imposes upon the divine. We always softly chuckled when the grim-looking Dr. Crenshaw referred in lecture to one of his books, *Whirlpool of Torment*. His class was indeed just that for many of us, until we learned better.

After three semesters at Duke, every student was required to fill out an extensive questionnaire, in addition to writing several essays about how we were growing, changing, and learning as a result of our experience at the divinity school. Each student had to pick a professor to evaluate our questionnaire, essays, and transcripts. A sit- down visit with the professor was also required as part of this "halfway there" rite of passage. The evaluator professor had the right to require the student to do remedial work. It was a big deal. It was a huge decision each student had to make in choosing which professor to work with.

Dr. Storey's roster of students was completely filled within minutes after we all got the e-mail. Dr. Willimon's roster was the same way. Deflated, I was paralyzed with dread for a couple of days. Finally, I made my decision. To be honest, there weren't many options left. Dr. Crenshaw was willing to work with me.

My essay work for the evaluation included a great deal of self-reflection. To my understanding, that is what the assignment called for. I can't even remember what the exact question was, but I remember going on for paragraphs and paragraphs about my self-consciousness about my voice, describing incidents where I was picked on in class in my junior high years.

I sat stoically in Dr. Crenshaw's office as he reviewed the notes he had jotted down in his reflections on my essays. I was sitting in the office of "Mr. Old Testament" at Duke. My friends and I always joked that, in his brilliance, Dr. Crenshaw probably knew the secret, full name of God the ancient Hebrews would never fully utter. We even got to calling him Moses. Here I was, sitting with Moses, in his office, while he — the author of many books — poured over my writing.

The years which have elapsed since that day have stolen my memories of the exact words Moses said to me that day, but I remember the heart of what he said. I write it here as conversation, with the understanding that it isn't a verbatim report of the professor's exact words.

"I think you are doing just fine here, Jeffrey, just fine," Dr. Crenshaw said at last. "Your grades are solid. You aren't going on for Ph.D. work. You are on a pastoral ministry path, and in light of that, you are doing just fine." I could feel my heart starting to soar. He turned the page of the little booklet of my writing that I submitted to him.

"The only thing I will say about your essays—you write well. Some of the things from your past you are really hanging onto though—your high-pitched voice, getting picked on in school, feeling alienated. I just want to say this about all of that. You are now in your mid-twenties. You are an average student at a prestigious university. You are going to be a pastor. In your cultural context, the young pastor of a church in a small town will be a big deal, an important person in the community, and more importantly, in peoples' lives. This stuff from when you were a teenager--it is time to let it go." He closed the booklet and patted it with his hand. "It's time to let much of this go."

I was elated. I had ascended Mount Sinai, and I had lived to descend the other side. I felt good. I appreciated what Dr. Crenshaw said. Now nearly pushing the ripe old age of forty, I am still struggling to follow his advice. I am still working on it, though.

The three years I spent at Duke truly did rush through my life like a mighty wind in green pines. I never dreamed they would, but they did. I can remember taking notes in class, and when a professor said something particularly poetic, prophetic, memorable, and momentous, I would think to myself, *Oooh...I will use that line in a church someday.* Then a corollary thought would rush through my brain-- *It is such a long, long way time before I will be the pastor of a church.* Well, it wasn't. To be honest, it probably needed to be much longer a length of time than it ever really could ever be. I had so much to learn. I had so much growing up to do. That time in seminary, like all time, flew by.

My graduation from Duke was a huge deal for me and my family. Everyone came. There was the general, huge graduation for the entire university on Saturday. The really meaningful service for divinity students, though, was Friday night in the chapel. The divinity school had a worship service and hooding ceremony. It wasn't a graduation with pomp and circumstance. It was a Christian worship service with liturgy and Sacrament. It was beautiful. I felt tears streaming down my cheeks when the dean placed my red, white, and blue master's hood on me. In the throng of people, I couldn't find my parents to make eye contact with them, nor my sisters or my grandmother. Right there in the row before me was my friend Turner, and when my eyes reached his, he gave me an assuring wink. I had never been alone for even one second of this journey. I wasn't alone now, as the journey ended.

I beat myself up now for rushing through my Duke years the way I did. When I was a student there, all I wanted to do was get back home to West Virginia. All I wanted to do was begin my life as a pastor. Now, with the tortured wisdom of hindsight, I know that West Virginia was always going to be there, and all the little churches I was perhaps destined to serve were waiting for me. God opened up so many opportunities for me, for all of the students at Duke. I wish I had taken more time. I wish I had been more conscientious. I wish I had been more appreciative of where I was, of what I was doing, of all there was in those hallowed classrooms to learn, of all there was in that "Gothic Wonderland" to experience.

Folks familiar with Duke and Duke's faculty may find it unbelievable I was a student there during Stanley Hauerwas's time, and I have written nothing of the legendary Stanley. Hauerwas's classes filled up so fast that I could never get in. My Christian ethics professor was a brilliant and lovely young woman named Amy Laura Hall. I loved her from afar. I was too shy to ever get close to any of my Duke professors. It isn't that I didn't want to get close to those brilliant men and women.

It's not that I didn't want them to know my name, to know something about me as a human being. It's just that every other student in every other class seemingly was seeking such a relationship with those professors, and to get close enough to speak to them after class required a self-esteem, a healthy self-consciousness, a self-worth I just didn't possess in those years. It also required, metaphorically (but maybe not metaphorically at all), a strong footing and a willingness to elbow others out of the way. I simply didn't possess that willingness in those years, and I still don't. I was entering Christian ministry in order to do work contrary to the Darwinian survival of the fittest, and I didn't have the heart for dog-eat-dog personal advancement in a school teaching me how to be a pastor for Jesus.

I wanted to have personal chats with Dr. Hall in particular, if for no other reason than she was an obviously brilliant, Christ-filled scholar and a pretty woman to boot. Of course, I never did. There were too many would-be Ph.D. students standing between us. I knew I would never get through, and I didn't have the strength to try. At least I got the privilege of hearing what Dr. Hall, and all my professors said to their classes each day. I was a student in their classes, and no one could ever take that distinction and blessing away from me.

One day in class, Dr. Hall told us she felt it was better for seminary students to not serve churches as student pastors while they were in divinity school full time unless they absolutely had to. She told us as Christians, we all have to offer our gifts to God on the altar of service. To her, at the stage of our lives when we were divinity students, the classroom, our studies, school, was our altar of service.

Dr. Amy Laura Hall was right. How often in the ensuing years have I wanted to return to that altar.

While I can never change the quantity or quality of myself — mind, body, and spirit — I laid down before God on the altar of my seminary education at Duke, I have feasted, and I continue to feast on the abundance of the gifts God placed on the altar of that school for me.

8 Senators and Ghosts

One of the most amazing experiences of my time at Duke, one of the coolest experiences of my life, period, was getting to work nights at Duke Chapel. If you've never been there, Duke Chapel is a neo-Gothic cathedral built right in the heart of Duke University's West Campus. Constructed from the same North Carolina stone as the rest of the academic castles, the chapel was a Depression-era project.

Anytime I ever got homesick, depressed, or overwhelmed during my three years in school there, I would make myself walk around campus, glance up at the spires of Duke Chapel, and remind myself just how blessed I was to even be there. It almost always worked. The few times it didn't, I just kept walking around campus until I arrived at the chapel. A few quiet moments alone underneath the flying buttresses and vaulted ceilings; a little timeout carved out within that sacred space, reading my Bible beneath the cavernous lights, illuminated by sunbeams radiating through stained glass of prophets, Christ, apostles, and saints, and I found enough emotional reserve and spiritual fortitude to fight through another day.

The path leading me to my humble, one-night-a-week position at Duke Chapel was to quote Lennon and McCartney, a "long and winding road." I was on a work-study scholarship at Duke, and I got fired from my first job. Yes. The audiovisual department of the divinity school let me go. It wasn't my fault. They were horrid. My supervisors took cigarette breaks out on the steps of the chapel. Yes, it was Duke. We were all receiving our wonderful educations, standing on the foundation of old Carolina tobacco money, but divinity students taking smoke breaks before the hallowed ground of Duke Chapel? Was nothing sacred?

I think I did two things wrong, which got me fired from this Duke gig. First and most seriously, I took a bank deposit bag to the wrong university department. It was so confusing. I had to take the red bus to the blue bus depot, and from there I had to take a blue bus to East Campus where I had never been before. From East Campus, I think I had to take a yellow bus to the Department of Development...or was it the Alumnus Department? No wonder I got confused! No wonder I got canned. I got horribly lost, trying to trek from one bus line to another. Duke's East Campus was completely foreign territory to me. I had never been there at all. I spent something on the level of two hours jumping from one mass transit bus to another. Finally, well past 5:00 p.m., exhaustion and sincere sorrow that I may never make it back to West Campus and the commuter parking lot again led me to just drop that money bag in the nearest Duke University drop-off box. Surely that money would get exactly where it was supposed to go in a matter of hours, if not minutes, right? Oh, but no.

It didn't take minutes or hours. It took a couple of days, days in which I unknowingly was responsible for who knows how much Duke money being missing. This department finally got it to that department, so they knew this little West Virginia hillbilly hadn't stolen it. They did know though, after that, that this little West Virginia hillbilly had no business being trusted with the transport of money from one university department to the other. I think I could have handled interdepartmental transfers, but this scenario of the buses and going across town from one campus to another? Oh, but no! It still gives me an anxiety attack even remembering it, to this day.

The second factor that got me fired from the audiovisual department was this. We taped the preaching class students delivering their sermons in the preaching labs. This was still the days of camcorders and video cassette recorders. Each student brought in a video cassette tape, and we filmed their sermon. After they delivered their sermons, the class critiqued them. So, in hindsight, I guess, I was technically supposed to leave after I had filmed the last preacher's sermon. There were other responsibilities in the audiovisual department, after all. Oh, but I got completely transfixed! I got completely transfixed by the sermons, and I got even more transfixed by the critiques.

I never heard a bad sermon in those preaching classes. Oh, I heard some flat ones, I suppose, some that were less inspired than they should have been. They were all solidly good, though. Some of them were downright brilliant. After hearing such sermons, I was in my own little world — a world of lofty theological insight, wonderfully astute exegesis, and poetic hermeneutics. My mind was nowhere near thinking about the next assignment in the old a and v (audiovisual) department.

The critiques of those sermons were something else entirely. Holy goodness! I still shudder when I think about some of them. Again, like the sermons, some of the critiques were uninspiring. Every student was required to critique each sermon, and every now and then it was obvious the critiquing student was simply "phoning it in." Other times though, the students had been as inspired by the sermon as I was. Their thoughtful analysis showed it. At such times, those preaching labs became holy jam sessions. One student preached a faithful, creative sermon. His and her fellow students responded with insightful, constructive critiques.

I remember one critique, though, that was just downright cruel. I don't know that I ever felt so bad for another student in an academic setting as I felt for this one guy as this lady critiqued him. Yes. She was critiquing *him* and not his *sermon*. The preceptor in the preaching lab attempted to intervene, but it was too late.

The preacher student in question was a chubby little guy, and like yours truly, he had a deficient number of hairs on his head. To be honest, he did sweat profusely as he preached, but to be fair, the room was hot because of the spotlights for the camera and the body heat with so many students in so small a room as the preaching lab was. Throw in the tangible stress of the situation, and to me, there was no wonder the poor guy was sweating. To be fair, we bald, or balding guys, also have the distinct disadvantage of not having a head full of hair where our perspiration can hide. This fellow was bald. This fellow was hot. This fellow was stressed. This fellow was sweating profusely, especially on his head.

"Your sweat really distracted me greatly," this female student told the little bald guy during her critique. "Your sweating was so disturbing to me, it got to the point where I wasn't even hearing your sermon anymore. Now, brother, I could understand your sweating so badly if you were doing something or preaching in a really exciting way. But you never moved an inch from the pulpit, and your delivery and voice were never at all exciting or energetic. I just can't get why you perspired as much as you did. Your sweat really detracted from your preaching as far as I am concerned."

I—the little stowaway from the audiovisual department sitting quietly in the back row—was shocked at this lady's comments. The teacher was shocked too. Again, he voiced a very weak response to the lady and uttered a feeble defense for the guy: "Well, I think perspiration is an involuntary biological function beyond our control." The young, bald, sweaty little student preacher was shocked, stunned, hurt, and humiliated. He didn't say a word. He didn't have to. It was all in the changing hue of his face, in the sudden mistiness of his eyes, of the sudden downward slope of his head and of his shoulders. It was like passing a car wreck, or two girls fighting. I felt horrible, looking at the emotional disaster, yet I couldn't turn away.

When I got back to the audiovisual department after the preaching lab was over, approximately an hour and a half after my filming duties were actually complete, the reception I received from my supervisor, Daniel, was not so peace, love, and Kum Ba Yah. He was also a work-study divinity student, a soon-to-be pastor, and a member of the Marlboro Light club. "Jeff, you had other things to do for us today besides taping those sermons," he said. "I understand you enjoy listening to the class discussion afterward, but you were supposed to come back here after everyone got done preaching. This can't happen again." I wondered if he knew the smell of Big Red chewing gum on his breath only made his cigarette breath smell like he had smoked a pack of Marlboros only to try to disguise it with one stick of Big Red. *How do you think emphysema breath will play with the little blue hairs in the Methodist Women, Danny Boy?* I couldn't help but antagonize in the privacy of my own thoughts.

That was on a Friday, and they fired me the following Monday. It was the sweetest, most Christian-like, passive-aggressive, oh-so-typical, non-offensive Methodist termination anyone ever received. I got called into the main supervisor's office, the lady on Duke's payroll to run the audiovisual department. After she explained to me I very nearly got her fired for misplacing thousands of dollars of university money in the campus mail, and that I had angered and antagonized the rest of the students on staff in the audiovisual department by camping out in the preaching labs all afternoon instead of trotting right back the way I was supposed to do, she asked me, oh so sweetly: "You really don't enjoy your work in our department, do you, Jeff ?"

"No, not really, ma'am," I squeaked back. I had been around enough passive-aggressive Methodists in my lifetime already. I knew what was coming. Therefore, I just had to add: "They are really hateful down there. There are going to be some angry churches here in a few years when those angry audiovisual people are their pastors."

She ignored that last comment. "Well, Jeff, you don't have to go into work today. In fact, we're just going to let you find another position somewhere in the school for your work-study scholarship." Then she smiled so I could see how truly relieved and happy she was to be getting rid of me. Then I smiled back so she could see how truly relieved and happy I was that she was getting rid of me. I hated those audiovisual people.

In about a week, I had landed the most amazing job of them all. I was the desk clerk at Duke Chapel from 6:00 p.m. to 11:00 p.m., weekdays. The prim and proper Miss Sally who was the supervisor of the desk clerks at Duke Chapel was an elderly southern belle whose roots probably touched the trunk of the John C. Breckenridge or John C. Calhoun family trees.

"Now, Mr. Jeff," she told me on that first day, "your job is to sit here at this desk. If anyone coming into the chapel or coming out of the chapel has a question, they will see you here and know you are here to answer their questions. You are not to engage them in conversation unless they engage you. Do smile and look friendly, but don't get all chatty. People come in here to meditate and pray in our beautiful chapel. If they want you to talk to them, they will speak to you. This is a chapel of reverence and not a tourist trap where you are trying to sell them souvenirs. Is that clear?" When I told her it was very clear, she showed me where the nearest exit was with a direct route to the university store just in case I should be asked where they could buy Coach K shirts or Reynolds Price novels.

It was positively the easiest job on campus. So long as I looked up and smiled every time someone entered the chapel, I was free to do whatever else I wanted to do at that desk. I read books for my classes, including the Bible. I read books for my pleasure, including Stephen King novels. In those days, I didn't have a laptop computer — only the Richie Riches did — so I worked on academic papers and creative writing longhand.

If someone entered the front door of Duke Chapel, I would look up and smile. The few who ever looked over at the desk at me generally did smile back. My job, as Miss Sally made abundantly clear, was to be available should anyone need me. My job was to be present; my job was not to make my presence known. I'm a pretty shy, reserved person by nature, so it was a perfect scenario for me. Having just come out of the horridness of the audiovisual department, I was grateful for such a low-key, low-pressure position.

In addition to all of that, it truly was an honor and a privilege to get to work in Duke Chapel no matter how trivial or menial the position was. There were times in that chapel, particularly in the early spring, when the air was electric with pollen and southern warmth, when sunset kept getting deeper and deeper into the evening, and blood red light in the west refused to yield to twilight just yet, when I could almost hear God whispering, occasionally whispering to me. It was something like magic. It certainly was holy. I did get a lot of praying done in those silent shifts in the chapel.

Of course, me being me, I also got quite a bit of my eyes full when spring weather also required the Duke girls to pull out their shorts, flip-flops, and T-shirts. More than once I was interrupted mid-petition when a few of the girls from the track team would come in for their own post-practice meditation and evening prayer. I never said a word to them. I was there at that desk if they needed anything, though! And of course, per Miss Sally's instruction, I looked up and smiled when they walked in.

There really wasn't any stress in this job, but the closest thing approaching normal stress occurred on Wednesday nights. Wednesday night was the busiest night in Duke Chapel. The choir practiced up in the chancel on Wednesday nights. All the undergraduate religious groups — from the Baptist Student Union to the Cardinal Newman Society to the Wesley Foundation; from the Jewish student ministry to the Muslim campus fellowship — met in the basement of the chapel for their weekly meetings on Wednesday nights. There was a huge amount of foot traffic. There was a moderate degree of legwork for me, too. It was the one time I was supposed to get up from the desk. The choir director and university organist liked the front of the chapel roped off during choir practice. Tourists were only allowed to get so close to the front of the chapel as the choir rehearsed. I thought it was silly, and I hated to do it. It wasn't like there were Broadway stars or classical music legends up there in the Duke Chapel Choir. It wasn't like there were ravenous paparazzi out in the knave waiting to capture an intrusive close-up of the third alto to the left on the third row.

I had already been fired from one Duke work-study job though, and I could not lose another one. Therefore, I dutifully put the rope out every Wednesday night around five forty-five, keeping the out-of-town folk throngs away from the holy of holies where the choir and musicians practiced for Sunday worship.

My bitterness at that little bit of academic, musical snootiness aside, the music on Wednesday nights was heavenly. Listening to the choir, pianist, and organist practice on Wednesday nights was my second favorite part of that job. My favorite part of the Duke Chapel job was simply watching the people with my eyes, letting my mind and my imagination wonder about them. The campus of Duke University also houses a major hospital, one of America's finest. Duke Hospital, and particularly the wing with all the oncology clinics, was within easy walking distance to the chapel. I knew many of the tourists I saw were actually family of patients in the hospital.

Each and every night, I knew I was seeing the moms and dads of sick children coming to the sacred space of the chapel to place their little babies into Jesus's loving arms. Each and every night, I knew I was seeing the healthy spouse of a dying mate who was in a room somewhere in the hospital — dying of cancer, dying of heart disease, dying of some trauma — coming into the chapel to try to bridge the gap between hard reality and hopeful faith, trying to sew a thread between medical science and divine grace.

I watched them. I saw them kneel in prayer. I heard many of them sob quietly to themselves. I wanted to hug them. I stayed back there at my desk. I was there if they needed to ask me any questions. I watched. I saw. I heard. I tried not to stare. I tried not to eavesdrop. I tried not to invade such sacred spaces. I tried not to contaminate such holy moments.

In the midst of truly Spirit-filled times, times where I was merely a silent witness to the humanity around and about me reaching out to God, I also experienced a freaky good old-fashioned spook.

Like most every other American who grew up in the

Appalachian Mountains, I grew up hearing family and community ghost stories. My step-grandmother, Mama, told two particularly frightening tales. One involved a little chant that went, "Lumber, lumber, lumber. Here comes one man kicking another man's head down the stairway." The other was a story Mama herself experienced about Big Mama.

My mama told her story of Big Mama masterfully. Big Mama was an obese, elderly woman who served as an adoptive grandmother for all the children in St. Paul, Virginia. Mama said she and one of her little friends used to visit Big Mama nearly every day, stopping to see her on their way home from school. Big Mama would always have something for the little girls to eat: fresh baked cookies, chocolate cake, or a pie. In warm weather, Big Mama would ask the girls to fan her. Mama and her friend always complied, and a sweating, panting Big Mama would always say, "I really appreciate you girls taking care of me like this. I will always be here to take care of you all too. Even when I die, I won't ever really leave you. I'll be here for you."

When Mama told that story time and time again for my sisters and me over the years of our childhoods, I always found that part of the story suspiciously hyperbolic: Big Mama professed eternal presence in two little girls' lives just because they had fanned her briefly on a balmy spring day. That little editorial critique of mine so stated, the story of Big Mama was Mama's story to tell.

Over the years of her young girlhood, the pattern persisted:

Mama and her friend would visit Big Mama. The old woman would have a sweet snack prepared for them. They would take her handheld fan and take turns cooling her. Big Mama would thank the little girls by weirdly promising to take care of them, forever, even beyond the grave.

The grave—Big Mama's grave—of course you knew the cemetery would be the ultimate destination of this story. When my mama was twelve or thirteen years old, Big Mama died. I don't think Mama ever included in the story what exactly took Big Mama out of this world. If she did, I have forgotten. I don't think I would have forgotten such an important detail, though. I am assuming the hefty old lady simply died of a heart attack, maybe in her sleep. The cause of her death wasn't important to the narrative of Big Mama as told by my Mama. It was her after-death that was so critical.

Big Mama had promised Mama and her little-ponytailed friend that she would take care of them, always and forever, even beyond the grave.

When Mama and her friend both carried a handful of wildflowers to place on Big Mama's grave, just a day after their elderly friend had been covered with soil and sod, maybe that loving but eerie promise was somewhere close to the forefront of their minds.

As they stood reverently, tearfully, silently at Big Mama's grave, both little girls heard distinctly, clearly, unmistakably, coming up from the ground beneath their feet — somewhere in the subterranean Virginia earth — moaning, groaning, hopeless sobbing.

"We threw those flowers far up into the air, and we took off as fast and as far as we could. We ran out of that cemetery just as fast as we could go, and we never, ever went back to Big Mama's grave again!" Mama would always conclude the story.

For a long time, my sisters and I just took the story of Big Mama at face value as truth, as art. As we got older though, of course, we had to ask questions. At one point, I think we all agreed Big Mama had probably been mistakenly pronounced dead and inhumanely buried alive. I think we had the good grace to never share this with Mama, but we all three shared just among ourselves our firm belief Mama and her friend probably really let Big Mama down on that one, leaving her quite literally dead, or should I say, almost dead, underneath a cold slab of stone underneath a blue sky looking down upon a green mound of grass showered with a scattering assortment of picked wildflowers.

I share that story with you only to prove my credibility. The tradition of living and telling spooky stories runs through my blood. It's in my family tradition, as well as in the heritage of my homeland. Call it Southern Gothic. Call it Appalachian folklore. Little did I know my employment on the evening shift at Duke Chapel would give me my own spooky story to live and live to share.

The chapel was completely empty that night, save me. Oh, there could have been any number of people downstairs in the offices, student lounges, and classrooms. There were entrances and exits on the basement level, so it was possible for other people to enter and exit the building, unbeknownst to me. Knowing that kept me from feeling totally lonely and alienated in the world, being alone in that capacious, drafty, gothic cathedral.

It was well past twilight, and the night blanketed the Carolina Piedmont with blackness. The lights in the chapel were dim, so in the night hours, the reverent spaces of sacrament and prayer were filled with shadows. It could be a depressive setting, Duke Chapel in the dark solitude, and I did find myself skirmishing with despair a few times there. I was sitting at the desk — my desk, the receptionist's desk — by the main entrance, about to turn the lamp on so I could see to read. Suddenly, rising out of the dark silence of the empty knave, like morning mist rising from the moist earth when the sun first bursts forth from the night, I heard organ music. It was faint at first, like muffled birdsong at dawn, when you're still in bed half awake and half asleep. At first, I attributed the organ song to my imagination. After all, my mind had the entire vastness of a medieval-style cathedral all to itself to fill with sounds, images, and memories. I was sure the sound of the organ was just a reverie until it kept getting unmistakably louder and louder and louder.

What was the song? I don't know. It wasn't any tune or melody I could recall. Though in those days, I was not exposed to classical music and to sacred choral. In just a few minutes, it was obvious someone was filling Duke Chapel with the haunting beauty of the organ. The sound was too vivid, too real to simply be confined to my brain, no matter how fertile a ground for fantasy and daydreams my head was.

"Wait a second!" After just a few moments of the beginning of an irrational freak-out, I was rationalizing a very plausible explanation. The university organist was a brilliant musician, and a prima donna kind of guy. This was a Thursday night, and I had never known him to come in any night except Wednesdays to play and rehearse with the choir. He was enough of an artist, living in the interior world of his art — the musical harmonies and chord progressions in his own mind and heart — that it would not have occurred to him that common courtesy and decency would dictate he let the lowly graveyard shift student receptionist know he was about to fill the joint with music at this unexpected, odd hour. It would be like him though to come into the chapel this late at night without speaking to me on his way up to the organ, I conjectured.

It was then the truth descended on me, hammering me down hard, body and soul, with the weight of the climax of a horror movie. He would have had to pass me on his way up to the organ. The organ loft was just above me, and the only way to get up there were either one of the stairwells, either over my shoulder behind me or right in front of me. I had not left my desk once the entire night. There was no way the organist could have ascended to his organ without me either seeing him before me or hearing him behind me.

Feeling a chill like death all over my body, my blood coursing like Arctic seawater, I got up from my desk. My destination was just a few feet into the chapel aisle to look up where the organ stood. My legs, my trunk, my entire body felt weighed down with lead or dread.

Those five or six steps were the longest of my life. What I saw when I finally reached my destination let me know every emotion and every sensation I had been experiencing, body and soul, were mere foreshadowing for what I was seeing, or not seeing, with my fright-filled blue eyes. There was no one up there playing the chapel organ. And though the sound of the organ was growing faint once again, I could still hear it.

I held up my trembling left arm to look at my wristwatch. It was a quarter till the hour. The chapel closed at the top of the hour. "Close enough," I said to myself. I determined my only response to the ghostliness going on about me was to lock up and get out of there as quickly as I could.

When I came back inside the knave after locking the massive front doors of the chapel, there was nothing but silence: still, soft, sullen silence on the enclosed, musty air. I was grateful. I locked all the side doors next. I waited until the very end of the evening.

I made it the very last thing to lock the door leading downstairs to the crypt. I had never thought anything sinister or creepy about the crypt before. It was simply the final resting place, the space for the entombed remains of several generations of Dukes and Terry Sanford, the former US senator, governor of North Carolina, and president of Duke University.

I walked into the foyer leading down to the crypt just far enough to turn the light out. The door of the crypt always moved outward toward you as you stood on the main floor of the chapel. Yes, I was emotional that evening. Yes, my arms and legs were still shaking and wobbly with fright. Yes, there could be a reasonable, scientific explanation for what I experienced next. I hope there is one.

I do not know what any of those explanations would be.

I only know what happened to me next.

As I pulled the crypt door back toward me to close and lock it, a sudden heavy force moved the door away from me, out of my hands, in the other direction. As bulky and as heavy as that door was, it simply flung like a loose feather on its hinges, hitting the opposite wall. When it hit the wall, the iron door came back to the proper direction back toward the knave. I was bracing myself to catch it as the sweat popped out all over my body as my eyes filled with tears. It simply stopped. The crypt door simply stopped, closing itself so I could lock it.

I did lock it.

I did run as quickly as I could out of there.

Nothing like what I experienced that night ever happened again in my employment at Duke Chapel. Nothing like what I experienced that night in Duke Chapel had ever happened to me before, or since.

I mentioned the name Terry Sanford. I suppose Sanford is buried in the crypt of Duke Chapel as a former Duke president, and his role as a senator and governor makes it all just that more impressive.

Even before I got the position at Duke Chapel, even before I started my career as a student at Duke, I was a Terry Sanford fan. I am simply a hopeless nerd, who has always followed politicians and writers the way most normal guys follow athletes or coaches.

My political hero has always been John Fitzgerald Kennedy, our martyred poet-president. I suppose my admiration for Kennedy means I have succumbed to the idealized, mythic, romanticizing of Camelot and the Thousand Days as Arthur Schlesinger forever memorialized the brief, brilliant administration of JFK. My love for John Kennedy goes far deeper than any cultural image or legend. My love for President Kennedy lies deep in my bones, planted far into my heart.

John Kennedy practically lived in West Virginia in April 1960. Leading up to our May primary, Kennedy didn't just barnstorm, or whistle-stop his way through the Mountain State. He truly spent time here. He truly took his time, getting to know the people here. To this day, there are no little towns where John Kennedy didn't stop and at least shake a few hands and listen to a few people. To this day, there are no little towns where at least a handful of people remain who don't remember shaking that hand, and who don't remember hearing that inimitable voice speaking their name. There are no hollows you can explore where people who remember 1960 won't speak fondly of hearing and of meeting John Fitzgerald Kennedy. Many of those people haven't voted for the Democratic nominee for the presidency in twenty years now.

My mother is one of those people who remembers John Kennedy in West Virginia. Momma was living in Wyoming County at the time. She was twelve years old. She was standing on the sidewalk, watching the little parade through the downtown of Pineville. Momma distinctly remembers the young, handsome, vibrant United States Senator John F. Kennedy, locking eyes with hers. My momma vividly remembers John Kennedy looking into her eyes, smiling and saying, "Hello there, little girl."

I love John Kennedy, in part, because that love is in my blood. Beyond that inherited reverence though, over the years I have read and studied Kennedy's life, and particularly his presidency. Early on, I came to admire him for the poetry of his words, for the humanity of his acts. In reading about Kennedy's presidency, particularly in Kennedy's brilliant speechwriter and friend, Teddy Sorenson's book *Kennedy*, I have found that when it comes to John Kennedy, the reality of his life is far richer and more beautifully complex than the American myth we have made him.

Terry Sanford was a John Kennedy Democrat when he ran for governor of North Carolina in 1960. Sanford won the governor's mansion. Kennedy won the White House. In the ensuing years, Sanford earned the reputation of being a moderately liberal, pro-Civil Rights Southern Democrat. He was the embodiment of the best connotation of the term *Southern Democrat*.

Many Kennedy biographies list Terry Sanford as high on the president's list of a potential new running mate if President Kennedy had decided to replace Lyndon Johnson from the 1964 ticket. Of course, that little nugget of very prevalent scholarship only enhanced the aura surrounding Terry Sanford in my heart.

After President Kennedy's murder, Sanford faithfully finished out his work as governor, but he was term-limited in North Carolina. He made his way to the presidency of Duke University, and as a capstone to his career, he served a term in the United States Senate as an octogenarian. Sanford had just died in 1998 when I arrived at Duke in 1999.

Needless to say, I was thrilled to be working in Duke Chapel where Terry Sanford was buried. Terry Sanford wasn't anywhere on my mind though, one evening when an elderly black gentleman came up to the receptionist's desk. It was one of the few times anyone ever came up to that desk to speak to me.

"Pardon me, sir, I am looking for Governor Sanford," the elderly man said to me. "I know Governor Terry Sanford is around here someplace."

My heart dropped. As I said, Sanford had just been dead a little over a year. This gentleman obviously didn't know Terry Sanford had passed away. How would I break the news to him Governor Sanford was, well, dead?

I opened my mouth and nothing but incoherent stuttering came out. "Well . . .I . . .ummm . . ." The frail, bent elderly gentleman looked at me with warm, pleading eyes.

"I know the governor is buried here in the chapel. and I just came to pay my respects."

Thank God! He knows Terry Sanford is no longer among us living. I don't have to break any sad, tragic news to this sort of sickly-looking elderly man.

"Yes!" I said, probably all too brightly and excitedly. "Mr. Sanford is buried down in the crypt with James B. Duke and all those Dukes. (One of my favorite jokes to this day is to say that in addition to the patriarch James B. Duke, Jessie Duke, Bo Duke, Luke Duke, and even Daisy Duke are buried down there too, but I had good grace and social mores to not utter that joke just then.) "Follow me, sir, and I will take you right to the governor's grave."

He thanked me, and the gentleman walked alongside me down the aisle of Duke Chapel. In a soft voice that started to get a little hoarse with emotion, he spoke to me as we walked.

"You see, young man, I used to work here at Duke. I was a maintenance man, and I worked here for over thirty years, including the time that Governor Sanford was our university president. Did you know that man would always stop me anytime he saw me? He would call me by name. He would ask me about my wife. He would ask me about my sons, by name. He would ask me how they were doing in school. He would ask me how they were doing in sports. When my oldest boy went over to Vietnam, Governor Sanford told me he would pray for my son, by name. When my wife died, yes, the university sent flowers to the church. But so did Terry Sanford himself. I just have always loved that man. When he died, I'm not ashamed to admit I cried, just like I did when President Kennedy died. Ever since, I have been wanting to come over here to pay my respects to my old boss, to my old friend."

He loved Sanford. He loved Kennedy.

I loved this little old man.

When we got to the doorway of the crypt, I debated on whether or not it would be patronizing to tell my new friend the steps were very steep, and he might want to hold on to the rail. In the end, I decided it would be very patronizing to tell him so. I determined, therefore, I would simply walk very slowly and gingerly, holding onto the rail myself. Since I was leading him, he wouldn't be able to go any faster, or fall down without knocking me down too.

At last, we made our way down into the crypt. One steady, shimmering sunbeam cascaded down through a stained-glass window toward the top of the vaulted ceiling. The light hit just shy of Terry Sanford's grave.

I motioned with my arm. "There he is, sir," I said with a choked-up voice.

The elderly black gentleman smiled at me, and he touched me on my shoulder. "Thank you," he mouthed silently. I decided I should leave my friend alone with this time, with this space. I knew it wasn't just Terry Sanford he would be spending time with, remembering. His wife would also be there, radiant and young. His sons would be there too, wet with sweat on basketball courts and baseball fields, glowing in their youth under the Carolina son. His son would be there, dressed in his fatigues heading to the airport gate, eventual destination: Vietnam. All these memories, I knew, would be clouded with tears.

"Hey there, Governor," I heard the elderly gentleman say in a soft, hoarse voice as I slowly made my way back up the stairwell.

By far, that was my best day working at Duke Chapel. I think it was my best day at Duke, period.

9 Good People

I am telling a story a little out of sequential order. This is a story about my relationship with some folks in one of my churches after I was serving as a pastor. I believe this story fits the overall narrative of this book because these particular pastoral relationships helped me continue to become a pastor. In that sense, this story shows how "becoming pastor" is an ongoing process, a perpetual journey following the selfless love of Jesus on the cross, as that cross forever points to the hope of the empty tomb of Easter.

I have replaced only one pastor whom the people of the church really loved. All but one of my pastoral assignments have been to replace unloved pastoral captains who were steering the ship of church right through a neighborhood of icebergs, ripping gaping wounds right through fragile hulls, which then started taking on untenable levels of seawater.

I don't know what this says about my fellow pastors. I don't know what this says about me.

"Send Kanode there. He is really good at plugging holes and steering churches back to safe waters."

"Send Kanode there. He is such a damaged vessel himself. It will do the least amount of damage if he goes down with that sinking church, which clearly cannot be saved or salvaged."

Welcome to the way pastors think. At least, welcome to the way this pastor thinks. I personally think it is the way most pastors think, whether they care to be honest with anyone else, even themselves. On my dark days, I have come to believe I replace failed pastors because the church hierarchy has already written those churches off, and I have been written off myself. On my better days, I have come to believe I replace failed pastors because I have developed a gift for healing wounds, repairing burned bridges, and revitalizing hopeless congregations. On any given day, I wonder which assertion is true.

Only once in my pastoral life has this question been null and void. Only once in my pastoral life did I enter a church where most of the church folk were grieving because the last guy left.

The folks at Sherman Memorial UMC really loved Ken, his wife, and their daughters. Ken was middle-aged, in midcareer, and he was really in the perfect place to be the perfect pastor for Sherman. He was the pastor of Sherman for three full years, and the bishop and cabinet placed Chelton UMC on a "charge" with Sherman. Now Ken was to continue being the pastor of Sherman Memorial, where he was well- established and loved, and Chelton UMC, a church with a rough, tough reputation. Ken never got established at Chelton, but Sherman continued to thrive under his ministry.

I recognized the dichotomy from the first day I served as pastor of Sherman and Chelton. At Sherman I would need to do some grief counseling and be aware the folks might be mourning for Ken for an extended period. At Chelton, all I needed to do was not be Ken, and I might just become beloved.

I was right on both counts. I was wrong in discounting the love and connection Sherman Memorial UMC and I would share together. Chelton was a tough church, and it nearly killed me over our four-year relationship. Sherman kept me alive. Even though those folks loved Ken and I wasn't Ken, they came to love Jeff too. Their love saved Jeff.

Preston and Dee-Dee were the power couple of Sherman Memorial UMC. Oh, every church has the power couple, or two, or three, or more. Every church has the power people, too. Generally speaking, power couples and power people usually recognize they do indeed have power. Preston and Dee-Dee never did. At least, they seemed to me completely unaware they yielded such enormous influence and carried such enormous weight in that little church. That's what made them all the more precious and special to their church and to me, their pastor.

Preston was wiry and feeble, in his early eighties. He walked a little crooked sometimes, and it always looked like he was on the precipice of losing his balance and taking a fall. He still had a full head of hair (which I always admire in a man since so much of mine was lost by my mid-twenties) though the snow-white mane was getting a little thin. Preston had eyes cobalt blue. They were piercing but gentle, tired but beautiful.

This little, feeble man, I soon learned, had "stormed the beaches of Normandy," as the boys said in the Stephen King book and movie, *Stand By Me.* Old Preston was a veteran of the Eighty-Second Airborne, and he served from the weather-beaten, summer sands of France to the tangled, dense forests of a German winter.

When I knew Preston in the winter of his life, his lovely wife, Dee-Dee, doted over him and almost protected him. Dee-Dee was some fifteen years younger than Preston, and I am sure in their early years, Preston had done the protecting and the doting. Now, age and love had turned those tables. Preston and Dee-Dee both had previous marriages behind them. Theirs was a marriage of second chances, a covenant of redemption. Preston's first wife had died of cancer some years before. He had been a widower for years before he met Dee- Dee. Dee-Dee was divorced after a difficult marriage to an abusive husband. Dee-Dee had no children. Preston and his first wife had three boys.

Preston wanted to pray with me each Sunday before church. Evidently, one of their former pastors from years ago had asked some of the men in the church to pray with him each Sunday. They would meet in the small chapel across the hall from the sanctuary. The pastor would kneel down, and the men would place their hands on him and pray. I loved the idea. It was just me and Preston. I kneeled down, and he placed aged, trembling hands on my head as he prayed for me. Often, he would also pray for America. This was 2003. We had just entered the war with Iraq on top of our war in Afghanistan.

I was moved when this little old man who as a young, scared, but brave American soldier had faced down death at Normandy prayed week- in and week- out in a voice growing weaker with time, but a voice still plenty loud enough to be heard, for "these wars to somehow come to an end, so our boys and our girls can come home and be with their families where they belong." He prayed those words at some point in his prayer every week, as he also prayed for me, his pastor. "Help Jeff give us your words, dear God: the words we need to hear to be better Christians. Fill him with your love and may he feel our love with him too." I always felt more peaceful, more hopeful, more confident, when I could stand behind the pulpit at Sherman, blanketed, anointed with a Preston prayer.

Preston's blue eyes would often grow misty hen he talked about World War II. I made it a point of never openly asking Preston about the war. I learned early on in our relationship that Preston's experiences as a young combat veteran in the Allied war against murderous Nazism was an engrained part of his humanity. The stories were pieces of Preston's soul.

He was friends with the chaplain of his company. This pastor, who had a congregation and a wife back home in America, risked his life on several occasions by entering into the line of fire-- which he was not required to do-- in order to pull and even carry wounded men to a safe place. "He was a preacher who helped men find sanctuary even in the hell of battle," Preston said.

I think his World War II chaplain symbolized for Preston, not only what Christian service meant, but also what Christianity should be. He didn't expect me, his current pastor in peacetime, postmodern America, to exhibit the same level of heroism and selflessness wrung out of one Christian chaplain's heart in the midst of war. The actions of that chaplain, though, were Preston's ideal of the true Christian heart and spirit.

Preston returned home to West Virginia after the war, and he proved himself a good husband, a good daddy, a good worker at a local chemical plant, and a good Methodist. Years went by. The scared but dashing Normandy beach- storming soldier slowly turned from a young to an old man. His springtime and summer all too quickly vanished into the leaves and snow of his autumn and winter. His sons grew to be their own men. His wife died. The chemical plant closed. In the frosty twilight of late life, God gave Preston some sunshine and warmth, some springtime and vibrancy when he met Dee-Dee.

They were married after a brief courtship, and their two lives seemed to gently flow into one. You would have thought they had been together for many, many years. They seemed so close, so connected.

Dee-Dee's previous married life had been as tumultuous as Preston's had been *Leave It to Beaver*. Her first husband was abusive, both physically and mentally. Over many years, Dee-Dee endured many seasons in darkness and in fear. The two could never have children. Dee-Dee then tried to build a positive life for herself with her job at a local bank and with a small group of girlfriends, most of whom she knew from the church. She was Baptist, and her Baptist church was just a stone's throw away from Sherman Memorial UMC, where Preston and his family attended for all those same years.

For all of those married years, for all of those pained, tortured years, Preston and Dee-Dee lived just a few paces away from one another's orbit. Preston didn't bank at the same bank where Dee-Dee's was employed, but he drove by it every day. Preston and his family didn't live next door to Dee-Dee and her husband, but they could have walked the distance between one another's homes. They probably ate in the same restaurants, more than likely at the same time, occasionally, over those years. They probably passed each other on the sidewalks of their town and never ever knew each other. Maybe, just maybe at some point in the midst of those years, they made eye contact with each other and just for a fleeting second shared a passing smile.

Dee-Dee wanted to leave her marriage many times, and with occasional bruises on her body, with constant wounds in her heart, God knows she would have been justified and righteous for leaving. She just didn't feel financially secure and independent enough to leave until she was in her early sixties. By then she had saved enough money. By then she was certain and peaceful enough in her own personhood to leave. She did.

Dee-Dee and Preston met when he started a savings account

at the bank where Dee-Dee worked as a teller. After a few months of innocent flirtation and getting to know one another from the safe space across the counter, Preston finally asked Dee-Dee out to dinner. They were married just a few months later. They had been married going on three decades when I served as their pastor.

Dee-Dee was as fun and vivacious as Preston was reserved and dignified. She loved to laugh and joke and gossip. Now, to be sure, gossip can be quite ungodly and deadly in a church, but gossip in Dee-Dee's loving way was neither. It was more informative gossip, more "did you know that so-and-so just separated" kind of gossip, without ever a hint of judgment or slander. What Dee-Dee gossiped about, Dee-Dee knew and could back up. What Dee-Dee gossiped about, Dee-Dee presented without judgment or prejudice. "So-and-so" may have just gotten separated, and Dee-Dee would let you know. She wouldn't speculate or judge on the *why*, though, who was at fault in the separation, or who did what to whom? Dee- Dee was the Walter Cronkite of small-town news, and maybe just maybe she was even more balanced than old Uncle Walt. There are some on the right, after all, who feel even he wasn't so nonpartisan. Dee-Dee for sure was completely nonpartisan. She just liked to talk and laugh and share what she knew.

She had a way about starting a conversation or sharing a juicy tidbit of information. Over the years, I have come to do it myself. It started by me lovingly mimicking Dee-Dee, but now I too share my gossip . . . er . . . information, the Dee-Dee way.

This lovely, stately lady with cheeks rosy red with rouge and hair brushed just perfectly, would get close to your face, so you could both hear her clearly and feel her breathe — which was always peppermint or cough-drop perfumed — and begin in a hushed tone, "Well, I heard that..." and she would always emphasize the *I* and draw it out.

Now I do it just that way. And I think of my Dee-Dee. Preston and Dee-Dee were the pillars of Sherman Memorial UMC, and there were many other solid rocks and steady stones in that faithful, loving church.

Tim and Nita were physically mismatched. She was petite and pretty; he was round and homely. As mismatched as they were physically, however, they were perfect for each other in spirit and in personality.

Nita had suffered from at least two strokes. These strokes left her with a halting walk accented with a slight limp. They also left her with slurred, stammering speech. Oftentimes I could see it in Nita's eyes. The words were there. The ideas were there. They were her words, and she could hear them. They were her ideas, and she could articulate them. Words and ideas just lived in her mind, though. Often Nita's brain couldn't deliver those words to her mouth, and she would grow frustrated with herself. When Nita was frustrated with herself, the slurring and stammering only grew worse. At such times, Tim was there with his gruff voice and his tender hand. He would say, "Slow down there, lady, you don't want to make these people as confused as we are," and he would place his hand on her shoulder. With Tim's voice and his touch, Nita would indeed slow down, regain her composure, and somehow articulate at least a fraction of what she was thinking.

Tim physically and emotionally supported Nita. She was proud, and she chafed at help. I noticed anytime Nita had to go up steps or walk up an incline of any kind, Tim nonchalantly and unobtrusively placed his hand underneath her arm to steady her. His voice was often gruff, but her smile back to him as he walked alongside of her with his steadying hand, or as he held her flank in conversation when she got caught up in a briar patch of speech impediment stroke aftermath, told me they had understanding. They had love. I could clearly see and understand that Tim was supporting Nita physically and emotionally now. She had been supporting him in every way for many, many years.

She called him Timmy. She doted on him. Often in church, I could see her putting her hands on his shoulders as she walked behind him at church potluck dinners or hotdog sales. Nita would straighten Timmy's tie when it had gone eschew, and sometimes she would rest her head on his shoulder during the sermon anytime Tim seemed to be growing restless or bored during the service.

Nita and her Timmy had one daughter, Tina. She was

incredibly accomplished and scholastically astute in high school, and for her accomplishments, she won a full scholarship to West Virginia University. Tina's college career opened up a whole new world for her loving parents. Nita and Tim became true-blue, loyal WVU fans who attended every home football game. Even after Tina graduated, got married, and moved to another state, Tim and Nita continued being loyal fans to WVU. When I visited their home for the first of many times, the first thing Nita wanted to show me was a large photograph of the WVU Marching Band taken on the football field, with all the band members positioned to make the outline of our state. "Me and Timmy were at the game when they took this picture," Nita said to me with pride.

I watched as Tim and Nita grew feebler over the four years I spent with them as Sherman Memorial UMC's pastor. Tim's walk grew slower, his back got more crooked, and his patience got a little shorter. Nita's walking became more labored, and her speech became more slurred and halting. Their love for one another didn't change at all. I think maybe it grew. Although Tim could be a little gruff with Nita at times in conversation—when she messed up a fact about family history, for instance—his protective actions toward her seemed to grow with tenderness. He seemed to hold onto her just a little more tightly as she climbed steps. He seemed to clutch her hand as they sat together in the pew more often than I had remembered him doing in the past. Nita too seemed to dote more on her Timmy, if that seemed possible. She bathed him with such sweet companionship so completely before that it was hard to believe she could have anymore to give, but somehow, she did.

When I left Sherman to take a new assignment in another Methodist church far away in another part of West Virginia, Tim and Nita were still clinging to one another, still willing each other to stay well and alive.

Little ole Jack was the jewel of Sherman Memorial UMC. I don't know what his prognosis ever was. We all suspected he was mentally challenged. Word from Dee-Dee and other folks who had been around for years was that Jack's family never even allowed him to attend school. His mother cared for him at home all his life. Tragically, Jack's mother died when he was in his mid-thirties. Responsibility for his care fell to his older sister and her husband.

Jack was a short, little man with white hair and a little fuzzy white beard, more like the unshaved peach fuzz of a young teenager, really. Every Sunday he came to church just as soon as Preston unlocked the door. He always had a sucker in his mouth. He always raced up to the organ to play for a time before church.

He played the organ well. Jack didn't read music at all, but he could play hymns he had heard his whole life. I always wanted to get Jack to play in church, but he never would. As a matter of fact, Jack would only play until a certain number of people arrived for church. He would then quit, sometimes abruptly. I never figured out if there was a particular person Jack refused to play in front of, and when that person arrived, he just decided to stop. I also

231

wondered if there were an actual number of people in the sanctuary that Jack was comfortable playing in front of, and when that number was surpassed, he intuitively knew and just stopped.

I don't want to overplay or oversell Jack's organ playing talent. He wasn't a gifted genius at the organ, but he played pretty well — well enough a congregation could sing along with his playing. I learned Jack's mother had been a music teacher early in life. After she resigned her teaching position to care for Jack full-time, she still offered lessons to children in her home. According to Dee-Dee, his mother never offered Jack formal lessons. We just surmised Jack picked up how to play what he played simply by what he heard and what he observed all of those years in his home.

Little Jack had a circuit he made every day through the town. He would go to the dollar store first at around eleven in the morning. His sister and brother-in-law had an understanding with the management of the store. They kept an envelope of cash at one of the registers marked Jack. Every day, when Jack came in, the cost of whatever he purchased came out of that envelope. The sum of money in the envelope would generally last a good while because generally Jack bought one item a day: a stick of chewing gum, a bag of mints, or a candy bar.

From the dollar store with his new purchase in hand and at least part of it usually in his mouth, Jack would walk to the Wendy's just down the street. Now this wasn't just any regular Wendy's fast-food restaurant. This Wendy's was the official hangout of a group of senior citizen ladies from Sherman Memorial UMC with a few friendly Baptist ladies thrown in for good measure. Jack would join them at least for as long as it took him to wolf down a cheeseburger and a few fries. Once again, Jack's family had an understanding with the management. They would prepay a month's worth of kid's meals for Jack.

Several of the ladies of this senior citizen, ecumenical "lunch bunch" tested the limits of Wendy's management to the outer reaches. Ruth and Jenny routinely came into the Wendy's dining area with their fish, fries, hush puppies, and soda from the Long John's Silver next door. Jack ate and ran pretty quickly to be sure, but the ladies did not. Lunch began promptly at 11:30 a.m., and it was usually not over before three in the afternoon. At least six, sometimes as many as nine or ten seats, and two or three of Wendy's prime tables were occupied by the ladies. It was comical. I always tried to buy a little extra in the way of an extra order of fries, or a Frosty when I joined them. I felt bad for Dave Thomas's employees, and being the pastor of the church where most of these ladies attended, I felt semi responsible. I also greatly appreciated how good the Wendy's staff was to Jack. Like the dollar store folks, they couldn't have been more gracious and patient.

Summer or fall, winter or spring, Jack dressed in a thick green Marshall University coat. The Marshall hat was optional in the ensemble, but the coat was nonnegotiable. In the summer heat, Jack clearly burned up with the sweat often pouring off his little balding head and his glowing face. Still, he had to wear his special green, Marshall Thundering Herd coat. One winter I bought Jack a green scarf to go with the coat. From then on, he wore that scarf too, in twenty-degree snows and in ninety-degree humidity.

Conversations with Jack were always quick and hurried because Jack was always hustling from one place to another. After he left the dollar store, he was hustling to get to Wendy's. After lunch at Wendy's, he was hustling to get home because his sister strictly made him return long before afternoon school and rush hour traffic. At church on Sunday morning, as soon as he entered the sanctuary, Jack was hustling to get up to the organ to play. When whatever triggered in his mind telling him it was time to stop playing, Jack was hustling to get away from the organ to sit down in his pew.

In the midst of all his hustling and moving, Jack developed a connection to me, and I to him, as well. Dee-Dee told me often that Jack's sister told her how much Jack loved his church and his pastor. I deeply appreciated hearing that because I never felt like I gave Jack the attention he needed and deserved. He was a little white haired, balding, green little streak bouncing from one end of the town to the other, bearing a lollipop in his mouth. Most everyone knew Jack, and Jack was, thankfully, looked after, and Jack was safe.

There were good people in that town who loved Jack. There were good people in that church, Sherman Memorial, who loved me and who loved each other. I would say they worked hard being the church: the family saved and bound together by divine love; the group of people given the holy, fearful, humbling title — the Body of Christ. I would say Sherman Memorial worked hard being the church, but then again, they did it so well that maybe, just maybe, it came naturally, as a gift of grace.

It has been seven years since I left Sherman Memorial as pastor. I am blessed because the church I now serve is only forty-five minutes up the interstate. Several times a year, I meet a group of those lovely people for lunch or dinner. Preston has become a shadow of his former vibrant self, but he still glows with brave manhood and Christian gentleness. Dee-Dee has lost weight, and now a once strong woman sometimes stumbles as she walks. Even Tim's gruff voice is weak today, and he is as unsure on his feet as Nita is. Still, the last time they came to our lunch, he walked protectively beside her, offering his beloved wife his hand. Nita still rested her head on her husband's shoulder, and though she struggled to speak, and a pained look sprung up in her eyes, she still smiled and joined our easy, friendly banter. Jack never comes to our reunion meals, but occasionally when I am passing by on the interstate, I will pull off the exit and drive through town, hoping to see him. Every now and then on these little mini-pilgrimages of mine, I do see Jack. I wave to him when I see him hustling — still the little man in Marshall green, rushing in the routine of his daily life.

These were always, these will always be, good people. They were, they are, the best of people.

10 My Biggest Fan

Next to her family, my grandmother loved her church more than anything else in her life. In the final era of her life after she was retired, widowed, and alone, except for a son and his family who lived close by but who lived their own busy life, Grandmother found her friendships, her activities, her life, really, at Bluecreek United Methodist Church.

She was an alto in the church choir. Her singing always reminded me of the *bah-bahs* of a sheep, and I made that observation secretly as a loving grandson. I wonder what fellow members of the choir—technically no relation in the technical sense of the word—thought, or maybe even said, about Grandmother's singing. She also played the piano, but never really for public. She played occasionally at home. In the years when I was around her, arthritis had crippled her hands so much that her playing ability was limited with many bad, sour notes interspersed with the occasional good ones. I remember once we tried to sing the old hymn "Beulah Land" together, and it sounded nothing like the song of the same name I had just heard Grandpa sing on *The Waltons*. Grandmother was an avid Bible study participant at Bluecreek, too.

In the late 1980s and early '90s, a new Bible study program called *Disciple* became all the rage in the United Methodist Church. In *Disciple 1*, students read through most all of the Bible in a thirty-four-week period. In all the subsequent *Disciple* classes, the curriculum zeroed in on smaller segments of the Bible, each class lasting the length of an academic year, usually September through May. I think *Disciple* was designed to bring biblical literacy to Baby Boomers and Generation Xers, the rising generations whose biblical literacy did not come close to the scriptural knowledge of the Depression and World War II generation, the Greatest Generation, as Tom Brokaw christened them.

My grandmother, of course, was a part of the Greatest Generation, and she already knew her Bible through years of faithful, devoted Sunday school attendance and study. Grandmother was typical of her generation with both her breadth of scriptural acuity and depth in church involvement. Church truly was a family; church truly meant something to my grandmother, and to her generation. Grandmother wasn't the target demographic of *Disciple*, but even if she had known that, she wouldn't have cared. It was a chance to learn about God. It was an opportunity to be with her friends in the church. Grandmother took every *Disciple* class offered during her lifetime. I think by the time she died, there were three courses in existence.

Today all of Grandmother's *Disciple* workbooks are in my possession, and I cherish them. Each day of the week, there are Bible readings to do. The workbook features little blocks for each day, so students can record their observations and thoughts about the day's reading. I have now taught through the *Disciple* program three times. I confess there are many weeks when the little blocks in my workbook don't even contain complete sentences. Sometimes blocks will contain just fragments, or a few words. Here and there, entire blocks are blank in my *Disciple* workbooks. My little grandmother crammed her blocks jam-packed full of her summaries, her questions, and her thoughts. She never ever left a day's reading undone, and she never failed to faithfully record her observations. I bet some of those tiny blocks contained at least a hundred, maybe more, words. Grandmother was so incredibly faithful to those *Disciple* Bible study classes. More than a few times over the years, I have carried Grandmother's, and not my own, workbook into class. I have taught many *Disciple* Bible study sessions with my grandmother's words and work sitting before me at the table, guiding me.

She was a retired school teacher. Grandmother taught second grade for over thirty years. In her humble, self- deprecating way, anytime someone asked her opinion on a matter, or anytime she offered an unsolicited opinion on a topic, she would end her comment with, "But what do I know? I spent thirty years in the second grade."

I suppose we often take our family member's professional talents and accomplishments for granted. I never really thought much about what kind of teacher my grandmother had been. I guess I just assumed she was sweet and good in the classroom with her school children just as she always was with my sisters and me.

It wasn't until my grandmother died that I finally got to see her in the full reality of her being. Grandmother wasn't just *Grandmother*. She was a gifted, professional educator whose students praised her and expressed love for her upon her death. I remember one young guy in particular, a guy around my age, who attended Grandmother's church, but who knew her first and best as his second-grade teacher. He came up to me at her wake, and he told me all kinds of little tidbits of wisdom Grandmother shared with her class — little nuggets of love from Mrs. Kanode, my grandmother, that this guy had carried with him all his life. I was profoundly moved with pride and love. I was also profoundly shaken with guilt and remorse. The waters of my grandmother's soul, the reservoir of her life, were so much deeper than I ever realized, and that life teemed with life like I never imagined.

The praise and love for my grandmother from her former students, so many of whom I don't even know, went on long after her death. Just last year, the daily newspaper back home asked readers to submit the names of their most beloved teachers. The paper then published the names of those teachers like a roll of honor. Lillianne Kanode, my grandmother, was right there on that list. I read her name through tears.

Grandmother was such a sweet, selfless person, she was easy to take for granted. She was easier still to marginalize. I never saw her mad. I never knew her to lose her temper. I made her cry once, that I know of, when I was a teenager. I didn't grow up gracefully. Do any of us? I think my "growing edges" were more jagged and sharper than most, though. Of course, my family bore the brunt of it. Of course, the sweetest, most selfless person among us suffered through the worst of the worst.

Ever since I was a very little boy, I would spend the occasional Friday night at my grandmother's home. To be honest, I really can't remember anything we actually did during those extended visits. I guess we just did the usual things. When I was very young, Grandmother would read to me. As I grew older, I would read my book as she read her book. We would watch a little television together. Grandmother would make a wonderful dinner capped off with a marvelous dessert.

As I grew older, and the little boy became the young teenager, spending the night with my grandmother became something I felt forced to do and not something at all I wanted to do. Oh, it wasn't like I had all these exciting things going on at home: friends to hang out with, extracurricular activities like team sports, or Boy Scouts to occupy my time. No, to the contrary, I had my books, my television, and my music. I had the cocoon of my bedroom, and I had my easy routine. At Grandmother's, I had to blend into her routine. I could "disappear" at home. I could spend hours alone in my room reading a book, or out in the den, watching television. I couldn't vanish like that in Grandmother's house. She would come hunting me. She wanted, she expected, my company. It wasn't that she didn't value my need for privacy as I got older. It's just that, for her, I was a little boy, a child, and a child needed an adult around to care for them, to watch them, to tenderly be there with them.

I was twelve or thirteen years old, filled with resentment and teenaged bile because I was being forced to spend the night at my grandmother's. I can't remember now what she asked me and what I smarted off about in reply to her. What I can remember, what can never ever be erased from my mind, was my grandmother's ocean blue eyes welling up with tears as she said, "I still love you, and I always will. But you just aren't my little Jeff anymore." Writing those words and reading them, I can hear her voice again. It still hurts.

It hurts me even more to remember that in the last year of her life, Grandmother didn't even have her grandson's phone number. I had been transferred from Clutchler to Chelton. My mother asked me one day, "Jeff, is it okay if we give your grandmother your new number?" I am ashamed to say that I said, "Oh, Momma, I wish you wouldn't. She calls at the worst times, and you just never can get off of the phone with her." Momma said she understood, and she promised she wouldn't give Grandmother my new number. Dear, sweet Jesus forgive me. I am certain Mom never told Grandmother she couldn't have my number. I just assume when Grandmother asked for it, Momma stalled, maybe saying she didn't have it close and would have to hunt for it. I just pray Grandmother never caught on.

I loved Grandmother! I did. We all did. It's just . . .sweet Jesus. She got on my nerves. She was so good. She was so sweet. She was so predictable. She was so boring. Conversations with Grandmother could go on for many minutes, even hours, and never meander outside the confines of Bluecreek UMC, or our own family. Grandmother's goodness made her almost unbearable to be around sometimes. It wasn't what you think either. Many really good, many maybe even holy, godly people have an air about them. Call it self-righteousness or heightened self-awareness of how much rarefied, sacred air they breathe. Grandmother didn't have that at all. In fact, a humble personality, a meek demeanor, helped define my grandmother's character and personhood.

I don't think she ever really understood how truly good she was. No. What made Grandmother sometimes hard to be around was simply that she was so good, because she was so Christian, because she was such a lady that conversations with her seemed forever stuck in the 1950s — the Ward Cleaver and *Leave It to Beaver*-sanitized 1950s, the 1950s everyone romanticizes now. Grandmother would never speak ill of anyone. Therefore, she would never engage in gossip or contribute new details or storylines to a juicy thread of slander. Grandmother was such a lady that you felt like you had to be on your toes around her because she was so genteel and gracious, and you simply were not.

She would never correct you, though, or make you feel bad if your conversations went into negative places. She just simply would not go there with you.

Grandmother was also always incredibly naïve. She watched the news, and she read the newspaper, but so much of what was going on culturally zoomed right past her. Looking back on it now, I wonder if this wasn't another sign of Grandmother's deep humanity. She simply refused to waste God's sacred gift of time and life down in the gutter and in the dirt. Back in the day though, it simply annoyed me that Grandmother didn't know The Beatles from The Backstreet Boys, and if they weren't on *Hee Haw* or *The Love Boat*, Grandmother just didn't know (or care) about one actor, one performer, from the next.

I guess it all comes down to this. My dear, sweet little grandmother very much lived in her own little world. It was a good world. It was a humane world. It was a wholesome world. It was a stained glass–tinted world. It was a very unexciting world. It was a very mundane world. At least, I thought all those things before God had grown me up enough to appreciate the wonder my grandmother truly was. By then, I could only visit her in the cemetery or talk to her in my prayers.

Even in the darkness of my teen soul, where I both felt and reflected deep shadows, there were moments of light. There were moments of grace. One of my best moments was the day I asked Grandmother to take me down to McDowell County and show me all the towns and places important to her. I was in ninth grade, so I was just beginning to drown in confusion, but I wasn't yet completely submerged. Grandmother was thrilled with the opportunity to share part of her heart with her only grandson. It was a holy, golden day. It was an extraordinary day of human connection between grandmother and grandson. It was a day, one of the few days when I was the grandson my grandmother deserved — a grandson who truly cared, who truly showed he cared about her life, about her world, about her heart and all the mysteries and wisdom therein.

I took our family camcorder along with me that day, and I documented almost everything. I wished to God I still had that video cassette, but I do not. I remember most of what was on it, though. The train whistle echoing out of Elkhorn hollow as the camera watched Grandmother slowly walk up the knoll to the post office — where the little postmistress greeted her with a huge "Well, hello there, Miss Lillian!" — haunts me still.

Like so many old West Virginia coal towns, Elkhorn was built in whatever space people could find to plant their little town. Cradled by craggy, brushy hills with a railroad track and a creek running like arteries pulsating blood through the center of town, Elkhorn was neither unusual nor mundane. It looked like a dozen other old dusty coal towns dotting US 52, yet it looked just distinctively itself, somehow unique, as well.

Elkhorn contained three essential, sacred spaces for

Grandmother. One was the bridge leading across Elkhorn Creek to the Elkhorn United Methodist Church. One was Creed Hall. The other was an old, dilapidated three-story house with a wraparound porch.

Grandmother held onto the rail of the bridge carefully as we walked across it. Below us, Elkhorn Creek gurgled and danced. About halfway across the bridge, Grandmother stopped. She turned to me slowly, very deliberately, almost dramatically.

"This is where I met your granddad, Jeff," she said to me in as soft a voice, in as girlish a voice as I ever heard my grandmother use. "This is where I met my CH."

"Wow, Grandmother," I replied with a frog in my throat and with a pure, authentic sense of awe. Even in my teenage angst, anything about my grandfather captivated me. This ground was sacred even for fourteen-year-old me. Thank God even amid the adolescent angst growing in my soul, I still had enough heart, and my mind had enough wisdom to guide my mouth to say, "Tell me the story, Grandmother. Tell me your story."

With a sparkle of life in her old eyes, Grandmother started sharing a tale I had never heard before, one she had kept private, safe, in her heart and memory. It wasn't as dramatic or made-for-television movie as I had hoped for. I was happy to hear the story though, because it was her story.

Grandmother, a young seventeen-year-old Miss Lillianne Creed, had been in the sanctuary of the Elkhorn Methodist Church, playing the piano. She did that occasionally because her parents didn't own a piano. Her father, Walter Creed, was downstairs in the church fellowship hall, waiting for a man he was scheduled to meet. As Grandmother ambled across the bridge, young—but thirteen years older than her—Cleo Henry "CH" Kanode came approaching from the other side, heading toward the church. With a little blush on her wrinkled face, Grandmother told her little grandson, "I knew I didn't know the handsome stranger walking my way, and I knew I wanted to."

According to Grandmother's report, CH Kanode wanted to know her too, because he stood on the bridge with her for fifteen minutes, foregoing promptness for his meeting (unbeknownst to either of them at the time, a meeting with her father, Walter, who was waiting in that church basement) in favor of flirtation. It was springtime 1940. Flowers and trees were blossoming all around them as a train rumbled by and children played. Both young hearts were ripe for love.

CH finally came to his senses, smitten by Lillian as all of those senses were. He realized he was late for a meeting with the mine superintendent whom he was interviewing with for a position managing the Elkhorn Company Store. Grandmother said she was sad as they parted company that first day; after all, she only knew the young man's name and the briefest of details about him. She had no way of knowing if she would ever see him again. As it turned out, Granddad knew the chances were good he would get that job, and he also knew the chances were very good he would run into young, pretty Lillianne Creed again.

Less than a week later, the mine superintendent invited the new company store manager to his home for dinner. The young manager, it turned out, did not need to be introduced to the superintendent's only daughter. She blushed and called him out by name as soon as he entered the front door with her father, that daughter told me over fifty years later.

Lillian and CH were married in that same Methodist Church, the pretty white-walled church across the bridge on the other side of Elkhorn Creek in the springtime of the next year. In the springtime of 1942, Grandmother became a war bride when Granddad left for the war in Europe. Six years later, heart-deep in the deferred passion and pinned up romance resulting in the baby boom, Grandmother brought a little baby boy into the world, a little baby boy with CH's eyes and his hair. They named him Greg, their one and only. Many years later, that son would have two daughters and one son, me — the grandson who at least had the grace to listen one springtime day to the golden narrative buried deep in his grandmother's marrow, a narrative which would someday lead to his own existence.

Creed Hall seemed to be quite shabby, feeble, and tired when Grandmother took me there later on that precious day. Still, I tried to close my eyes halfway and imagine the building as my grandmother remembered it. Creed Hall was a lively building of dances, band concerts, beauty pageants, community theatre, and civic meetings. Creed Hall was named in honor of her father, Walter Creed, the longtime mine superintendent of Elkhorn.

Grandmother was sad when we found the doors of her daddy's hall were not only locked but padlocked. Two of the front windows were broken. "I just can't look in, Jeff," she told me in a trembling voice. "You are welcome to peek in if you want to, but I want to remember it as it was." I respected the autonomy of my grandmother's memory enough to not violate it with my own peek into the building, which would have imparted on me only shadows of reality on the sunshine of the past she shared about Creed Hall.

Her and Granddad's wedding reception was there. They shared their first dance there as a married couple. During the war, Grandmother and all the ladies of Elkhorn gathered there to help sew blankets and quilts for the boys overseas, and they organized events like talent shows and chorales to keep morale up among those wives, girlfriends, children, and parents left behind. Over the years, there were a thousand wedding and baby showers there, and birthday parties, family reunions, and town homecomings. There was laughter. There was happiness. There was life there in Creed Hall. Grandmother remembered far more than anyone else ever could, standing in front of that shell of a building, that building which bore her daddy's name.

The old Creed home was across Elkhorn Creek, and

Grandmother decided we would just look at it from the distance. Like the old hall, the house was looking pretty ragged. There were two or three old junked up cars in the side yard, cultivating weeds around their tires. Children's toys in sundry states of use or abuse were strewn across the porch, porch stairs, and yard. The white paint of the entire structure was peeling and fading terribly. I noticed the plain outline of Christmas lights still strewn upon the pillars of the porch, also reaching down to a couple of wild, straggly bushes whose ancestors were once, Grandmother noted, well- manicured pieces of shrubbery.

Her observation about the shrubs was the only sad or negative words Grandmother offered about the house. She didn't say much. I suppose the current state of what once was her home, coupled with the conditions of Creed Hall, simply choked her words out of existence. She did say in a hoarse voice, "Jeff, you really can't see it from here, but that porch reaches all the way around the house. We were really proud of that porch. Daddy had men's prayer meetings on the porch, and Momma's brother, Arthur, had a little string quartet, and they would practice around back. When they got really good, they brought their playing up front, and we would have practically the whole town in the front yard for free, unexpected concerts. Now it looks..." Her voice faded off into nothing, and she reached in her purse for a tissue.

As I say, my camcorder tape of that journey into my grandmother's life is long lost. I wish I still had it. I would love to play it now. Every moment, every second, every dancing sunbeam, and every cloud racing past on a sea of blue sky is emblazoned forever in my mind. So are Grandmother's smiles, her laughter, and her tears from that day.

In her last couple of years, Grandmother slowed down a great deal. I wasn't around by then, nor was I in touch very often. My mother told me Grandmother would call her every morning when she got out of bed. She would even call Mom before she brewed her pot of coffee or made her breakfast of oatmeal or scrambled eggs. At first, Mom admits Grandmother's every-morning, early-morning phone calls got on her nerves. "Then it dawned on," she said, "although she would never say it, your grandmother was calling me to let me know she was safe and okay first thing in the morning. She knew the day would come when she wouldn't be."

That day did come in late 2003. As per usual, Grandmother called Mom first thing in the morning. On that day, Grandmother's breathing was heavy and rushed. Mom came right out and asked her if she was okay. "My chest does hurt a little, I suppose," Grandmother told Mom.

Mom called Grandmother's doctor, and the doctor directed her to call 911 for an ambulance. Grandmother was in the hospital in Bluefield for three days before they transferred her to a larger hospital in Charleston. Chelton was very nearby, so my parents and sisters stayed with me in my parsonage. We all visited Grandmother for hours at a time, and all the visits were good,

251

especially since we were all together like a family reunion around Grandmother's bedside. While all the visits were good, and while it was wonderful having all the family together, there is one visit I cherished and still cherish the most. It was a Saturday night visit, and it was just my grandmother and me.

Grandmother was scheduled for valve replacement surgery the following Monday, very early in the morning. My sisters and parents decided they would go home for the weekend and return Sunday night. We would all visit with Grandmother the night before her surgery, and we would all wait it out together on Monday. Saturday night was my time to be with Grandmother, and my time alone.

It was a sacred Saturday night.

We watched an old episode of *The Lawrence Welk Show*, perpetually in rebroadcast on our state public broadcasting station. I always made fun of Grandmother's *Lawrence Welk Show* viewing in the past. This time I sat and watched it with her. I watched the whole show with her, from start to finish. I liked it, too. I liked it because I knew she did. She smiled. She laughed. She even sang along to many of the songs. She told me all the cast members' names. I held her hand and squeezed it every now and then. She always squeezed back. Several times she said, "I am proud of you, Jeff. My Jeff. My little grandson. My little pastor."

I still love you, and I always will. But you just aren't my little Jeff anymore.

Thank you, Grandmother, for those words on that Saturday night when I visited you in the hospital, and we held hands and watched Lawrence Welk together.

Looking back, Grandmother's voice had an ageless, faraway quality that night at the very end of the show when she joined Lawrence and all the cast as they sang,

> *Good night, good night until we meet again*
> *Adios, au revoir, auf wiedersehen 'til then*
> *And though it's always sweet sorrow to part*
> *You know you'll always remain in my heart*

Grandmother was bright and happy Monday morning. She was so happy to see us all together: Mom, Dad, my sisters, Monica and Heather, and me. She wasn't scared at all or didn't seem to be, anyway. If she was nervous, you couldn't tell. Grandmother was so positive that she was so naïve in the most beautiful way. I really don't think she ever comprehended the gravity of her situation. An eighty-two-year-old woman was going in for valve replacement surgery. She possibly wouldn't come out of that surgery alive.

Really, she didn't.

Grandmother did survive the initial surgery. Shortly thereafter though, her body started retaining fluid. Another surgery was needed. Nothing went right. In the end, my prim, proper grandmother was bloated to probably three times her normal size. She was never conscious again. In the end, she was on life support. After a couple of days, as a family, we decided to have the life support withdrawn.

That graceful, grace-filled, sweet, generous life slipped out of this world in a far less dignified way than she would have ever agreed to. We were all appalled at how such a good life ended. We can be the writers of our own story only to a point. Our pens, our imaginations, our wants, and our desires are not supremely almighty.

Grandmother's pastor then was a strange monster-size of a man not many other church members liked, but Grandmother never said an ill word about him. He liked her, and he was good to her. I always appreciated that. At her wake, this pastor came up to me and said, "You know, Jeff, you just lost your biggest supporter, your biggest fan. She adored you."

Indeed, she did.

Indeed, I had.

Grandmother loved the fact I was a Methodist minister. More than anyone else in our family, she was thrilled when I announced, "God has called me into the ministry." I don't know anyone else in the family understood what I meant by those words. Grandmother did. She understood, and she cherished them. Grandmother was so proud, so thrilled that her little grandson was a Methodist pastor.

Grandmother's pastor asked me if I wanted to do a eulogy for my grandmother at her funeral. I told him I needed to be sitting with my family throughout the service. I needed to be with my family, a brokenhearted grandson, not a wounded pastor. I wish now I had done a eulogy for my grandmother. If words and speaking are the talents or gifts God has given to me, then I should have used them in a final act of love for Grandmother. I suppose these feeble words I write over ten years later are that eulogy.

The Bluecreek UMC Choir sang at Grandmother's funeral. She had been a member of that choir, an alto, for over fifty years. They had her choir robe draped over an empty seat, bearing a single red rose.

I was, I am, forever, Lillian C. Kanode's grandson.

On a Saturday night, I stay as far away from the television as I can. Even just a few seconds of *The Lawrence Welk Show*, and I...I just can't watch, not even for a few seconds, surfing on through to another station.

I thank God I will always have the sound of a train whistle thundering off the hillsides of Elkhorn Hollow, with the vision of an elderly woman forever climbing the steep incline to the post office door where she was greeted by a friend. I thank God I will always have the sound of an alto voice, maybe baa-baaing like a sheep singing, and the touch, the squeeze of an elderly hand accompanying every note.

> *Good night, good night until we meet again*
> *Adios, au revoir, auf wiedersehen 'til then*
> *And though it's always sweet sorrow to part*

You know you'll always remain in my heart

11 Sherman Marching

Being the geeky little guy that I am, I have always loved history. Although I took a class or two in college, I consider myself woefully uneducated in world history. American history is my mistress though. I adore it. Specifically, the time period of American history I am most enamored with is the Civil War. I suppose I would consider myself a Civil War buff. I have read many books. I have traveled to battlefields. I have the Ken Burns *The Civil War* memorized. I adore Shelby Foote.

When I decided to empower myself by "naming" or "owning" my depression, I decided I would do that by literally naming my depression, giving *it* a nickname. There was only one logical choice. My depression marched through my heart and ravaged my soul the way William Tecumseh Sherman marched and ravaged the South from 1864 to 1865. My depression, then, is named Sherman. When my depression hits, I simply live with the fact, deep within my soul. After all these years with acceptance now but never resignation, I tell myself, "Sherman's marching."

When Sherman marches, all I can do on the home front is put everything into my survival. Sometimes I have to hide in the cellar. I just have to disappear in the subterranean places of my psyche whose lights, shadows, and contours are known only to me. In my cellar, I read books. I write. I daydream into existence a happier day. When Sherman marches, often I emerge out of my cellar only as often as I have to in order to stay employed, or earlier in life, to get the grade.

Sometimes when Sherman marches, putting everything into my survival means digging trenches and then manning those trenches with as many positive memories and poetry and daydreams as I can in order to at least put up some type of frontal defense against the terrible, brutal onslaught. In the trenches, defending myself against Sherman, I go to the gym and work out. I force myself to survive by taking my reading, my writing, out of my shadowy, solitary home and into the light of a coffee shop or a café. There, I may still be alone in my words, within my despair, but I am still surrounded by humanity. Just being surrounded by people, even in my solitude, I am firing a volley Sherman's way. Sometimes it impedes his assault for a day or two and softens the impact of the damage he wreaks on the landscape. A few times it has forced his retreat for entire seasons.

I think they called Ronald Reagan the Teflon President, and Bill Clinton was the self-proclaimed Comeback Kid. For most of my life fighting old Billy Sherman, I have been like Teflon too, perpetually bouncing back. Like a comeback kid too, I have kept coming back, again and again, even though most everyone around me didn't even know I was getting knocked down anywhere to come back from.

Only once in my life did I question whether or not I could get up. Sherman was marching, and I was pinned down pretty well, heart up a hollow and back to a raging creek. It was in Clutchler, my first little parish, in an impoverished coal camp in southern West Virginia. I really don't remember any of the triggers, any of the causation for my depression that time around. To be honest, there may not have been anything specific going on around me to cause my depression. There was enough of a storm inside of me to yield a little ground to Sherman, and that was all the depression needed to start the war up again.

While I don't recall all the details, what I do recall terrifies me to this day.

I woke up on a Sunday morning. It was already after eight o'clock. For the first and, to date, the only time in my life, I couldn't get up out of bed. There was nothing physically wrong with me. I wasn't sick. I simply could not move. I was paralyzed by the most overwhelming feelings of hopelessness, guilt, self-hatred, and anxiety that I have ever known. I didn't see it coming. I don't know what specifically brought it on. It just came. It just happened.

Even lost in such a thick shroud of dark despair, thankfully my brain still worked well enough to reason and plan. I looked at the clock. I needed probably just fifteen minutes to shower and dress. I would need another fifteen minutes to drive from Clutchler to my first church service up Dove Cry Mountain at the Haven United Methodist Church. I lie there in my bed, unable to move but at least able to calculate in my mind *the last possible moment* I could stay in bed, immobile, before reality's necessity dictated I had to get up to shower, dress, and drive to my first church service.

Worship at Haven starts at ten o'clock. I need fifteen minutes to get up there. That means I can leave here as late as nine forty- five. I need fifteen minutes to get ready. That means I need to be in the shower by nine thirty.

And so, covered up to my nose in a thick blanket on a warm April spring Sunday, I was just lying there in bed. I wasn't sleepy. I wasn't tired. My mind was racing. My thoughts were sharp. I just felt overwhelming guilt, like I had murdered someone. I just felt anxiety like I was going to die. I just lay there, staring at the ceiling, occasionally peering down at the clock. I just lay there until nine thirty. At nine thirty I got up, I showered, and I dressed. By nine forty-five, I was in my car, rushing down one mountain, racing through one hollow to plow my way up another mountain, to pierce my way through another hollow. I made it to church on time. I prayed. I preached. I visited with my church people. Everything was fine. I was fine. I made it through two more church services that day.

After church, I ate a sandwich and watched NASCAR. That night I had a youth group meeting to lead. The paralyzing depression I survived that morning stopped dogging me somewhere on my commute to the first church service. It didn't return. It has never returned. It still haunts me, though. I still fear it. What will I do if some morning I awaken, and it is back? What will happen if some morning I awaken, it is back, and this time, I can't get up? What happens to me then? That paralyzing depression was Sherman burning Atlanta, I suppose. God helped me feebly rise out of bed that day and saw to it I could crawl out of the flames. Someday I fear Sherman will penetrate my defenses so thoroughly that my resolve to fight will be lost. I won't be able to get up, and the flames will consume me. There will be a church filled, or more likely semi-filled, waiting for me to burst through the door with a smile and a sermon. I just won't show up. What happens to me then?

Over the years, I have solicited professional medical help to save me from Sherman's marching. When I was a student at Duke, I availed myself of the university's wonderful health care system. Students at Duke had access to mental health care as part of their tuition. I thought it was a wonderful thing then, and as time has gone on, my admiration for the program has only increased.

My therapist at Duke was a young intern. He was new and not quite as polished and smooth as other therapists I would come to know over the coming dozen years. This guy had talent and ideas though, and he gave me a strategy I use periodically to this very day.

He homed in on all the voices from my past: those nagging, hurtful, killer voices which bounced back and forth in my brain like the particles of an atom. He told me it wasn't just that I still heard those voices in my memory. Over the years, he theorized I had started believing the voices, and I had even adopted the voices. The voices, he said, were no longer the voices of other people from my past, or fresh voices from my present. The voices had become my voice. I had taken all the poisonous word from so many years, and I had come to believe them as truth. Those words from all those voices morphed into my own voice. Now the many voices had become my own voice. It was deadly. My young Duke therapist called it negative self-talk.

"You have been conditioned over time to hear these voices and to replay them over and over again in your mind," he said. "You have come to believe everything you have ever heard negative about yourself. Now, we need to recondition you to love yourself. Since you love to write, I think we can use your writing to help you value yourself and love yourself." The idea was simple in practice, but profound in principle.

My therapist told me to start keeping a journal and fill it with nothing but positivity about myself. "Every night before you go to bed," he instructed, "write down five or ten positive affirmations about yourself. Don't include any other person or any other issue. This must be all about you. It must all be about your goodness and value. The last voice I want you to start hearing every night before you sleep is your own voice. I want your voice to speak respect, value, and love for yourself." Of course, I smiled and agreed with his theory. I told him that I bought into his plan. That is just how I am. I am naturally agreeable, and it is not in my nature to question or buck back. In my mind though, I was thinking, *Spending the last part of the day writing down great things about yourself sounds incredibly narcissistic, the epitome of self-consumption. I want to feel better. I want to beat back Sherman forever. I just don't know about this deal, though.*

Despite my trepidation, I tried it. I purchased a little spiral notebook, and I put it on my nightstand. Beginning the first evening after the therapist told me to try, I began. Oh, how hard it was coming up with five to ten good, wholesome, positive things to say about myself! At first, most of my positive affirmations related to how I interacted with other people.

I am nice to people.
I am friendly.
I try to be friendly and nice to everyone I meet.
In social settings, in church, and in work with children in particular, I try to look out and figure out who is being ignored, who is being left out. I try to go and hang out with that person, that lonely elderly person, that little child.

The list, even that first evening, grew in complexity the more I wrote. As my young therapist expected I would, I started learning more about myself. I started gaining some self-awareness. Although I had not previously articulated or even understood it, "there was a method to my madness," to use a tired old cliché. Although I had never identified or recognized it, there was a theology, a belief system behind the way I was living. I did care about people. I did purposefully try to reach out to people I saw being ignored or abused.

Through that first list, I remembered all the children in the Salvation Army program I used to mentor. Through that first list, I remembered the children I was currently working with through Duke's chapter of America Reads. It was true. I intentionally gravitated toward the kids I knew to be poor, the kids I knew who were probably coming out of abusive families, and the kids I didn't see anyone else spending any time with, the kids who were alone. I could also see that I was taking that same approach, that same strategy, and that same way of being into my work as a pastor.

Then suddenly it dawned on me. It was something of an epiphany, not nearly as dramatic as the Wise Men, or Saul on the road to Damascus. It was a moment of grace, a moment of light, and a moment of enlightenment, sacred and God-given.

I am a good person.

I really am a kind person. I really do love other people.

I really do try to be compassionate and loving.

I am more sensitive than most of the people I meet.

God must love me.

God must love me. That may sound so simple to you, or you may say that fact should have always been a given for a young man who had grown up in the church, who was currently enrolled in school to be a pastor. For me though, it was an earthshaking, sunlight-blazing awakening. My heart was saying, "You know, I am doing okay. I really have tried. God must love me."

It sounds a little "works righteousness," I know. I was coming to believe God loved me based mostly on a list I had made of good, selfless ways I interacted with others, a list which basically mostly came down to "Do unto others, as you would have them do unto you." It sounds as if I had concluded in my list of positive affirmations that I had found enough evidence of goodness in me for God to love. I can't really argue the point that theologically that is probably where I was in that moment in time. But it was a beginning for me. It was a beginning to end self-hatred. It was a beginning to embrace the genesis of self-love, self- respect, and self-dignity.

I came to realize too that my list of positive affirmations were not like how many push-ups I had done that day, or how many people I had visited lately, leading them to Jesus. My list was very basic stuff. "I smiled and flirted around a little bit with the overweight cashier tonight at the store because the guy in front of me had been so rude to her." As the days wore on, my lists of positive affirmations were usually nothing but sentences like that. I came to realize such things were just, are just, engrained into who I am. It's just who I am. I am not going to be rude. I am going to be friendly. I am not going to belittle or cut down. I am going to praise, and I am going to build up. It's just who I am.

Those of us who have bled from wounds recognize the

bleeding of others, and we know what to do to at least stop that bleeding. It's called human decency. It's called humane interaction with others. Like Jesus, these things save.

Finally, I realized I had a good start. I had a pretty decent foundation for understanding, for appreciating, for loving, and for working to grow my humanity. After over twenty years of living, I could finally see I was a human being I would want to know if I were another human being. If nothing else, I knew I would be a person who would be sweet and kind to someone else. I had lived long enough to know not all people are like that. I finally decided those simple virtues were enough to help me love myself.

One incident I recall seeing in the waiting room of the Duke mental health department has stuck with me all these years, and it brings me to the next chapter of my life we need to discuss.

The waiting room to see a therapist or a psychologist was packed. There were Duke students from across every spectrum of age, race, and style. There were boys and girls embracing the grunge look: ponytailed girls in ball caps, and unshaven boys with their caps on backward. There were slightly older students who were probably master's or even Ph.D. students in khakis and skirts. There were the little preppy kids too: polo shirt–wearing guys with sleeves showing just enough forearm we could see some muscle; skirt-wearing ladies whose skirts were just short enough to be excitable to a guy and sexy feeling for the lady.

It was a lady like that who did the thing I will never forget.

She was a very attractive young lady, clearly an undergraduate no more than twenty-one or twenty-two at the oldest, and possibly as young as eighteen or nineteen. There was a radio on in the waiting room: not an expensive central stereo system but a simple old boom box radio, '80s style, sitting on a table with the prerequisite waiting room magazines. The radio was tuned to Top Forty pop. This was the late 1990s, early 2000s, so there were lots of Britney Spears, Christina Aguilera, Backstreet Boys, and NSYNC tunes assaulting the air. My mind was drifting away to a thousand other places, but I remember drifting back into an awareness of what was going on around me as a song on the radio ended and a commercial began.

The first commercial was for a local car dealer who was having this amazing springtime sale. The next commercial was for a weight loss product: "Do you want to lose ten pounds in ten days? Now is the time to start thinking about getting that bikini body back for the beach this summer." All of a sudden, this very pretty, very thin young Duke undergrad dressed to the nines stood up, rushed over to that radio, and angrily punched the power off.

A few of us looked up and looked at her, mostly I think, out of surprise.

No one said a word to her.

No one dared to get up to turn that radio back on.

Over the years, I had wondered about that young Duke

undergraduate, and I have wondered if perhaps some kind of eating disorder or body image issue brought her to the therapist that day. If so, it still confounds me she couldn't perceive how beautiful a person she truly was. I hope she made it through her course of therapy. I pray she made it out of college healthy and whole. I trust now she has the world by the tail, and she is living her dreams.

Although I didn't know the young woman, I felt every piece of the cutting glass which was shredding her heart that day in that waiting room when she was assaulted by that weight loss commercial.

Twice in my life, I have lost profound amounts of weight. Twice in my life, the weight loss was tied to Sherman marching, and twice the weight loss entirely consumed me. I don't know if I was trying to commit a long, very public suicide — *Watch me disappear into nothing right in front of you* — or if I just got obsessed with losing weight because my weight was a life circumstance I could control. I had reached that point we all get to at various ages, where I was finally realizing how much in my life was so much out of my control. Where am I going to be assigned by the bishop? When am I going to finally meet a good girl who will love me? The state of my physical body became supremely important to me because I knew, unlike so much else, my food intake and my body weight were variables very much in my control. I just don't know. All I do know is, twice in my life, I lost upwards of fifty and sixty pounds in a very short amount of time. Twice in my life, I looked skeletal. Twice in my life I really liked it.

The first period of weight loss was during a very difficult period of my ministry. I was serving as the pastor of the Chelton United Methodist Church. It wasn't all them. It wasn't all me. It was just a bad situation for both parties: church and pastor. I really do believe the church-pastor relationship is like a marriage. Sometimes the love doesn't last. Sometimes one loses their love for the other. Sometimes one party simply grows and evolves, while the partner does not. Sometimes the marriage just was never meant to be because compatibility between the parties was always nonexistent. What was the case between Chelton and me? I am not entirely sure. I just know the marriage was not healthy and whole. I became very unhealthy and far from whole. In fact, I was in pieces.

My weight loss started very innocently enough, with dual causes. First, I had a terrible dental problem which left me unable and often unwilling to eat. Second, in the course of a couple of years, I had put on a good deal of weight. I was never overweight per se, but I weighed more than I ever had before. I came to believe I needed to shape up and firm down a bit.

The dental problem was a horrid nightmare. I was born with a genetic quirk where two of my permanent front teeth never came in as they should have. My dentist, who took care of my entire family from my boyhood on, fixed me up with veneers—

essentially little fake teeth bonded to the fragments of my baby teeth and attached to those roots.

When Dr. Lawson did this work in my early teen years, he said, "Jeff, this should get you out of high school. When you start to college, we'll look at getting you implants." My high school graduation came and went, and those little fake teeth held firm, as strong as ever. "Jeff, these little teeth should get you through college. When you graduate from college, we'll look at getting you implants." I told Dr. Lawson that sounded just fine.

My college graduation came and went. I went on to seminary. I graduated from seminary, and I was living in my first parishes in the first years of my ministry. I was by now in my mid-twenties. My little fake teeth, my little fakers, still held firm and strong.

In the Chelton church, there was a young couple. She was the granddaughter of one of the church mothers. Her husband was a freshly graduated, hotshot dentist. For months and months, he begged me to start coming to his practice. "Jeff, it is silly for you to drive all that way back to your hometown to see your dentist. I can take care of you right here."

I am not saying the young man wasn't being sincere and earnest. I am sure he truly wanted to help take care of me because I was good friends with him, his wife, and her grandma. (It wasn't all a broken marriage in that church.) Still, my taking him up on his offer to provide me with dental care set up a chain of events that very nearly wrecked my health completely.

The young dentist decided my little fake teeth just had to go. "Jeff, you just barely have any of those baby roots left. I just don't see what is holding them in. Let me pull them, and we will put in a bridge."

He wanted to do a bridge with the two teeth holding on to my strong, sturdy front teeth with like a piece of metal. My insurance company, he reported, would not pay anything for the far more expensive implants.

All that nicety and humility on my list of positive affirmation came back to haunt me. Of course, I wouldn't say no. I agreed to let the young dentist pull out my little old half-veneer, half-baby teeth which had lasted me at least a dozen years, and replace them with two bridges, two little false teeth that would hold inside my head only by the little metal prongs connecting them to my healthy front teeth.

A nightmare unfolded like a horrible cut spilling blood across the very fabric of my life.

One night, at the Hanging of the Greens potluck dinner at Sherman United Methodist Church (which, you will recall, I also served while I was assigned to Chelton), a simple bite of baked steak brought one of those damn little bridges right out of my mouth. I was horrified. I rushed to get to the privacy of the men's bathroom, so I could retrieve the fake tooth from the sinews of half-chewed meat I had conspicuously spit out in my palm.

The horror was magnified a thousand times when I anxiously

pulled myself before the mirror. I can still feel the weight of my head — like it weighed a hundred pounds — as I used every ounce of strength I had to lift it so I could see my face in the mirror. I looked like a goober. I mean, I was missing a front tooth. It was awful. With my hand over my mouth, I told the church folks I had gotten very ill. I had been in the bathroom for a very long time, so the story of sudden sickness was more than plausible. It wasn't a lie either. I was sick. I was becoming deeply, profoundly emotionally, mentally sick. When I said I needed to go home immediately, of course, any number of those dear people offered to drive me home. Sherman was a great little church. I told the folks I appreciated their kind offers, their sincere compassion, but I really thought I wasn't so ill I couldn't make the fifteen- minute drive back to the parsonage at Chelton. I didn't need or want to be with anyone at that moment. I needed to be by myself. I needed to cry profusely. I needed to cuss badly.

The other bridge fell out that very night when I tried to eat a cracker. I put both little teeth in a cup. I called the young dentist. He and his wife were out of town at a college football game at their alma mater three hours away. Clearly distracted by the revelry of either the game or the postgame kegger, he rather heartlessly instructed me to "go to the Dollar Store, buy some Fixodent, and come see me first thing Monday morning."

I have always been an extraordinarily self-conscious soul: self-conscious of my voice, self-conscious of my hair, self- conscious of my small build. Never in my life had I ever been, or have I ever been, as self-conscious as I was the following day at church. Preaching at both Sherman and Chelton, I was just certain both of those horrid Fixodent adhered little teeth were going to come flying out of my mouth as I preached, as I prayed, or as I talked. I was equally afraid to eat. So, I didn't eat at all that day.

The young dentist did indeed professionally reconnect the bridges into my mouth that next Monday. And they kept coming out. I would get maybe two or three days out of each reconnection procedure. In the meantime, I spoke as little as I could get away with. I ate only what I needed to keep the hunger pangs from tearing my stomach apart. Mostly I ate soup, deep in the confines of the privacy of my little parsonage. Within a couple of weeks, I had already lost a noticeable amount of weight. It just got worse.

I was losing the weight because I was eating very little. I was eating very little because I was afraid of my cursed teeth coming out. It wasn't long, though, before people started commenting on my weight loss. And I liked it. I liked it a lot. I liked the attention. I liked the fact I was losing a noticeable amount of weight.

I had gotten a little bit, just a tiny bit, chunky. When you're a pastor, you have to work really hard to keep your weight down. So much of what we do revolves around food. You go to someone's house for a visit, and they have cake or pie there waiting for you. You know you'll offend them if you don't have some. You have a church potluck dinner after church on a fairly regular basis. Two people make salad, and everything else is either fried or loaded down with carbohydrates. You go to a committee meeting either in your local church, at your local ministerial association, or in your state conference. Of course, they have coffee and donuts.

Pastors are surrounded by really bad food on almost a daily basis. One could say I am making excuses — as Americans, aren't we all surrounded by horrid food each day? Well, yes. But no one has the vocational pressure to eat badly like a pastor does. If we don't eat a piece of fried chicken and chocolate cake, we'll hurt Granny's feelings. We can't hurt Granny's feelings. We can't afford to hurt Granny's feelings and keep our job. So, we eat Granny's fried chicken and chocolate cake. She sends us home with fried chicken and chocolate cake wrapped up in aluminum foil, too. To maintain a good, healthy weight, a pastor has to be very self-conscious and work hard to stay in shape. In that era of my life, I hadn't been very disciplined, and I had gained weight to the point I was the heaviest I had ever been in my life. I wasn't fat Elvis, but I was chubby John Lennon, circa *Rubber Soul* and *Revolver*. Now all of a sudden, I was truly delighted. I was losing weight and folks could tell it. A few Chelton folks had not hesitated to tell me that my face had filled out in the previous months, so when I was told by numerous people that they noticed I was losing weight, I reveled in it.

When my mother saw me at Christmas, she cried. She said I had lost too much weight. She said the bridged teeth looked hideous. "They didn't take the time to make them blend in with the shape and shade of your other teeth, Jeff," she said tearfully. I didn't know what to do. By then, losing weight was a game, an addiction, a drug I was really into. I wanted to see just how much I could lose. Like Mom, I hated those two fake teeth, but I didn't know what to do about it. I couldn't afford anything else. Not eating very often was helping the durability of the bridges, too.

One day, early in the new year, my mother was at a dental appointment with dear Dr. Lawless. He asked about me. He had been, after all, my dentist pretty much my whole life.

In answer to Dr. Lawless's question, "How is Jeff ?" my mother burst into tears.

Between her sobs, Mom told Dr. Lawless the cogent points of the painful, hideous story I have thus far shared with you.

Dr. Lawless just shook his head. "Please tell Jeff to call me right away. I will get him in as soon as he calls. Please tell Jeff to come here and see me. He needs me."

In the coming weeks and months, Dr. Lawless did for me the greatest series of deeds of compassion and grace I have ever experienced. First and foremost, he took me back into his care without question. In so doing, he fitted me with a retainer with two little fake teeth attached to the front. The retainer was two-fold in function: first, it contained two little fake teeth to replace those horrid bridges; second, it helped bring my two good front teeth back into line. The pressure and the weight that those bridges had placed on my two good, beautiful, pearly white front teeth had caused the two to flare out and grow crooked. The retainer would fix all that. Next, Dr. Lawless set me up with an oral surgeon. The oral surgeon began the many-month process of preparing me for two permanent implants. In the meantime, I wore the retainer, which was giving me two unnoticeably fake front teeth, and slowly repairing my damaged, unaligned good teeth.

During this time period, I still lost weight. I could eat with the retainer in if I was in public. At home, I could take the retainer out while I ate. Dental woes were no longer the cause of my refusal to eat much. I had simply become addicted to weight loss. I had become, I believe, undiagnosed anorexic.

I never purged. I never became bulimic. I just simply didn't eat. Typically, my practice was to eat once a day, usually at the Chelton Shoney's. I would go there at around two or three o'clock in the afternoon. I would get the salad bar and eat approximately half of the salad. I would then get a chicken salad sandwich and eat exactly one-half of it. That is how I ate. That is all I ate every day, day after day after day. That is how I survived for months.

I got down to around 120 pounds and maybe even less than that. I see pictures of myself now from that time period, and it is truly sickening. I looked sick. I could have passed for a cancer patient deep in the midst of chemotherapy. I could have been an

AIDS patient slowly wasting away. I wasn't either. I was a perfectly healthy – physically – young man who had fallen in love with attention and had become addicted to losing weight. It was horrible. I was wasting away. I could barely live a normal life, I had such little energy. In previous years, I could mow the parsonage yard in three hours. In the spring and summer of my anorexic period, I was so weak that I could only manage to mow for maybe twenty minutes at a time. I would then need to rest and nap for an hour, sometimes more. What had taken me three hours of hard, solid, sweaty work was now taking a full eight-hour day to get done.

I was so mentally ill. I was so obsessed with what was happening to my body, the destruction I was bringing upon myself. I loved the transformation of my body. I got a rush out of seeing my sunken cheeks or looking at myself in the mirror with my shirt off, seeing ribs, bones, and not a tubby tummy. Today, all these years later, I know now just how sick it was that I loved it so. But I did. I was very, very sick. The attention, the being in control – being able to cause such profound, tangible change within myself, with my body, was as addictive as any drug a junkie burglarizes or prostitutes for.

I so related to that young, attractive, well-dressed young lady at Duke who slammed off that radio.

How did I survive? How did I ever get back into my right mind and start eating again? I hate to disappoint you, but it was nothing dramatic. Family and friends didn't gather for an intervention. I didn't collapse and nearly die. It never got to the point where I was forced to either wake up, get help, or die. I wasn't institutionalized. The natural ebb and flow of daily life saved me.

I got transferred out of Chelton to become the associate pastor of the Lewiston United Methodist Church. The Lewiston Church was so busy, and my job was so demanding, I found myself eating more because I simply needed the strength to keep up with the pace of the church and do my work. Lewiston was not Chelton, either. I loved Lewiston, and in just the first few weeks there, I was happy. I wanted to live again. I wanted to eat so I would feel good. My two little fake teeth were rock solid, drilled, implanted right into my bones. Within a couple of years, I gained twenty or thirty pounds. I looked good because I was happy. Sherman wasn't marching nearly that often when I lived in Lewiston.

Life was so good in Lewiston. I found myself with a true circle of friends probably for the first time in my adult life. My work as associate pastor was demanding and rewarding. Also, for the first time in my professional life and maybe in my life, period, I found myself a member of a team. The Lewiston UMC was the fifth largest Methodist church in the state, and with the wealth and resources of that lovely town behind it, the church had a full staff of very talented, dedicated people. There were full-time secretaries working every day from eight to six. There were activities in the building, sometimes multiple activities, every night of the week. That church was alive. It was a vibrant community to be a part of. As the associate pastor, I had the honor of being an integral part of it, too. I finally cared about myself enough to want to care for my body and my mind. I finally thought enough of myself to really honor and care for my work.

Life was so good in Lewiston. I found myself with a pretty active dating life. For the first time in my life, I actually had choices to make: which lady to see and date seriously; which lady to see just as a friend; which lady to trust with the emotional intimacies of life; which lady to hold at arm's length with a wink and a smile.

Life was so good in Lewiston. In time, I fell in love, and for the first time in my life, she fell in love with me, too. The story of that love affair — the first great, true experience of love, relationship, intimacy, and companionship in my life — is also the story of destruction, wreckage, violation, alienation, near-death, and finally, in the end, resurrection. It is the story of the second great period of weight loss in my life. It is the story of how Sherman came up from the rear, launching an attack I neither expected nor feared — an attack so surprising and vicious that it cut my lines of communication and nearly tore the army of my being in two. It is the story of another day and another book.

Suffice it to say for now, even as I write these words, Sherman still marches.

I still countermarch. I still entrench. I eat. I still survive.

12 On the Air

He is hyper. He is joyful. He is innocently flirty. He is so hyper that he makes me look lethargic. He is so joyful that I am almost depressive by comparison. He is so flirty that I am a wallflower standing beside him.

He is my dad, and in so many ways, I consider myself a continuation of his soul. We are so alike that one of us has to take a little step back when we are together, or our combination would be just too much hyperactivity, joy, and flirtation. In social interaction, I am usually the one to take that step back, although I have noticed as I mature and age, often now, Dad will dampen his own light a bit and let me shine.

I adore and respect Dad like I adore and respect no other. Today, when I come home to visit, we kayak or take long walks in our town park. We talk politics — I bucked the conventional wisdom of political scientists who say most Americans adopt the political philosophies of their parents: Dad was a Nixon Republican back in 1960; I fell in love with the myth of John Kennedy; my first political love was, and remains the man from Hope, Arkansas — and we talk church and family life.

As much as I treasure my time with Dad in our current evolutionary state, the image of my dad I conjure up most in my mind is him as a young man in the late 1960s and 1970s: wavy brown hair, stylish brown sideburns, red mustache, dressed to the nines in his business suit, the handsome little stud.

The essence of my dad's soul shines out in such pictures. A handsome, charming salesman and a gifted, bright disc jockey with a high-pitched but professionally modulated voice radiating passion and joy — that was my dad in his professional heyday. He carries those characteristics to this day as he eases into the slower retirement phase of his life.

I am my dad's third child, the last, the youngest child. I am his only son. As such, I have been adored, protected, coddled, and comforted. I define both manhood and fatherhood through the example of my dad. My mother was a divorced, single mom when she met my dad. Dad has always said he fell in love with my mom, and he fell in love with a glorious little girl, my sister Monica.

The story of how my parents met is one of my favorites. I suppose that whole thread of narrative strikes a chord within all of us. There is even a television show now, *How I Met Your Mother*. All of us are fascinated, I suppose, with how our parents met. Their courtship, how those two souls initially came together, provided the genesis for our lives, the seed of our very being.

My mom and dad met as a result of a bar fight. No, they were not in the bar at the same time. Neither of them was directly a part of the fight either. Dad was at a bar in Bluefield with a buddy. Meanwhile, in the other part of town, as the cliché goes, my mom was working triage for the emergency room of Bluefield Hospital. My dad's friend got into the fight with some dude. I can't imagine my dad being any help in the fight at all, or actually being involved in the fight in any way, shape, or form at all, either.

Dad's role in being a friend to his bar buddy consisted of helping the poor dude off the floor, giving him a tissue for his bleeding nose, and taking him to the hospital. The hospital Dad transported his fighting friend to was, of course, Bluefield Hospital, where a pretty little surgery tech named Dianne, my mom, was working triage.

I guess this is how God works God's creative genius: the wink and the nod from the God of the universe, what some folks call fate, and what other folks call pure chance. Mom's job usually consisted of assisting doctors and registered nurses in surgery. She had never worked triage in the emergency room at all. She would never work triage in the emergency room again.

It just so happened (was Jesus laughing, or was it just some meaningless happenstance?) the ER was full that night. The staff was overwhelmed. There were no scheduled surgeries at night, with no emergency surgical cases coming in, and the powers that be sent a pretty surgery tech out to work triage in the emergency room.

Into that room strutted a well-dressed, local celebrity, a nighttime disc jockey at WKOY Radio who called himself "your little buddy, Greg K." He style was stunted only ever so slightly by his fairly well-beaten buddy on his arm. Amusingly, Greg K himself had obviously escaped, perfectly unscathed by the carnage his friend fought through valiantly. In just an instant, my dad had forgotten all about his whipped friend, and his universe became the pretty young nurse who was taking that friend's blood pressure and cleaning up the blood on his face.

There were too many people in that emergency room on that hectic night for Dianne, the young, pretty little surgery tech working triage, to make or feel any connection to the young, hyper disc jockey, Greg K. For her, the connection began to be made the next day when the same well-dressed young radio man showed up at the hospital just to say hello. He would have missed seeing her entirely—the emergency room was, after all, not her regular department—had he not pulled into the parking lot at just the same time she was getting out of her car to clock in for work.

"I wanted to see you again," he told her in his best radio voice, "but I was just afraid I couldn't convince any friends to get into another bar fight. Without a bloody friend to bring to the hospital, I didn't know how else to see you again, except to just come by." She was flattered, and she promised him she would tune in to his radio show when he promised to play a song just for her around midnight. She was also flattered when he asked her out to dinner. She said yes, she would tell her son years later, not so much because she was infatuated or even interested in him at that point. "Your dad was just really sweet, Jeff," she said, "and I got the impression he was going to keep showing up until I did say 'yes,' so that was just the easiest thing to do."

Greg K played the Beach Boys' "Good Vibrations" just for Dianne, the pretty little surgery tech, that night on his radio show. It wasn't the romantic ballad she had perhaps expected, but for him, the song hit just the right chord of hope and excitement for what the future might hold. He took her out to dinner that next Friday night. Soon, he would meet her little daughter, Monica. Greg K fell for the little brown-eyed, dark-haired girl just as profoundly, but in a far different way as he fell for her pretty mommy.

Dad would always say ever after, he fell in love with Mom, and he fell in love with Monica too. At the age of twenty-three, my dad became both a husband and a daddy, all at once. He cherished both roles. He fulfilled them both, ably and lovingly, ever after. Many years later, my sister Monica would write a paper in a college English class where the assignment was to describe how you met an interesting, intriguing person who changed the course of your life. Monica wrote a paper describing how she met a man when she was five years old, and how he immediately became daddy to her.

They were married in 1971, and by 1972, there were two little girls in their family, sharing the tiny trailer they called home. My sister Heather was born in the early spring, and brown-eyed, dark-haired Monica had a green-eyed, blonde- haired little sister to adore and torment.

In January 1978, Dad lost his beloved father to a stroke. In

May, his last child, his son, was born. A family friend who was there in the waiting room with Dad has always told me Dad leapt up in the air and let out a great, joyful "whoo-hoo!" when the doctor came out and told him that both his wife and his son were doing just fine.

Earlier on that day, my birthday, when my mother went into labor, Dad was out on sales calls for the radio station. In those days before cell phones, the only thing Mom could do was call the radio station for them to give Dad the message that his wife was going into labor. He always called in to check his phone messages periodically throughout the day.

The disc jockey who took Mom's message decided her message was too urgent to wait around for Dad to call in. The deejay knew Dad would be in and out of his car as he went from business to business, trying to procure ads for the station. The disc jockey also knew FCC regulations forbid (and I expect still does forbid) person-to-person personal messages to be broadcast on the public airwaves. Surely the deejay telling my father his wife had just gone into labor met the criteria for a person-to-person personal message.

This Bluefield disc jockey was a maestro of broadcasting. He figured out a way to deliver the message to Dad perfectly — and perfectly legally. He played, "When a Man Loves a Woman," the original, raw, real Percy Sledge version of that song and not the dishwasher Michael Bolton version of much later. When Percy was done, the deejay opened his mic to speak to the world, and he said, "When a man loves a woman, there are many things a man will do for her. For instance, Greg K, he might go the hospital in Princeton immediately when she is about to have his baby. It's about fourteen past the hour. Now for the two Virginian's weather…" It was brilliant. It worked. Dad heard it. He made it to the hospital to be with Mom when I was born.

I got my dad's blue eyes, and as I have mentioned, I got his spirit and his personality too. Although I have suffered from depression for years, at the root, at the very rock-bottom foundation of my heart and soul, I have Dad's abiding optimism. My dad's greatest bequeathal to me is hope. Without it, Sherman's marching would have wiped me out when I was in high school, if not junior high.

If my dad ever suffered from depression at any point in his life, it didn't last long, and I have never detected it. Dad's inherent positivity always buoys him right out of it before it ever has the chance to start. Dad's sense and spirit of hope reminds me of what F. Scott Fitzgerald, my all-time favorite writer, wrote about Gatsby:

…it was an extraordinary gift for hope, a romantic readiness such as I have never found in any other person and which it is not likely I shall ever find again.

Dad's determination to forever live out God's gracious gift of hope is one of the thousand reasons my dad is my hero.

While I cherish the memories of watching my dad interact with his daughters over the years, my favorite memories are of Dad and me, one-on-one, alone together, father and son, especially at the radio station.

Dad started working in radio when he was just sixteen years old. That first radio gig was at WTZE in Tazewell, Virginia. After his high school graduation, Dad worked at WKOY in Bluefield, West Virginia, for many years. He started out there working part-time and, in the summertime, while he was in college. Dad actually got a degree in teaching, following Grandmother into the education system. He taught school for two years, doing his radio deejaying part-time. When a position opened up full-time at the radio station, O. C. Young, the station owner who loved my dad like a son, offered Dad a position encompassing a sales position, an on-air show, and a place in the station's management. Radio was Dad's first professional love. He couldn't turn the opportunity down.

By the time of my early childhood, Dad was the operations manager of the station, and the sales manager. He did some guest disc jockeying, but no full-time show anymore. He did often work "remote" broadcasts, where the station would broadcast several hours from a local business or civic event. These "remotes" were either extended commercials Dad had sold to the business, or they were public service broadcasts the station was donating time to for the community.

My dad loved his work, and he loved sharing that work with his little boy. I would often accompany him to his Saturday remote broadcasts, and I loved it. My favorite part of the day though — my favorite part of the event — was going with Dad both before the remote and after it, to the radio station studio.

The studio and offices for WKOY AM and WKMY FM were located in downtown Bluefield. It was a five-story building, nondescript on the outside, except for the glorious neon sign shining out *WKOY* and my most vivid memory of its interior is of the steps. Upon entering the front entrance of the building, you encountered those stairs going straight up — a straight shot up to, for my young heart, what was the magical world of my dad's broadcasting dream. At the top of the stairs on a table clothed in light were stone letters painted bright blue and red, alternating with each letter: WKOY-WKMY. I loved it. For me, being there with my dad at the radio station was akin being in heaven.

Beyond those call letters down the shag-carpeted hallway in a haze of ever-present cigarette smoke pouring out of the studio, faceless radio voices assumed human shape as my heart burst with pride in Dad and with joy in the world I was discovering — broadcasting, my dad's world. The studio was the heart of the radio station. For me, it was the coolest place on the planet. Being there with my dad made it almost a sacred event for me, like being in church on a Sunday morning. Watching the various disc jockeys spin those forty-fives on a turntable was like sneaking a peak at sunbeams dancing with the prism of the stained-glass windows during the sermon.

The disc jockeys of Dad's radio station were as interesting a cast of characters as I have ever encountered. Some of them were local radio legends. All of them were local celebrities with something of a following in the Bluefield-Princeton area.

Big Jim Stevens did an all-request show from seven until midnight each evening. Each song he played had at least five dedications, and the station telephone rang nearly constantly during Big Jim's show. Old Jim fit the category of legend; he also fully lived into his nickname. He was big of stature, big in weight, with a big beard punctuating his expansive face. I still laugh when I recall Big Jim's booming baritone voice saying, "All right, old son, we're going to send this next song out to Darlene from Billy, the man who loves you, Sugar Cube. We are also going to send it out to Roscoe from Wilma, from Chester to Dede (Chester says he'll see you after work, sweetheart), and to all of our friends working out at the Maiden Form factory tonight. Here's Merle Haggard and 'Let's Chase Each Other Around the Room Tonight.'"

I would also get cracked up at the five or six requests and dedications nearly nightly for "If I Said You Have a Beautiful Body, Would You Hold It Against Me?" by the Bellamy Brothers, and "I Can Tell You've Never Been This Far Before" by Conway Twitty, with the incomparable 'Bum, bum, bum' from old Conway, punctuating his verdant urgency to his virginal lady friend.

Fred Jennings was probably my favorite of the jockeys, and he was probably the reddest and the wildest of the lot. He had the midday show, and he came the closest among all of those local jocks to sounding like someone who truly could have been a nationally syndicated radio star. Freddy had a deep baritone voice, which was still sharp enough to inflect and reflect expression in tone. He was witty too—he was extremely funny in an improvisational way, which was never too much, or never not enough. Freddy hit that balance just right. For all of his talent though, Fred evidently lead a very broken and ragged life. Off the air in conversations with Dad, which I often overheard (until Dad realized that I could hear everything and asked Freddy to tone it down), Freddy often spoke dismissively of his wife, the "hell witch," and spoke in a dreamy, breathless voice about "my long-legged girlfriend." Freddy would eventually, tragically in my mind, leave the radio business for good to drive a tractor trailer. I say the career switch was tragic, not because tractor trailer drivers don't provide a wonderful, essential service, literally driving our economy, but because Freddy was so naturally gifted on the radio that I hated to see that radio station and any future station lose him.

Rick Woodly was the deejay among those Bluefield radio titans who took the most interest in me and attempted to pal around with me. Rick always made me feel super cool the way he let me sometimes "run the board" during his show. I got to spin my own choice of records, provided my choice fit the format of the station, and play commercials (or "spots" as Dad taught me the folks in the business called them) and public service announcements. Sometimes Rick led me take the helm of the station for upward of half an hour. He was always right there, of course, in case anything went wrong, and I messed up catastrophically. At least he gave me the allusion I was in charge when it was me sitting in the big chair at the control board with Rick sitting — now that I really look back on it — on the edge of the leather sofa just across the way.

I never spoke on the air during Rick's show. He never offered, and I never asked. Being my dad's son, though, I got plenty of chances to speak on the air over my childhood and teenage years.

The first time I ever remember being on the radio with Dad was on a commercial for a local department store at Christmas time. Dad was the voice of Santa Claus, and I played the role — quite naturally — of a little kid.

"What do you want for Christmas?" Dad-as-Santa asked. I replied, "I want a new He-Man bicycle and Atari games, Santa!"

Then Dad jumped in with his regular voice, "When Santa needs help filling the wish list of all the good little boys and girls, he goes no further than Kirkland's Department Store, my friends and your friends, serving Bluefield since 1911 from their location on Main Street."

I can also remember helping with a public service announcement. My big line for that one was, "Here comes Smoky Bear. He's not scary at all. He's our friend. Forest fires are scary though, and we need to help Smoky stop them. Right, Smoky?" And then Dad inserted the voice of Smoky Bear from the nationally distributed audio.

Often friends from school and sometimes even teachers from school would hear me on the radio, and their recognition always made me feel good. My exposure on live, local radio with my dad was nothing but positive for me emotionally and spiritually. It was nothing but positive for me socially and spiritually, at least through elementary school.

When junior high school rolled around, my cute little squeaky voice was no longer cute. When everyone else's voice changed to fit the new season of our lives, and mine remained the same, stuck in the early spring days of grade school, my voice became not a source of recognition, but a cause for scorn, bullying, and ridicule. I refused to talk on Dad's radio station anymore somewhere around the seventh grade. I don't think I talked live on the air with Dad again until I was an ordained Methodist pastor up in my twenties.

Dad dealt with all of this graciously and lovingly. He used to tell me there was nothing wrong with my voice. I had a good, well-modulated, very expressive voice, Dad said. Dad used to also point out, "My voice isn't all that much deeper than your voice,

Jeff K."

Jeff K. That is what my Dad calls me to this day. His on-the-air name was Greg K. Dad has always called me his one and only son, Jeff K. I love it. I also love the fact my dad's full given name is Gregory Creed Kanode, with Creed being my grandmother's maiden name. At Dad's insistence, Mom and Dad named me Jeffrey Creed Kanode. I just love the universalism, the continuity, the constancy between Dad's name and my own. I have always thought — and I hope my wife agrees — it is only right, if we ever have a son, for his name to be *Something* Creed Kanode.

The quality in Dad's soul which has always made him so unique and so special, is how he treats people. I have been a witness to this humane beauty all my life. I pray I have learned from it, and if I have learned or inherited just a portion of Dad's humanity, I am a much better person because of it.

It was the early 1990s. This was the age of Garth Brooks, Clint Black, Reba, Travis and Alan. This was the age when country was truly cool on a national scale like it had never been before.

One of the deejays at Dad's station routinely referred to Vince Gill as *Vince Gills*. It was always, always, always, "Here's a new one from Vince Gills," or "That was a former number one from Vince Gills." The mistake made the jockey sound foolish, and it made the station sound bad. It wasn't just an occasional thing. It was every time the man had to say the name "Vince Gill," he rechristened him "Vince Gills."

The owner of the station, a dour, red-faced, silver-haired man named Harry Bonnet finally got wind of the "Vince Gills" screwups. He told Dad to fix it, or the Vince Gills– playing disc jockey would lose his job. I remember sitting with Dad on the back porch as he agonized over how to handle the situation. He smoked cigarette after cigarette, openly verbalizing his options. It reminded me of an episode of *The Andy Griffith Show*, watching Andy go to such great lengths to protect Barney's feelings and dignity.

"I don't want to hurt his feelings," Dad said and took a great drag from his Winston. "If I don't correct him, he will lose his job, though. So I have to correct him." Dad looked over at me and smiled. Then he gave me a lesson in humanity I will never forget, and one I have carried with me always. "You see, Jeff, you can never tell a man he is doing five things wrong without first telling him five things he is doing right. Sometimes that's an easy thing to do, and sometimes it is really hard. Easy or hard though, it's the only way to keep someone's morale up, you know, help them keep their pride. If you take that away from someone, you're just being cruel." Dad exhaled a long plume of smoke, and he sat silent for a couple of minutes. I watched him closely. I could see his mind working in the way his blue eyes twinkled. "I have it," he said with a grin. "I have it." He picked up the cordless telephone and started dialing a number.

In the following moments, I witnessed true magic, true

compassion, true graciousness. "You know, bud," Dad told the hapless joc who had no idea his job was even in danger, "I am just sitting here at home watching television, and you know, the funniest thing just happened. Vince Gill is on a talk show. I always thought his name was Vince Gills, but as it turns out, his name is Vince Gill! I had no earthly idea. So how are you doing? I was listening in to your show earlier. Everything is sounding good."

Within the hour, the disc jockey introduced a new song called "I Never Knew Lonely" by "that sweet voice we all love, Vince Gill."

Dad handled things perfectly. He always has.

My dad is not what you, or me, or anyone would call a real masculine man. I am not, either. I simply don't think it's in our DNA. Still, for many years, I never witnessed my dad cry. He would grow really sad and treat my sisters and me with great tenderness whenever we had fallen and gotten hurt. Dad could be so empathetic and always naturally merciful. But I never saw a tear fall from Dad's blue eyes until I was twelve years old. He was picking me up from basketball practice. I was in the seventh grade.

I was in the seventh grade, and I was enduring one of the craziest, most confusing times of my life. I have described part of this narrative earlier. I never played any kind of team sport. I didn't like ball, and I had no desire to ever play ball. In my loneliness though, in my alienation, with full awareness that at school I was very much alone, and I didn't want to be alone anymore, I decided I would go out for basketball. I didn't belong there. I didn't enjoy being there. I opened myself up to a whole new battlefront of bullying, belittlement, and criticism. I was simply trying to *not* be alone. In that righteous endeavor, I nearly let my soul get smashed and slashed almost irreparably in an effort to fit in somewhere.

In that painful, confused context, Dad picked me up from basketball practice that rainy November day. There was loneliness and shadows covering my heart. The trees all around were seemingly dead. My dad had the pained task of being forced by the cycle of life to tell his only son more shadows were falling upon me and my family.

My great-grandmother, Mama Creed, Grandmother's mother, had been in the hospital for a few days. We drove home in Dad's little red Honda Civic pretty much in complete silence. I never, ever remember Dad being silent. I knew something was up. I was afraid to ask. Mama's condition was not in my mind as a reason for Dad's silence. I was in such survival mode within myself. I think I was oblivious to everything, even my own beloved great-grandmother, beyond the next breath I was willing myself to take.

Dad and I finally pulled into our driveway. He put the car in park, shut it off, but he didn't get out. I waited for my dad to say or do something. I could feel something--tension, melancholy, drama, thick in the air. Finally, after many pregnant seconds, Dad spoke. When he spoke, he started to cry. For the first time in my life, I saw my dad cry.

"Jeff K," he said softly in tears, "your Mama Creed passed away today. I know how much you loved her. She loved you too so, so much."

I started to cry. Dad moved close to hold me. Together, father and son cried in each other's arms. Sitting in our driveway, sitting in Dad's little red Honda Civic, father and son cried in each other's arms.

The next time Dad cried in front of me, he was walking me to my car. We had just bought the car together—a blue Chevrolet Cavalier—and it was time for me to drive away for my high school graduation. I can't remember exactly what Dad and I said to each other, except he said he was very proud of me, and he loved me. He started to cry. I started to cry. Father and son embraced each other below a dark blue sky as birds sang in the trees, as children laughed and yelled in the yard next door, and as the sun flooded down with the blessing of the abiding spirit of spring, with the promise of summer only a few steps behind.

I didn't know what would come next for me. I knew I had survived to see my graduation day. I knew I had survived in no small measure because of the love, the safety, the humane spirit of this man, my dad, who hugged me so tightly. I had survived, and I would go on surviving. I was my dad's son.

I do adore my dad like I adore no other human being. I am not so innocent or so naïve anymore to see or think about Dad as being perfect. No human being, not even one who loves so dearly, who is loved so dearly, is perfect. He's not perfect. He wasn't even the perfect father. No man can be. He was, and is, a good father though: a loving father, a gentle father, a positive father, a compassionate father.

When I think about my dad, I think about that young, want-to-be-stud strutting into the Bluefield Hospital emergency room with his drunken buddy. The young, hotshot disc jockey who fell so immediately, and so intensely in love for the pretty little surgical tech is the essence of my dad, to me. When I think about my dad, I think about the young romantic discovering in his heart that he could be, and deeply wanted to be, a young daddy when he met Mom's little girl, my sister Monica. When I think about my Dad, I think about him tan and healthy with his shirt off, glorying in the heat and light of the sun, playing like mad with his little daughters and his little boy at Myrtle Beach. When I think about my dad, I think about his music: the oldies were always playing at our house, or in our car. Dad was always still being a disc jockey, and he will always be a jock, loving those songs, especially the Motown of the 1960s.

When I think about Dad, my family is all together. The Supremes are singing in the background. It is a brilliantly bright summer day. We are at the beach, and Dad sings as he spends time with each of his children, building sandcastles, playing in water, or just strolling down the shore. When I think about my dad, I think about all these things. All these things are illumined by summertime light and heat, all choreographed by the hopeful, joyful hits of the '60s, and all wrapped up in love. Dad's love is hyper and youthful. Dad's love is wise and humble in its knowing. Dad's love reflects the human being Dad is, and I am grateful to be his son. I am grateful to carry his stories in my heart, in my blood, and in my words.

afterword

I opened up this book by lamenting the fact maybe only a narcissist could write about himself or herself for over two or three, let alone three hundred pages. Now that the journey of writing *Becoming Pastor* is complete, I am still lamenting that maybe only a narcissist could do this.

I hope not.

I truly did not write this book as a self-conscious, self- aware narcissist. But then, are narcissists even self-conscious and self-aware enough to know they are narcissists? I am a pastor, not a psychologist, so I don't know. Oh dear.

Becoming Pastor seeks to explain how one human soul came to become an ordained pastor. *Becoming Pastor* tries to answer how someone so picked-on and bullied, how someone so tormented with negative voices and harassed by hateful ghosts, survived this life—surviving to come to the place where he knows that God loves him.

God loves *me*. God lovingly calls me to serve God. God lovingly calls me to serve people and to serve them lovingly through God's love.

All my life I have wanted to write. Writers, professors, experts, whomever *they* are, always say, "Write what you know." And so, I have written what I know. I have written of my family. I have written of my childhood. I have written of my adolescence. I have written of my coming-of-age. I have written of my experiences in church. I have written of my epiphanies of discovering Christ's love.

I hope you don't mind, but as I did in my first book, *A Young Pastor*, I have changed the names of some people and some places. I have done so for people's privacy. I have done so for my own protection.

In "On the Air," my parents lovingly dispute my story of how they met. I swear one of them, or maybe one of my sisters, told me that story just as I wrote it, once upon a time. Recently my folks told me they met at a drive-in movie theatre. My story is better. I will always lovingly contend someone told me that story, and it is true. At least, it is true for me.

In that same chapter, for simplicity and narrative flow, I condensed Dad's working life into one radio station, WKOY-WKMY. He also worked at J-104 in Bluefield, WAEY in Princeton, and he ended his full-time career and is gliding into retirement working for our dear friend Bob Spencer, who now owns several radio stations in southern West Virginia.

My prayer is that I have not written my story in vain. If one tear has fallen, if just a subtle chuckle has floated upon the air, then I am glad I have taken this journey. I am glad — no, I am grateful that you chose to take the journey through these pages yourself. Thank you, and I hope we can meet again like this someday.

Every Sunday we tell the story

And the story is old

And it is new.

The story is well known

Memorized. Recited.

The story sounds foreign to most honest ears

Certainly, most hearts especially, the authentic

Even the ones who think they know

Every scene, all the plots, every character's heart.

I tell the story

Though you know, and though I confess

Sometimes I stutter and every so often

I doubt

That story

Of mud made human by Spirit

That story

Of perfect beautiful divinity becoming human

To save every human.

From a manger's seeming poverty

To a cross's seeming defeat...

The impossible reality, the impossible- to-deny Resurrection

Crying women, running disciples, scared soldiers

A gathered throng speaking different words

Words they claimed heaven whispered

To them.

To tell That story

Embodied in every winter

Melting into every spring

Confirmed by every gentle deed

In a violent world.

And your stories… And my stories… We find it all

We find ourselves, all of us somehow

Wrapped up, wrapped within

That story.

The story which we tell

Or try to tell

Every Sunday.

Works Cited

"Adios, Au Revoir, Auf Wiedersehen" Lyrics by Jack Elliott, Music by George Cates. Recorded by The Lawrence Welk Singers. Copyright 1969.

"Blessed Assurance." Lyrics by Fanny J. Crosby, music by Phoebe P. Knapp. Originally published 1873. From *The United Methodist Hymnal*. Abingdon Press, Nashville: 1988.

"East River Mountain." By Dr. Raymond T. Hill. From *The West Virginia Encyclopedia*. The West Virginia Humanities Council, Charleston, WV: 2006.

"Getting Better." Lyrics and music by John Lennon and Paul McCartney. From *Sergeant Pepper's Lonely Hearts Club Band*. Apple, 1966.

"Losing My Religion." Lyrics by Michael Stipe, music by Bill Berry, Peter Buck, and Mike Mills. From *Out of Time*. Warner Brothers, 1991.

"Season Suit: Spring." Lyrics and music by John Denver. From *Rocky Mountain High*. RCA, 1972.

The Epistle of 1 Peter. 1 Peter 2:4–5.

The Great Gatsby. By F. Scott Fitzgerald. Sribner and Sons: New York, 1925.

"The Monster." Lyrics and Music by Marshall Mathers. From *The Marshall Mathers LP2.* Aftermath Records, 2013.

"The Long and Winding Road." Lyrics and music by John Lennon and Paul McCartney. From *Let It Be.* Capitol, 1970.

Various Lectures from Dr. Peter J. Storey, Duke Divinity School. Spring, 2001.

We are all a story. We are all the little stories, sewn together, quilted into the story of each of us, in all the sacredness of our humanity.

This is a story of a squeaky voice and running down the basketball court the wrong way. It's the story of bullies whose voices echo forever, voices only love can reduce to powerless whispers. It's the story of faith discovered, and faith's insistence that a human life must survive.

It's a story very different from your story.

It's a story that is the same as your story.

It's a story, one person's story, and it is nothing more, and nothing less.

www.ingramcontent.com/pod-product-compliance
Lightning Source LLC
Chambersburg PA
CBHW030155070426
42447CB00031B/288